From the James Beard Journalism Award-Winning Publication

FOOD STORIES

WRITING THAT STIRS THE POT

THE BITTER SOUTHERNER

MENU

Orange Is the New Peach
by James Murdock
p. 6

How Hot Chicken
Really Happened
by Rachel Louise Martin
p. 20

Immigrant Spaghetti
by Farhan Mustafa
p. 44

Beans & Rice: More Than
a Poor Man's Meal
by Nikesha Elise Williams
p. 60

The Last Oyster Tongers
of Apalachicola
by David Hanson
p. 68

The Man Behind
the Counter
by Sayaka Matsuoka
p. 82

The Elusive Roots
of Rosin Potatoes
by Caroline Hatchett
p. 92

This Last Earthy Sweetness
by Chelsey Mae Johnson
p. 118

The Woman
Who Ate Atlanta
by Wendell Brock
p. 126

A Hunger for Tomatoes
by Shane Mitchell
p. 144

The Short & Brilliant
Life of Ernest Matthew
Mickler
by Michael Adno
p. 170

Southern Hustle:
Houston Hip-Hop &
Chinese Chicken
by Alana Dao
p. 192

My Old Friend
Natty Light
by Mickie Meinhardt
p. 204

They Like That
Soft Bread
by Chelsey Mae Johnson
p. 220

Killings
by Daniel Wallace
p. 242

The Driest State
by Alice Driver
p. 252

Country Cooking:
Minnie's Corn Pudding
& Tammy's Better Than
Sex Cake
by Jennifer Justus
p. 264

The Creature Comfort
of Aunt Jemima
by adia victoria
p. 276

Lemon Meringue Pie:
A Lesson in Love, Hate
& Bravery
by Kathleen Purvis
p. 284

Tamaleando
en Tennessee
by Keitlyn Alcántara
p. 292

He Could Have Been
a Colonel
by Keith Pandolfi
p. 304

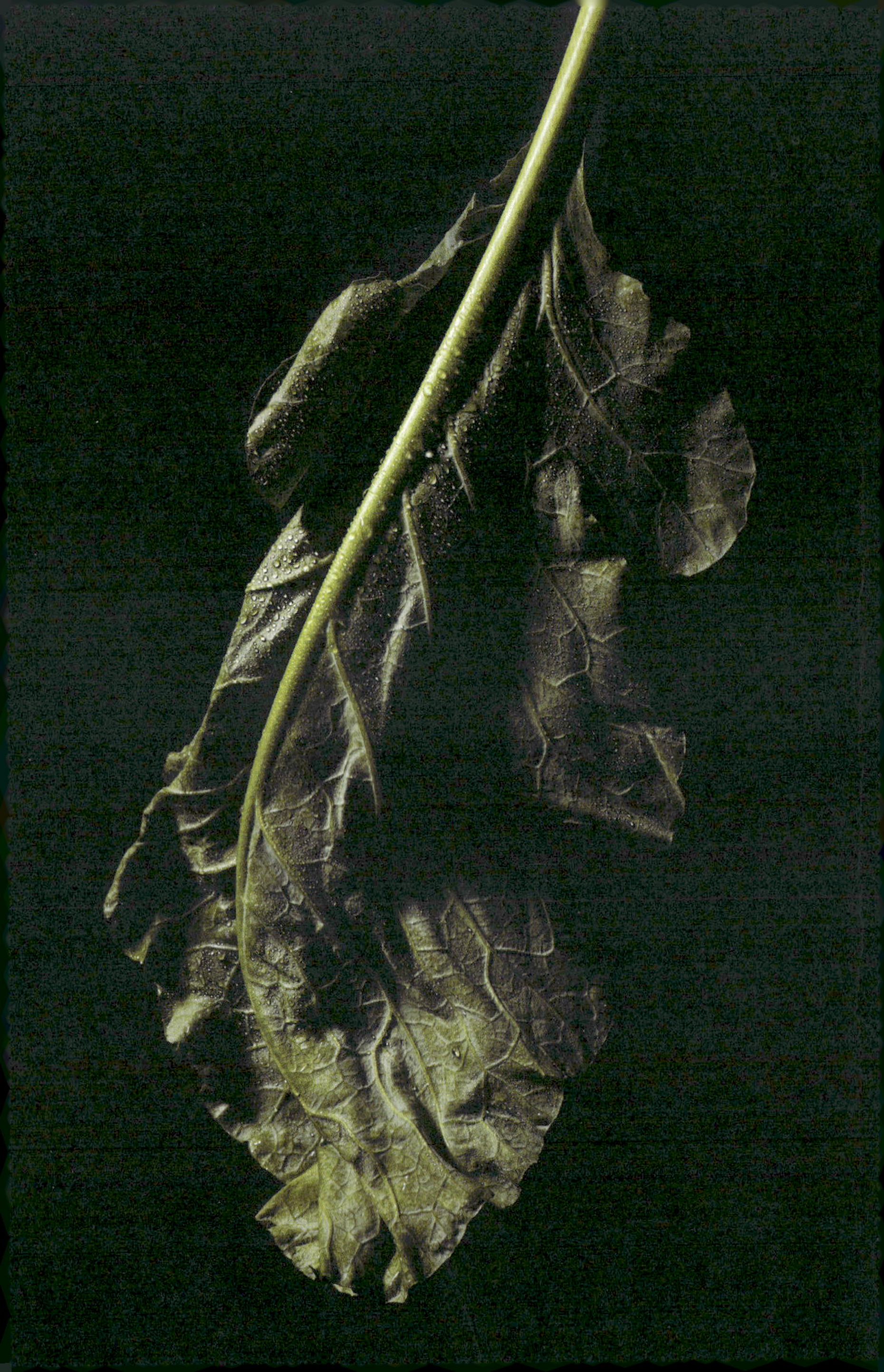

FOREWORD

—

MAY 2023

Food stories are often about so much more than what's on our plate.
    For 10 years, working with the best writers anywhere and always through the lens of a better South, we've published stories about the foods of our region. Some of those earned our writers nominations and wins from the prestigious James Beard Awards. Last summer, The Bitter Southerner brought home the big prize for Food Coverage at the awards ceremony in Chicago. Rest assured, we celebrated big that night with both food and drink.
    Inside this anthology are 21 of our favorite stories from the magazine's first decade. You'll read about oyster tongers, fried burgers, white trash cooking, a legendary food critic, rosin potatoes, Natty Light, farmers facing climate change, making sorghum the right way, steamed sandwiches, Houston hip-hop and Chinese chicken, beans and rice, historic lunch counters, Tennessee tamales, lemon meringue pie, country music cookbooks, our complicated love affair with tomatoes, and the demise of a chicken.
    Writing that stirs the pot. Dig in.

ORANGE IS THE NEW PEACH

—

by James Murdock

Photo by Gregory Miller
This story was originally published January 5, 2021

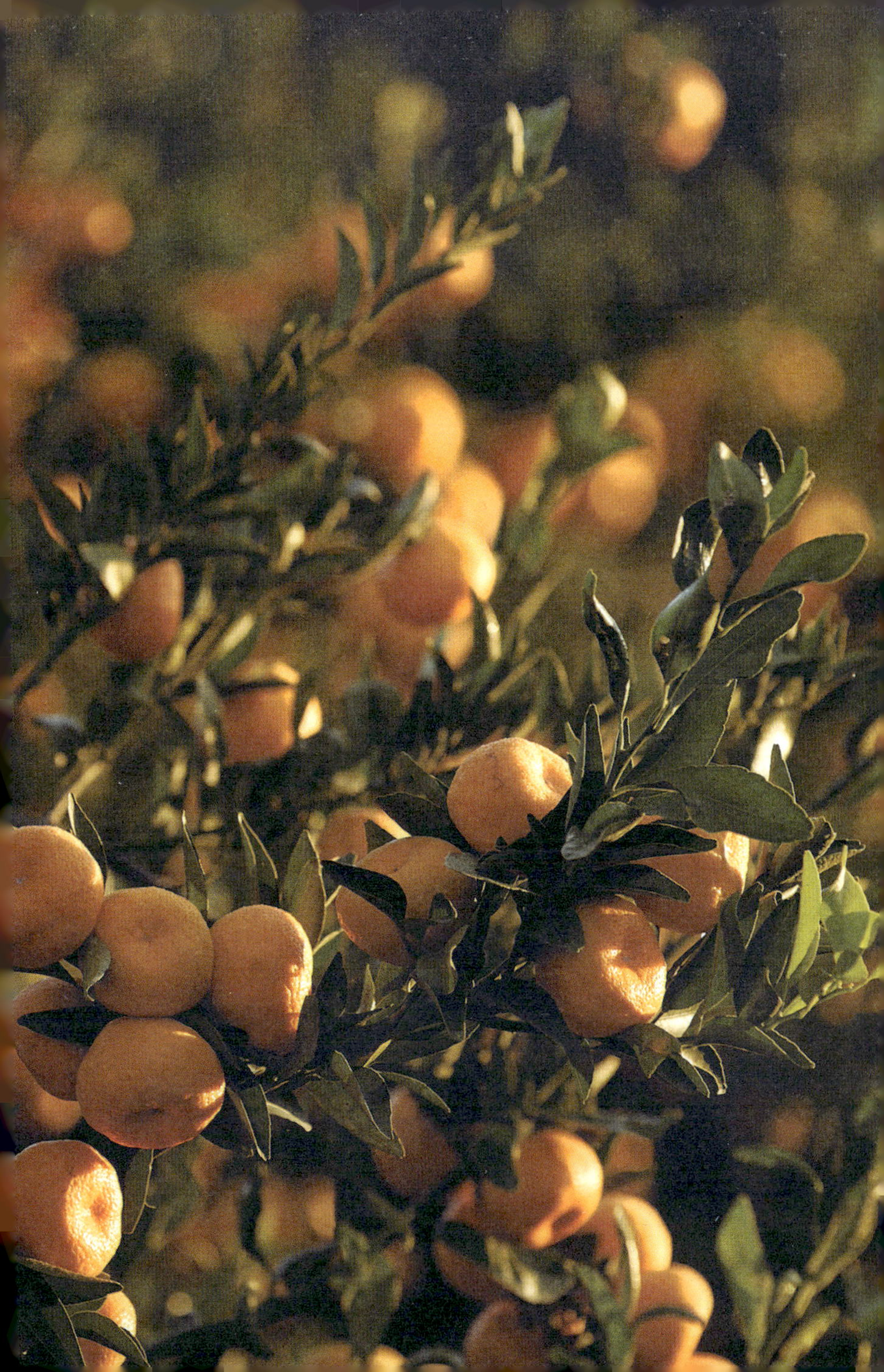

Orange Is the New Peach

> *"There's nothing in south Georgia, people will tell you, except straight, lonely roads, one-horse towns, sprawling farms, and tracts of planted pines. It's flat, monotonous, used-up, hotter than hell in summer, and cold enough in winter that orange trees won't grow."*
>
> —
>
> Janisse Ray, *Ecology of a Cracker Childhood*, 1999

A blaze of orange, a tropical tone in winter, glowed from a dark corner of my mother's kitchen. Tiny heads of fresh citrus formed a delicious mound in a ceramic bowl. Lively leaves perked from their stems as if still reaching toward the sun. Too lively, I thought, to have made the trip from Florida.

"Where'd you get these?" I asked.

"A man in Statesboro grows them," Mom said. "He's got a stand on 301."

"A man grows these here?"

"Yeah. I guess we can grow them here, now."

I spent the first 18 years of my life in South Georgia and never saw a single orange tree. I thought Mom must be mistaken, but she assured me. Confused by this, I kept a suspicious eye on the fruit. And I ate a few. Each tiny segment, robust with sweet, tangy juice, enticed me more.

My hometown of Metter lies in Georgia's upper coastal plain, 100 miles, as the crow flies, north of Florida. Though the region is part of a landmass that falls gracefully from the hilly Piedmont to the ocean, it is nowhere close to the traditional citrus belt of central Florida.

Each time I glanced at the fruit, Mom's words, *I guess we can grow them here, now*, roamed around my brain like a moody raccoon. A feeling of dread, but also curiosity, arose. I needed to talk to that farmer out on U.S. Route 301.

• • •

The bottom of Joe Franklin's shirt pocket holds an ink stain; his mind moves too busily for bleeding pens. He sports white tennis shoes and a scruffy mustache, from which a strong septuagenarian voice pushes patient words. When I asked to visit in his free time, he said, "When you work with citrus, there is no free time."

Still, he welcomed me on a Saturday in mid-harvest.

When we meet, Franklin is agitated. A delivery driver flaked on him, and the clock ticks at a market in Savannah. His blue eyes squint over a cellphone as he paces, and I know to stay out of the way.

Franklin's office, a tin building doubling as a packing center, swims with relics of fishing expeditions. I examine some color-drained photographs, groups of men smiling behind bounties of pickerel, and I'm drawn toward an open sunny garage door to inspect the scenery on the other side of the office.

The sky is cloudless, and an aroma of peroxide and citrus peel lingers in the warm winter air. Out in the light, long rows of glossy trees disappear into a backdrop of sycamore and pine. I have entered a strange dimension, I think, where two typically distinct environments merge into one bizarre ecotone.

I imagined finding a few ugly trees clinging to life. What I discover is a full-scale citrus farm where citrus farms do not belong. As far as I can see, trees gushing with bright globes bask in the sunlight. Voices interrupt my trance. A younger reddish-blond-haired man breaks the tension with news that the driver has come and gone. Franklin breathes, knowing his citrus will make it to Forsyth Farmers' Market in Savannah.

The morning is born again.

"This is Billy," Franklin says, introducing me to his farm manager, Bill Renz, as the three of us head outside.

We walk into an open-ended hoop house where a jungle of fully grown orange and grapefruit trees press against one another, jockeying toward the sunlit ceiling. A country ringtone blares from Renz's phone. Franklin begins to tell his story while Renz disappears into rustling branches.

In the spring of 2009, Franklin and his fishing buddies headed to Louisiana seeking redfish, but he found his destiny. Folks sold Satsumas from nearby family orchards out of the backs of pickups. Curious, having never heard of the sweet, loose-skinned mandarin orange, they pulled over to buy a bag.

"It was the best piece of citrus I've ever put in my mouth," Franklin says. He pulls an orange from overhead and opens his pocket knife.

When he returned home, he researched how to raise the trees, which have been cultivated for centuries in Japan. No information on growing Satsumas in his climate zone existed, but Franklin's curiosity would not let up. The next spring he bought 200 Satsuma seedlings, for $21 each, and planted them himself on a small plot of his family farm.

This was no meager experiment, considering the price for the trees alone added up to over $4,200. With site prep, irrigation, and fertilizer, Franklin's little experiment cost in the ballpark of $10,000. Having no research-based information on how the trees might react to this environment, on what chemical regimens were required here, on how weather patterns might affect the tree's production, this project was more gamble than investment. Satsumas take three to four years to produce edible fruit. Years would pass before Franklin could taste the fruit of these young trees. He rolled the dice anyway. If there was a chance he could grow what he tasted in Louisiana, it would be worth the risk.

In his younger years, Franklin raised beef cows on the land that he inherited. In 1979, he purchased an additional 100 acres, bringing the farm to a total of 450. After the beef trade became more heavily regulated, he leased his fields to local farmers, who grew peanuts and soybeans. Franklin tried his hand at growing soybeans once, but was never crazy about growing crops that came with prices dictated by global markets. He always searched for something else.

Franklin passes me a slice of a Page orange, and Renz explains that these oranges must be cut open — the peel contains oil that corrupts the eating experience if the fruit is broken by hand. Renz is a reservoir of citrus knowledge. "Page oranges were popular in the '70s and '80s," he tells me. "They fell off because they're seedy and hard to peel. And because of the oil. Breeders use them these days to sweeten things up; they cross other oranges with Page to try and pass on its flavor." The Page slice tastes so sweet, it reminds me of orange-flavored candy — like it's sprinkled with processed sugar. I bite and juice pours out of the corner of my mouth.

Franklin points at trees and says names I've never heard. Oroblanco grapefruit from Israel, Dekopons from Japan, and Australian finger limes. He cuts open a finger lime and squeezes it over my palm. Luscious little morsels fall like tiny pearls into a pile. These limes sell for up to $174 a pound online. "Citrus caviar," Franklin says.

Renz explains that the hoop house is both a site of experimentation and an insurance policy. If a killer winter storm rolls in, the houses provide backup fruit. But they mainly serve as research centers. Franklin and Renz are not just farmers, they are effectively scientists.

Renz grew up in citrus country, in the small southwest Florida town of Alva. As a kid, with 30-foot orange trees in his yard, he'd whack fruit with a baseball bat into fields to feed cows. A decade ago, about the time Franklin planted his first trees, Renz and his family moved to Statesboro, Georgia. He had just landed a job managing a local nursery that grows flowers and ornamentals.

One fateful summer day in 2010, Franklin wandered into the nursery to browse plants, not in search of anything citrus related. Renz struck up a conversation that eventually led to Franklin telling him about his little experiment. Renz was fascinated and drove right over after work to check it out.

Within weeks, Renz became a citrus consultant for Franklin, sharing valuable knowledge as the trees grew. He started helping on weekends, and soon Franklin hired him as a part-time farmhand.

"The first pickers were me, Joe, and a couple of his buddies," Renz says, laughing. "We were like, 'What the hell are we going to do with these things?'"

Recently, Franklin gave Renz half the business and made him a partner. As the farm adds thousands of new trees a year, Renz oversees the expansion, as well as everything from shipping to marketing. His teenage daughter, Shaylee, takes pictures for the farm's social media sites, and his wife, Lauren, works markets on weekends.

Renz kept his job at the nursery, but after 10 years of managing the store, he's taken on a new role of coordinating landscaping projects. He manages a team, based out of the nursery, that implements his designs. This role provides Renz more flexibility now that Franklin's Citrus is expanding. Still, during the three-month harvest, he works 70 to 80 hours a week, half at the nursery, half at Franklin's.

Renz strategizes how to deliver their product to larger retailers — raising Franklin's from farmers markets and its roadside stand on U.S. Route 301 to grocery chains across the country. The farm supplies a variety of citrus — Kishus, Tangos, Satsumas, lemons, and grapefruits — to more than 20 small produce vendors and to markets in multiple states. Drivers who buy truckloads of citrus from Franklin's deliver their fruit as far north as Philadelphia and as far west as Oklahoma.

Outside of the hoop house lies a serene morning. It's quiet for midharvest, and I search for teams of roving pickers in the orchards. With more than 6,500 trees, 53 acres of citrus, plenty of work awaits. A few songbirds fly by; nothing else moves.

The 25 people who pick for Franklin's Citrus are all members of the Ventura family, who live in a nearby community. They work six days a week during harvest, from sunup to dusk, loading citrus into large, front-heavy bags strapped to their shoulders. They cut kishus, what Franklin calls "Georgia Kisses," from branches with needle-nose clippers to keep the tiny, delicate fruit from slipping out of its loose-skinned peels. They pack thousands of boxes a week. But not on Saturdays, even with retailers calling. As Seventh Day Adventists, the Venturas will not be photographed and spend the daylight hours of their Sabbath in worship.

...

In the late 1880s, Satsumas became popular in the Gulf, thanks to an Irish-born painter named Anna Schoyer. While on a cultural mission in Japan during the Meiji Restoration, Schoyer met two loves, Robert Bruce Van

Valkenburgh, the U.S. Ambassador to Japan, and the lovely, palm-sized fruit "unshu mikan" on Kyushu Island. We call the fruit Satsuma because of Schoyer, who named it for the samurai-ruled province where she first tasted its sweetness.

After marrying in Japan, Schoyer and Van Valkenburgh had a two-story Carpenter Gothic abode built overlooking the St. Johns River outside of Jacksonville, Florida. Schoyer longed for the fruit she had tasted while abroad, and soon after the house was finished, in 1878, she had 75 Owari Satsuma trees delivered from Kyushu Island to her doorstep. She and her husband planted the trees directly behind their house amid long, drooping branches of live oaks on their 18-acre estate.

Satsumas became a celebrated centerpiece at the couple's dinner parties, and soon news that the seedless mandarin was cold-hardy enough to grow in north Florida spread. The fruit gained popularity among consumers for its sweet taste and easily peeled skin, and growers across the Gulf sought to meet new demands. By 1890, more than a million Satsuma trees stood in groves from Florida to Texas. A group of growers established the Gulf Coast Citrus Exchange, built solely around Satsumas, which delivered the fruit as far north as New York.

But this young boom would lack the hardiness required for survival.

Several brutal winters, beginning in the late 1890s, swept through the region, killing trees. Growers learned quickly that the cold-hardiness of Satsumas had limitations. After the 1890s, the industry rebounded, but more devastating winters hit in the 1910s. Then more in the 1930s. Each string of deep freezes decimated groves across the Gulf and crippled the young industry. Growers were resilient; the trees were not.

"The winter of 1935 did them in," Franklin says, as we stand among his Satsumas. He speaks about this in a pleasant tone, like what happened then is somehow unrelated to the trees that make up the majority of his farm. I wonder if he shouldn't be more disheartened by this story.

"You're not worried that could happen again?" I ask.

"One thing that encouraged me to plant citrus was the warming trend," Franklin says. "Climate change."

I suppose climate is a natural place for any discussion about citrus in

Georgia to go. Why is this fruit being grown successfully farther north than it has ever been before? Hearing Franklin, an older south Georgia farmer, say the words "climate change," affected me more than any scientific report I had read.

"When I was growing up," Franklin went on, "back in the '50s and '60s, not often, but maybe once a year, we'd have 8 or 10 degrees here. I remember Thanksgiving, going deer hunting, and we'd have to build a damn fire. It'd be freezing cold even during the day. It's not that way anymore. Weather patterns are changing. Now we have colder weather in the latter part of February and in March."

Franklin is right; weather patterns are changing. The 2010s were the warmest decade ever recorded in the Southeast. According to the U.S. Global Change Research Program (USGCRP), the current southern climate zones are projected to shift one to two zones northward by 2070. The traditional fruit crops of the South face unprecedented challenges. In 2017, Georgia peach farmers lost 85% of their crop. Warm temperatures in February caused trees to develop early buds. When a late freeze hit in March, the buds, and the promise of Georgia peaches, withered.

The Florida orange industry currently lies in ruin as a result of climate-related factors. For over a decade, an insect-borne invasive bacteria, huanglongbing (HLB), has ravaged Florida groves, causing citrus greening, which prevents fruit from ripening. The invasive psyllid that spreads the bacteria thrives in climates with nighttime temperatures ranging from 60 to 80 degrees. Two-thirds of Florida orange growers have closed their doors — a hard blow to a $9 billion industry and a loss of over 34,000 jobs.

Winters on Franklin's Citrus Farm seem to be ideal for Satsumas, which need some cold weather to ripen. Will the climate still be ideal here in another 10 years? I ask Franklin about the possibility of citrus greening spreading north if climate zones continue their shift. He thinks it's still too cold — for now. At the moment, he is in the right spot: not quite hot enough for the bacteria-spreading psyllid to thrive, and not quite cold enough to kill trees.

"That's not to say that one of them clippers from Canada can't come down and wipe our ass out," Franklin says. "But things are changing."

Schoyer enjoyed the fruit of her Satsuma grove for several years before she passed in 1887. She did not live to witness the apocalyptic destiny of her trees. 1899, the coldest winter in Florida history, with temperatures as low as minus 2 degrees Fahrenheit, spelled the end of America's first Satsuma orchard.

...

As we stroll down a sunny open lane, I cannot help but notice the buzz of life around us. Bees bob on wildflower heads, which fill the gaps between trees. Thrashers scratch for worms and retreat to the woodline as we pass. Grasshoppers leap, sugar ants march, beetles flitter, an ecosystem works.

The hum of this grove stands in contrast to the silence of nearby cotton fields. Cotton, like most industrial crops, requires high levels of pesticides, synthetic fertilizers, and herbicides, chemicals that pollute ground and surface water, expose workers to dangerous toxins, and disrupt natural habitats. Cotton, as well as other crops, requires tilling and heavy irrigation, a combination that contributes to the structural collapse and erosion of soils.

This orchard, on the other hand, provides food and shelter for life. While it might exist as a result of climate change, it may also combat warming. University of Florida researchers found that one acre of citrus trees consumes 23.3 tons of carbon dioxide and produces 16.7 tons of oxygen per year. Biologists have identified over 159 species that live in, and depend on, grove ecosystems. Large spaces between rows allow for natural small habitats to thrive. Rather than exposing soils with constant planting and tilling, the roots of trees hold the earth together.

I notice a white, cloudy substance on some leaves and ask if this is some sort of chemical residue. Renz says no, it's kaolinite, a clay mineral native to Georgia, used for all sorts of things. They spray it on the trees to protect fruit from sun exposure. As an added bonus, the clay acts as a natural insect repellent.

Franklin and Renz don't run a completely organic operation, but they use synthetic fertilizers and pesticides minimally. Renz says the best fruit comes from trees not overly fertilized, and they only spray for insects twice during the summer.

Franklin's grove doesn't experience a lot of the insect issues that plague growers farther south. Citrus farmers in Florida, for instance, spray constantly to suppress the psyllid that spreads citrus greening. Renz and Franklin have had to figure on their own what regimens work in Bulloch County — another way they represent the cutting edge of citrus research in the Peach State.

"It's hard for young growers starting out here, because all the information they get on chemical regimens is based on Citrus Belt research," Renz says. "Satsumas are a different animal."

The orchard teems with plant and animal diversity. A honeybee collects nectar from a Satsuma bloom. "Normal in winter?" I ask. Citrus trees bloom randomly throughout the year, Renz explains. Satsumas self-pollinate, but their flowers attract and feed a variety of flying insects. Franklin partners with a local beekeeper who jars Satsuma honey. The bee we observe helps to create that delicious serum.

"One more thing," Renz says as he points to the ground. "Drip irrigation allows us to use about one-tenth of the water most farms in the area use."

•••

In 2016, Franklin co-founded the Georgia Citrus Association, a nonprofit in support of education and research in the state's emerging citrus market. He did this to help provide information to his potential competitors and share what he and Renz are learning on their farm. In the association's first year, the number of citrus trees in Georgia doubled, from 21,000 to 42,000.

As word of Franklin's success spreads, more Georgia farmers experiment with citrus. According to the association, 300 South Georgia farms now grow citrus trees. Many of those are small trial plots, but some farmers plan for large expansions. Franklin says if he is still the biggest producer of citrus in the state, he won't be for long.

In Fort Valley, three peach-farming families joined to build a 77,000-square-foot packing facility dedicated solely to distributing Georgia citrus. Nurseries across south Georgia sell seedlings, recognizing the rising demand for trees. As Florida groves continue to struggle with citrus greening, Georgia growers look toward an emerging market with earnest curiosity.

Renz understands this blooming industry better than anyone. He looks to the future and knows farmers markets will not be able to sustain farms like Franklin's. "If I had a crystal ball," he says, "it would tell me that those markets will corrode." He sees the popularity of citrus now, grasps the reality of Georgia nurseries selling trees, and knows that Franklin's must seek the security of wholesale markets.

"Farmers markets have been great for building our brand," Renz concludes. "But we did not expand to this size only to supply roadside stands."

Franklin's Citrus Farm Fruit Stand sits on the side of U.S. Route 301, between Statesboro and Interstate 16. Customers file in and out, some with masks, some without, all leaving with bags of Satsumas or Georgia Kisses. A young man hauls bags of Satsumas to his family's car, as Shannon Jones, a longtime friend of Franklin's who works the tin-shelter stand, rearranges bags of citrus for customers. The shelves inside hold a variety of local products — homemade soaps, candles, jams, fruitcakes, cane syrup, and Satsuma honey. Jones works the register, smiles warmly, and greets guests. Beyond a couple of picnic tables, cars whiz by on 301 headed into or out of Statesboro, going to or from nearby I-16. Holding a bag of Franklin's Satsumas, I gaze out at the highway and think about all the places these sweet mandarins, this budding South Georgia industry, might go.

The farm stand is a display of Franklin's love of his community. As I acknowledge each product, he tells me who grows it or makes it. It turns out the brother of the cane syrup maker dates my cousin. "We're practically family," I tell Franklin, and we laugh.

The stand also remains a vestige of an experiment, a gamble, that has paid off exponentially. And though this stand is the beginning of a journey, the roads that lead away from it will carry the next chapter.

"You're going to see Georgia citrus become the next Vidalia onion," Franklin says. "Soon they'll be in every grocery store around." ◊

James Murdock is a writer, naturalist, and English teacher from Jasper County, Georgia. He earned an MFA in narrative nonfiction writing from the University of Georgia's Grady College of Journalism. Murdock enjoys writing about nature and agriculture and how such topics intersect with the human spirit. He published his first poetry book, Think, Dear Daughter, *with the help of friends, in 2019. Murdock lives on a farm an hour east of Atlanta with wife Jenna, daughter Tallulah, and many plants and animals.*

HOW HOT CHICKEN REALLY HAPPENED

—

by Rachel Louise Martin

Photo by Joe Buglewicz
This story was originally published July 7, 2015

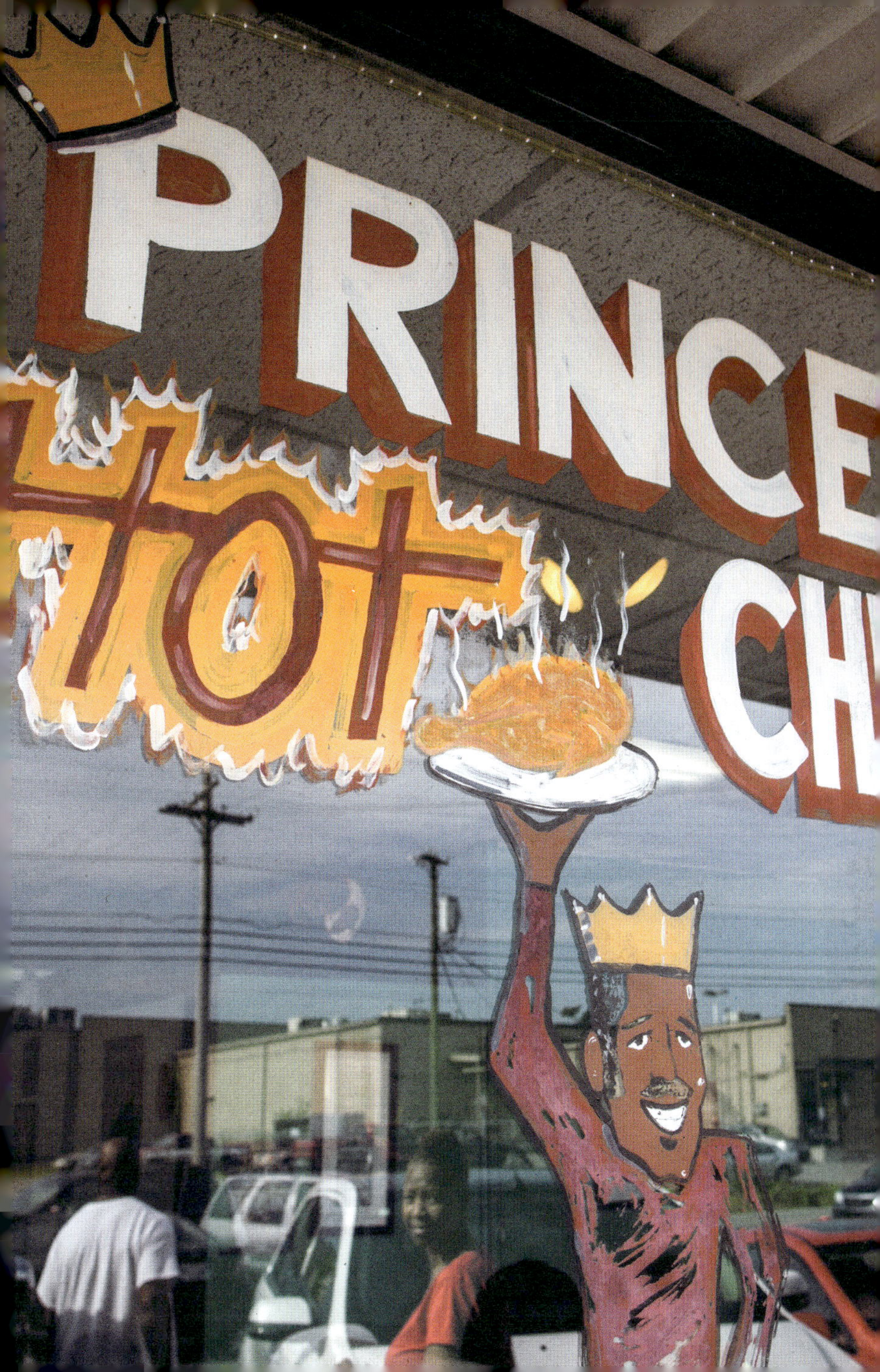
PRINCE
Hot
CH

How Hot Chicken Really Happened

Hot chicken.
It's on the list of "must-try" Southern foods in countless publications and websites. Restaurants in New York; Detroit; Cambridge, Massachusetts; and even Australia advertise that they fry their chicken Nashville-style. More than 12,000 people showed up for the 2014 Fourth of July Music City Hot Chicken Festival. The James Beard Foundation recently gave Prince's Chicken Shack an American Classic Award for inventing the dish.

But although I'm a second-generation Middle Tennessean, the daughter of a Nashville native, I had never eaten hot chicken — or even heard of it — before I moved away for graduate school in 2005. I came back eight years later to a new Nashville that eats new food.

The city is growing almost faster than developers can manage. Historic neighborhoods are being razed and renewed. The suburbs are expanding. Fields are being replaced by paved shopping paradises identical to those spreading across the nation. My friends have moved to the neighborhoods we grew up avoiding. They asked me to meet them for drinks or haute Southern cuisine in places I remembered as industrial wastelands. And everyone was eating hot chicken, a food I didn't know.

Embarrassed that I didn't know this food everyone else loved, I turned to Google. The web was full of photographs of fried chicken slathered with a hot sauce that somehow kept it crispy, served on a bed of white bread and topped by a pickle. Then, last summer, my friend Julie moved home. She called me.

"What's hot chicken?" she asked. "Have we been eating our chicken wrong all these years?"

I asked my dad if he had ever had it. "Nope," he said. But he taught school in the 1970s, and he remembered that some of the Black teachers carried their own bottles of hot sauce. Sometimes they'd prank him by spiking his cafeteria lunch.

Was this the answer? Was hot chicken a part of the city's history that had been invisible to me as a white woman? I asked Denise, an older African American woman in my church who was raised in the city.

"Of course you didn't eat hot chicken," she said, shaking her head at me. "Hot chicken's what we ate in the neighborhood."

I went to the downtown public library to do a very unscientific survey of what they had on hand. I sat in the second-floor reading room, surrounded by stacks of cookbooks, just to see if I could find a recipe to prove that in Nashville we didn't choose our chicken style based on race. I walked away with several new ways to fry a chicken. One of them added some black pepper, but none of them made it spicy.

Sure enough, as I started investigating, I discovered Denise was right. For almost 70 years, hot chicken was made and sold primarily in Nashville's Black neighborhoods. I started to suspect the story of hot chicken could tell me something powerful about race relations in Nashville, especially as the city tries to figure out what it will be in the future.

...

I hate it when people date everything Southern back to the Civil War. But in this case, that's where my story starts. That is when Nashville became a segregated city, a place where there were white neighborhoods and Black neighborhoods and very little shared public space.

Before the war, about 700 free Black people lived in Nashville. Their houses were clustered in small enclaves, mostly on the northern side of the city. But there were over 3,200 people of color who were enslaved in the city. Most of them could not choose where they lived.

Many enslaved African Americans used the war to claim their freedom. They left their homes and moved to the edges of Union camps. The places where the freed people lived became known as contraband camps. Some of these were migrant communities following the soldiers as they campaigned. Others were permanent settlements where residents plotted streets, built wood cabins, and organized churches.

Federal troops captured Nashville in February 1862. The first Southern state capital to be taken, its early capitulation meant that the city became a key Union base. African Americans from across Middle Tennessee fled there, and contraband camps sprouted up around the military installations perched on the eastern, western, and southern borders of Nashville.

After the Civil War ended, the people living in Nashville's contraband camps had a choice: return to the places they had lived before the conflict, hoping to negotiate new contracts with the whites who'd once claimed to own them; strike out for somewhere new, gambling that they would find more opportunity in the North or the West; or stay in Nashville, building a new life in the growing city. Many chose to remain. Between 1860 and 1870, African Americans grew from being 23 percent to 38 percent of the population.

One of the largest Union camps had been Fort Gillem, north of downtown and near where the free Black people lived before the war. When the Union army pulled out, Fisk Free Colored School took over the grounds. Rechartered as Fisk University in 1872, it became a leading institution of African American higher education. The wagon road through the fort was renamed Jefferson Street. A prosperous Black business district grew up along it, and houses popped up around it.

Several other large African American neighborhoods developed around former camps located in what is now known as East Nashville, just across the Cumberland River from downtown. Like the Jefferson Street area, these were neighborhoods filled with professionals, businesspeople, and skilled laborers.

Another Black neighborhood grew up a few blocks northwest of the capital. Known as Hell's Half Acre, it housed the poorest African Americans in the city. It had unpaved streets and no sewer system. The city's disinterest left the area open to trouble. It became known for saloons, prostitution, and other vices. It also had some of Nashville's oldest Black churches and schools.

• • •

Over the last decade or so, the story of how hot chicken was invented has become part of local mythology, the sort of tale Nashville residents can recount with dramatic pauses and wry chuckles.

It happened this way: Back in the 1930s, at the height of the Great Depression, there was a man named Thornton Prince. He was a handsome man, tall and good looking.

"Beautiful, wavy hair," his great-niece Andre Prince Jeffries tells me. He was also a bit of a womanizer. "He was totally a ladies' man," she laughs. "He sure had plenty of women."

Women handle cheating partners in all sorts of ways. Some look the other way. Others walk out. A few get even.

One of Thornton's women got fed up with his philandering ways. He had stayed out all night and come home expecting breakfast. She wanted retribution. That morning, just like all their other morning-afters, she got up before him. And she didn't make him dry toast or gruel. Oh, no, she made him his favorite. She made him fried chicken.

Then she added the spiciest items she had in her kitchen.

No one knows what went into that first hot chicken. "She couldn't run to the grocery store to get something," Jeffries muses. By the time the bird was cooked, she was sure she had spiced it beyond edibility.

As Thornton Prince took his first bite, she must have braced herself for his reaction. Would he curse? Whimper? Stomp out?

But her plan backfired. He loved it. He took it to his brothers. They loved it, too.

The woman disappeared from his life, but her hot chicken lived on. The Prince brothers turned her idea into the BBQ Chicken Shack.

"We don't know who the lady was that was trying," Jeffries says. "All the old heads are gone. Gone on. But hey, we're still profiting from it." She pauses. "So women are very important."

How Hot Chicken Really Happened

Jeffries has an easy explanation for the chicken's popularity. "My mother said, if you know people are gonna talk, give them something to talk about," she says. "This chicken is not boring. You're gonna talk about this chicken."

Jeffries tells me this sitting in a bench at Prince's Chicken Shack, the business founded eight decades ago. She is about 70, with carefully applied makeup, a Farrah Fawcett flip, and a contagious laugh. She moves a little stiffly, but she's still the one who runs the restaurant. As we talk, she keeps a close eye on her employees, many of whom are either family members or longtime friends.

I'm at Prince's early on a Thursday evening, so most folks are picking up to-go dinner orders. Customers file past our table. Some stop to share their own memories. They walk by us to the back of the restaurant, where a plywood wall separates the dining room from the kitchen. A window has been cut in the wall, and a woman sits there, ringing up the orders. Occasionally, she yells a number and hands over a brown paper bag of food. The chicken's grease and sauce quickly saturate the paper, so most customers grab a white plastic bag off a nearby counter. A young man is stapling strands of yellow, white, and red Christmas lights around the window.

Of course, a few folks say that before there was Prince's BBQ Chicken Shack, there was a place called Bo's. But who wants to mess with a good story?

• • •

By the time Thornton Prince opened his restaurant, segregation governed Southern life.

Reconstruction had seemed to offer African Americans new opportunities. Black men got the vote, and a handful were elected. Schools opened, educating children and adults alike. People hoped for land ownership and fair wages. But the abandonment of the federal government and violent opposition by groups such as the Ku Klux Klan let white Southerners "redeem" their communities. Jim Crow laws hardened the divisions between Black and white people, making inequality part of the legal code. Lynchings, riots, rapes, and other attacks terrorized Black communities. Many people left the region, hoping Chicago or New York or Los Angeles would be more peaceful and profitable for them. Others fled the countryside for Nashville and other cities of the upper South.

Jefferson Street gave Black Nashvillians places where they could shop, eat, learn, and worship safely. Thanks to these new migrants, the area around Jefferson Street continued to grow and prosper. In 1912, the Tennessee Agricultural and Industrial and Normal School — now Tennessee State University — moved there. That same year, the city built Hadley Park, the first park Black people could use. Restaurants, music venues, and speakeasies opened. Country music dominated white Nashville's music scene, but Jefferson Street became an important haunt for jazz and blues musicians. The Ritz Theater let African Americans watch movies without having to climb into a segregated balcony. Motels and hotels gave travelers options. Similar districts grew up at the heart of the Black neighborhoods in East and North Nashville.

But the city developed a "pyramid" zoning code, which meant that land was zoned according to its perceived value. Property zoned for residential use was of higher value, and so it was protected from the incursion of commercial interests. Property zoned for commercial or industrial use could be used for single-family dwellings, but at any point, a developer could come into the middle of the neighborhood and start building anything he or she desired.

Most white neighborhoods were zoned as residential areas. African American neighborhoods were zoned as commercial and industrial properties.

In 1949, the city administration claimed 96 acres in Hell's Half Acre. They justified it by saying they would rid the city of vice. The plat included six historic African American churches, a business district, schools, and other sites of community life. The city replaced the neighborhood with the State Library and Archives, a large office building, a six-lane parkway, terraced parking lots, and green space. They announced that they would replace the rest of the neighborhood with a planned municipal auditorium and private development. Few provisions were made for the people who lost their homes.

How Hot Chicken Really Happened

There was "a view that Nashville had held for some time that suggested that one of the major problems with downtowns was people," former Mayor Bill Purcell explains to me as we look out the window of his high-rise downtown law office. "That if you could eliminate the people, then the city would be successful. ... They banned vices; they banned activities that they felt were detrimental to civic life, and they banned residential living."

Urban redevelopment accelerated over the next several decades, and it bore down upon other Black neighborhoods around the city. The 1954 Federal Housing Act offered to pay up to 90 percent of the cost if Nashville would raze unwanted buildings and replace them with superhighways. The city planners cleared the edge of East Nashville for a new interstate. They emptied another 400 acres for warehousing and industrial use. Another highway was routed through Edgehill, a lower-income, predominantly minority community. Black leaders began worrying that urban renewal would become "Negro removal."

New suburban developments popped up just outside the city's limits. The interstates proved to be effective walls between the new developments and the city's centers. Neighborhood covenants controlled who could buy the houses, and so these areas were up to 98 percent white. Nashville grew increasingly segregated.

...

Over the past 80 years, Thornton Prince's hot chicken business has wandered through Black Nashville. The first BBQ Chicken Shack sat at the corner of Jefferson Street and 28th Avenue, near Tennessee A&I's campus and just down the street from Jefferson Street Missionary Baptist Church.

From the beginning, the restaurant was an unusual place. It was not the Princes' primary source of income. Thornton had a farm. His brothers worked for the post office or at other restaurants.

"It was just a little substitute to try to get over," Andre Jeffries tells me. "Try to get some more bills paid."

Since they had other jobs, they opened the restaurant after their workday ended, and they stayed open later than any other restaurant in town: midnight during the week and until 4 a.m. on the weekends.

"That's one tradition that I try to keep, being open that late," Jeffries says. "It's grown on me. I'm a night owl now."

Because the restaurant was a late-night place, Jeffries and her siblings didn't grow up eating there.

"My father would bring it home and put it on the stove on Saturday night," she remembers. "When we'd get up on Sunday morning, getting ready to go to Sunday school and then to church, I'd always see that little greasy bag on the stove. Hey, we were tackling it because he wouldn't bring more than one or two pieces, and that would make us mad."

After a few years, the Chicken Shack moved downtown into Hell's Half Acre and close to Ryman Auditorium, home of the Grand Ole Opry in its heyday.

"When he drove to the Opry on Saturday nights, he could smell something really wonderful but couldn't figure out where it was coming from," said Lorrie Morgan, the country singer and daughter of George Morgan, a Country Music Hall of Famer who was a regular on the Opry stage from the late 1940s through the early 1970s, in the cookbook *Around the Opry Table*. One night he tracked the smell to the BBQ Chicken Shack. He loved the food and the hours. Pretty soon, the Opry stars were headed there after every performance.

Segregation complicated the restaurant's new popularity. The Princes needed a place to seat their white celebrity clientele without alienating their Black customers. They constructed an ingenious compromise. They built a separate room for their white guests, but it was at the back of the building. Whites walked through the main dining room and the kitchen to reach it.

"It was quite a nice room. ... We sat out front on these benches," Jeffries says as she rubs an unpadded white booth that looks like the church pews I grew up sitting in. "I don't know how old these benches are, but I remember them when I was a child, and I'm almost 70 years old.

"Black people have never been segregated from the Caucasians," she continues. "Caucasians separated us. ... As far as segregation is concerned, that is a Caucasian problem." She claps her hands together and shakes her head. "Have mercy!"

How Hot Chicken Really Happened

The BBQ Chicken Shack was in the middle of the Hell's Half Acre urban renewal project. The Princes relocated. Their new space was too far from town. They moved again, choosing a block building at 17th and Charlotte, the heart of a Black community north of downtown. It sat "just about where the Krystal's is," Jeffries clarifies for me.

• • •

Desegregation was a two-edged sword for many African Americans. Racism severely limited their lives and opportunities. They had poorer school systems and fewer good job options. They were prohibited from moving into the best neighborhoods. They were denied loans and mortgages. They were expected to treat all whites with deference, even as they were mistreated. Any challenge to this system was punished with violence.

At the same time, segregation gave African Americans even more reason to develop separate businesses and community centers. Black schools, churches, and businesses became sites of resistance where the next generation learned about Black heroes and Black history. The BBQ Chicken Shack might not have lasted if it hadn't first been fostered within Nashville's Black neighborhoods.

In 1954, the United States Supreme Court ruled that public schools had to desegregate. They could have announced a time frame for it; instead, the justices said desegregation had to happen with "all deliberate speed."

Many communities used that wishy-washy language to push desegregation off for years or even decades. In Nashville, a young Black man named Robert Kelley walked past all-white East High School, over the Cumberland River, and through downtown to all-Black Pearl High School. His family filed a lawsuit in 1956, arguing the city should open East High to him. The Rev. Henry Maxwell filed a similar suit because his kids were bused from south of Nashville to the other side of the city, a 45-minute ride. To settle these cases, the courts announced that beginning in the fall of 1957, Nashville public schools would desegregate one grade per year in what became known as the "Nashville Plan."

The school board gerrymandered the school districts so that only about 100 Black first-graders were eligible. Nine enrolled. White "segregation academies" and white flight further undermined efforts to integrate the schools. Seven years later, fewer than 800 Black students were in formerly all-white schools. Black teachers and principals faced demotions or layoffs as the city consolidated the system.

The next stage in Nashville's Civil Rights struggle happened in February 1960. A few weeks earlier, students in Greensboro, North Carolina, had sat at a downtown lunch counter and demanded service. Inspired by their example, students from Fisk, the American Baptist Theological Seminary, and Tennessee A&I organized similar protests in Nashville. Black shoppers boycotted downtown businesses.

Local Civil Rights attorney Z. Alexander Looby headed up the team of lawyers defending the arrested students. His house was bombed in mid-April, though no one was injured. In response, several thousand protesters marched from Fisk to downtown. The mayor met them on the courthouse steps. Diane Nash, a Fisk University student who would help found the Student Nonviolent Coordinating Committee, demanded, "Mayor West, do you think it is wrong to discriminate against a person solely on the basis of their race or color?"

"Yes," he replied. He added, "That's up to the store managers, of course." The Tennessean newspaper left out his addendum in its coverage. The "Whites Only" signs came down.

Compared with many other cities, desegregation was relatively peaceful in Nashville, but this may have been because residential segregation and urban renewal had already separated the races from each other. Official, or de jure, segregation may not have seemed as necessary when interstates and building codes had ensured Black and white people would not live, study, eat, or work together.

...

When Thornton Prince died, his brother Will took over. His wife, Maude, ran the business when he passed.

How Hot Chicken Really Happened

Prince's first real competition happened because the family had a falling out with their cook, Bolton Polk. In the late 1970s, he left to open his own place, which he named Columbo's Chicken Shack. He served his own version of hot chicken. He added his wife's chess pies and potato salad. This launched a new debate among generations of hot-chicken devotees. Which restaurant had the better food? Which had the hotter chicken?

The first Columbo's was near Prince's in the same Black neighborhood off Charlotte Avenue. Polk eventually moved his business just across the river from downtown Nashville. That was where former Nashville Mayor Bill Purcell first encountered the dish.

"As soon as I had this hot chicken, I knew it was unlike anything I'd ever had," he says to me. "It was one of the best things I ever had."

By 1980, it was time for a new generation of Princes to take over the restaurant. Andre Prince Jeffries was a recently divorced mother of two. Her parents had been helping her raise her daughters, but her mother was dying of cancer. Her parents worried that Jeffries' job in city government would not be enough for her to care for her children on her own. Great Aunt Maude decided Jeffries should take over Prince's. Her mother told her to accept the offer.

Jeffries renamed the restaurant.

"I took out the 'BBQ' because this was never barbecue," she says. She also decided it was time to relocate. "When I took over, it seemed like every weekend we were getting robbed."

In 1989, Prince's Chicken Shack moved to its current location in East Nashville. It's in a strip mall that gentrification hasn't touched yet. On one side of it is Entrepreneur Clothing. On the day I visited, a deep bass rhythm pumped through the open door onto the street. Next to that is a customer-less Chinese restaurant and a nail salon. The parking lot is potholed, and when Prince's is busy, guests bump their way to an unpaved lot next door. The area is best known for prostitution and drug deals.

"You've got to earn the respect of the guys around here," Jeffries says, shrugging.

She talks about the memorabilia that used to be in the restaurant. Many pieces have been stolen, including photographs of her family, plaques and awards given to the restaurant, and a set of autographed plates from the celebrities who frequent Prince's. Jeffries had hoped to move the restaurant again, somewhere nicer and newer.

"We were supposed to move to 10th and Jefferson, but a lot of politics got involved," she says a little sadly. A new baseball stadium was planned for the area. "If I had it my way, we'd have a shack-type building, but upscale on the interior, with a big old potbellied stove in the center of it," she tells me.

"My mother always said, if you have what people want, they will make their way to your door," Jeffries says, patting the table in front of her. "You can tell this is certainly not an upscale bird place. This is my little hole in the wall, but people have made their way here from all over the world. All over the world."

Columbo's was also trapped by the improvements happening around Nashville. In the late 1990s, Nashville won an NFL football team. The Houston Oilers became the Tennessee Titans. Columbo's sat right where the new football stadium was supposed to go. Bolton Polk closed his restaurant, and he died before he could reopen it.

. . .

The public projects accelerated in the late '60s. I-40 was built in 1968, and it cut through the heart of Jefferson Street. Because the city had zoned the region as commercial and industrial, Black homeowners had few protections or ways to resist.

"We thought that we were saving the city," former Mayor Purcell explains to me. "But that wasn't going to save the city. There is no city that has been successful merely as a collection of suburban places."

"When the interstate was built, there were no exit ramps," Reavis Mitchell, a historian at Fisk University, told The Tennessean. Fifty percent of Jefferson Street's residents moved. One hundred twenty businesses closed. "All those major vital things within the inner city were blocked off. North Nashvillians were suspicious as to why they were being isolated and wondered if the interstate project was in response to the marches and sit-ins."

How Hot Chicken Really Happened

Demolition continued into the 1970s. Developers pitched ideas to tear down more of the historic neighborhoods, replacing them with public housing, industrial warehouses, and strip malls.

"I was still not sure about Nashville, and I'm not sure Nashville was sure about Nashville," Purcell says. "It was not clear what we wanted to do. ... There was a history and a practice of believing that if you did not have it here, we could go to Chicago or New York or Atlanta to buy it or see it or do it."

This was the Nashville of my childhood. Downtown was a handful of honky-tonks catering to tourists who wandered about, dazed by rhinestones, whiskey, and country cover bands. Then came the lawyers' offices, banks, and insurance corporations, which emptied as soon as business hours ended. Ringing all of that were strip clubs, car lots, and interstates.

The first big preservation fight occurred when a plan emerged to tear down historic Second Avenue and replace it with a skyscraper. The economy was not strong enough to support the development, and the preservationists won. People started debating whether progress meant erasing or celebrating the past.

"It's all well and good to want to be the Athens of the South and to be a center of learning, but it's the city's obligation to ensure that it's so," Purcell says. "A city has to be safe — the whole city, not just parts of it or neighborhoods in it.

"By and large — this is the late '80s now — downtown Nashville was suffering from Nashville's own decision that the future of downtowns was not certain and certainly not required," he summarizes.

We're talking in the conference room of his law firm, which overlooks downtown.

"We had made periodic efforts to salvage what we had and other competitive efforts to knock down and replace what we had."

Purcell beckons me to the window. He points out the places where there was once a garbage incinerator, derelict buildings, and empty lots, right in the heart of the city.

"Only about 900 people lived downtown," he says.

Before Bolton Polk passed, he taught his nephew Bolton Matthews to make his chicken. Polk never wrote down his secrets, and his nephew has supposedly followed his example.

"He's the only one that fixes the recipe," his wife and business partner, Dollye Ingram-Matthews, told an interviewer with the Southern Foodways Alliance. "I can just tell you parts of it are probably made from pepper bomb spray."

Ingram-Matthews made hot fish. In 1997, they combined their secret spicy recipes and opened Bolton's Spicy Chicken and Fish in a small, low concrete block building on Main Street. It's a block from East Park, where the annual Hot Chicken Festival happens.

"I think it's popular in Nashville because there are a lot of people living today that had ancestors stuck on pepper," Ingram-Matthews says. "Maybe they had hypertension and couldn't use salt, so they used pepper instead. ... A couple of generations like that, and you know you just got the clientele for hot and spicy chicken."

Then came perhaps the oddest venture in the hot-chicken story, hotchickens.com. It was started in 2001, when the internet felt new. It wasn't a hot-chicken delivery service; it was a restaurant. And yes, ".com" was part of the name and even on the building's sign.

The restaurant was founded by country music stars Lorrie Morgan and Sammy Kershaw. Morgan learned to love hot chicken by eating it with her father, George. Food writer John T. Edge described hotchickens.com as "a gingham-trimmed fast-food outlet that ... reflects the peculiar Nashville geek-in-a-cowboy-hat zeitgeist." Debts from the restaurant eventually drove Kershaw into Chapter 13 bankruptcy. Their marriage ended in mutual restraining orders. Morgan tried again, underwriting Lorrie Morgan's Hot Chicken Cafe inside a gambling resort in Alabama. That effort attracted a governor's office investigation.

How Hot Chicken Really Happened

...

When I came back home in 2013, Nashville was more than 10 percent larger than it had been when I'd left less than a decade earlier, and it's surrounded by communities that have grown by as much as 44 percent.

The tourist strip is busier and glitzier than ever. High-rise condominiums have popped up amid the business buildings. A new symphony center hosts concerts, speakers, and community events. The Nashville Convention Center and the Music City Center draw thousands of people to town every weekend. The Bridgestone Arena seats close to 20,000 people and is home to the Nashville Predators hockey team, which has shocked its hometown and become a competitive club. Unfortunately, the same can't be said of the Titans these last few seasons.

Even more surprising to me, my friends live in East Nashville, a region of the city I remember as having a few antiquated businesses, many abandoned houses, and large public housing complexes.

East Nashville's development was partially Mother Nature's fault. Tornadoes struck Nashville in April 1998. One of them swept through downtown. Another one devastated the neighborhoods of East Nashville. Three hundred homes were destroyed. A Regional/Urban Design Assistance Team formed to make suggestions for how to redevelop and rehab that quadrant of the city. It recommended creating public/private partnerships, building infrastructure tying the neighborhoods to downtown, creating design guidelines, and encouraging investment.

"The two greatest treasures East Nashville offers are its diversity and authenticity," the redevelopment team wrote in its final report. "Throughout the nation, new 'neo-traditional' communities are being planned and developed in the hope of replicating the feeling that this community offers."

Today, East Nashville's crime rates are falling. New magnet and charter schools are commandeering public school buildings. Some historic homes are being carefully restored. Others are being razed and replaced with new, high-priced developments. Restaurants and coffee shops and boutique clothing stores form the heart of new, trendy business districts catering to a hipster crowd.

The improvements are billed as helping the entire community, but they are coming at a cost to the people who have lived there for generations. Many of them are getting priced out of their homes. Some of the Black residents whose ancestors first settled East Nashville are being forced into the suburbs where white people used to live. Others are ending up in overcrowded, low-income pockets of the city.

In this era of change and loss, residents and visitors alike are anxious to celebrate what is historic about the town. Hot chicken has become shorthand for the area's various traditions, a de rigueur part of being from here.

...

Hot chicken has left the neighborhood. But new restaurants specializing in the dish are popping up across town.

"They're like pizza places — all over," Andre Jeffries tells me. "Everywhere you look, there's a new one opening."

The craze for hot chicken started in 2007 with the first Hot Chicken Festival. Mayor Purcell was stepping down after two terms. He still went to Prince's regularly, referring to it as his second office. He urged his friends and colleagues to try hot chicken, though when he brought new customers to the restaurant, he would pull Jeffries aside. "He'll tell us to give it to them hot, don't give it to them mild. You don't know if he's their worst enemy or what!"

Purcell also set Prince's up with free advertising, making them the face of the new hot-chicken trend. "Why?" Jeffries asks. "Because he knows I have to pay my bills."

Purcell was looking for a way to celebrate the city, which was approaching its bicentennial.

"Hot chicken is truly our indigenous food," he explains. "It seemed a way to convene the city around something special to us worth celebrating, but also allowed everybody to participate."

He founded a festival committee, and they decided to put the festivities in East Park, which is near the entrance to East Nashville. This meant it was close to downtown but wouldn't be swallowed up by other events happening in the city.

"And I was the mayor," Purcell adds, with a little smirk. "East Park was close to where I live."

The festival quickly grew in popularity, introducing people to the dish. Hot-chicken cooking contests became part of events around the city. New hot-chicken restaurants were founded, most of them run by young white men in popular gentrifying districts.

Isaac Beard was the first of the new generation of hot-chicken restaurateurs. He opened Pepperfire Chicken in 2010.

"I believe I was born to do something with hot chicken," he told food columnists Jane and Michael Stern. "I am a hot-chicken evangelist."

The most successful of these new ventures is Hattie B's, owned by Nick Bishop Jr. and his dad Nick Sr. The first Hattie B's opened in 2012 in Midtown, right in the heart of a new, hip area.

"Hattie B's is almost in both Music Row (the area where country recording studios are located) and the campuses of both Vanderbilt and Belmont universities, making it a much nicer area than Prince's seedy strip mall," food blogger Dan Angell wrote of his visit there. "The idea of being in a more protected area was appealing to us, and since you can't go through Nashville without having experienced hot chicken, Hattie B's was the choice." Soon the Midtown location had a loyal following. They opened a new spot on the edge of a rapidly gentrifying neighborhood once known as the Nations, which developers are trying to force us to rename Historic West Town.

I asked Andre Prince Jeffries if she's worried about losing her customers.

"My customers, they try all these different places that are popping up," she says. "They come right back here. Might take 'em a little while, but they come back to the real thing. They tell me all the time, 'You still got it.' 'Course, that makes me feel good. Have mercy." Her only question, she insists, is which family member will take the restaurant next.

• • •

Food Stories

Yes, I have now eaten hot chicken. I decided to start with the original, so I got a leg of Prince's the day I interviewed Andre Jeffries.

It was getting late, so I took my food to go like most of the other customers. By the time I placed my order, someone else was sitting in my booth. I stood along the wall, waiting for my food and balancing my recorder bag on my feet. A B-grade horror flick played on a flat-screen TV suspended on the wall across from me. I watched a plastic dinosaur chase stranded castaways down a beach.

Jeffries saw me standing there. I heard an argument start up in the back. She told them to rush my order. "But she just got here!" a woman said. "No, she's been here for over an hour," Jeffries replied. A young man came out with my sack of food a few minutes later.

There are people who order their chicken so hot that Jeffries sends them home to eat it in private. There are people who go with chicken one notch down. They sometimes ask for wet paper towels to lay over their eyes. Food reviewers warn hot-chicken newbies to wash their hands before using the restroom or touching any other sensitive body parts.

If you want to read the graphic details of what absurdly hot poultry can do to a person, what happens to your body when you eat food so spicy that you shouldn't be seen in public, well, I'm a wimp. I grew up in a household where adding garlic made a dish spicy. I ordered my chicken mild. I added a side of coleslaw, figuring I could use it to cut the heat.

It was very good fried chicken, moist and crispy at the same time, but it was warmer than I like my food. While I'd love to talk more with Andre Jeffries, I'm not sure I'll ever be the hot-chicken devotee so many Nashvillians have become.

• • •

One day in graduate school, I went to a meeting at the Center for the Study of the American South. The speaker had spent the past year photographing the U.S./Mexico border, recording the terror and danger faced by undocumented workers who fled their homelands for the opportunities the United States represented.

How Hot Chicken Really Happened

It was the spring of 2008, and North Carolina was in the throes of an immigration debate and newly awakened by the pending nomination of Barack Obama. Issues of race and equality were on our minds, but we were also historians. We could all riff on the discouraging realities of modern America, like the fact that public schools were more segregated than they had been at any time since 1965, and income inequality was growing. Our conversation grew increasingly cynical.

Then William Ferris chimed in. Ferris is a noted folklorist whose wife is a prominent foodways scholar. He is one of those public intellectuals whose list of achievements should make him terrifying, but he has a deeply kind streak that makes him a student favorite.

Ferris said that the popularity of Mexican culture encouraged him. He pointed out that Mexican restaurants are growing ubiquitous, and in each establishment, customers met people affected by the immigration debate. Maybe restaurant-goers would get to know their servers, fall in love with their food, dance to the music they heard playing over the sound systems, and thus learn to empathize with immigrants.

At the time, I vehemently disagreed with him. It was the only time I dared to do so. I used the African American experience as my example. "[White people] have eaten fried chicken for centuries now," I remember saying. "Segregation still exists."

But these days, I find myself hoping he was right. Is the hot-chicken craze helping Nashville create a new history? Or is hot chicken being stripped of its cultural meaning as it's moved out of the neighborhood? Can a simple chicken dish be trusted with healing the divisions that have taken generations to form? Or will it become nothing more than Nashville's newest hipster trend?

...

The ninth annual Music City Hot Chicken Festival happened on July 4, 2015. It was an unusual Independence Day for Tennessee, with a high of only 82 and an almost guaranteed chance of rain. Diehard hot-chicken lovers still braved the weather, ducking under golf umbrellas or into the beer tents when rain started falling.

Food Stories

I showed up for the mid-morning parade that kicks off the day's official events. I was supposed to be meeting a guy for a first date. I was counting on Andre Prince Jeffries' theory that this chicken would give us something to talk about. But as I got out of my car, I got a text from him saying he would be late. Then I realized I had forgotten my umbrella. It seemed an inauspicious beginning to both the relationship and the day.

I found a seat on a low concrete wall along the parade route and started making notes about the folks around me. Though the crowd's racial demographics didn't match East Nashville's neighborhoods or even the numbers in Nashville generally, it was the closest thing to a mixed gathering I've seen in Nashville (outside of a sporting event).

But very few individuals mingled with anyone other than the people they'd come with. I wondered if that was partly because the weather kept numbers low. Groups could sit comfortably distanced from everyone else.

The parade was what Momma would call "homegrown." Two police officers on motorcycles led it, followed by a small brass band. The rest of the parade was made up of: four antique fire trucks that judiciously chirped their sirens, trying to show off for the crowd without scaring the babies; a series of municipal candidates and their supporters, who hurled candy at bystanders; a couple of local businesses, with people tossing beads out the door of their company vehicles; one home-converted topless wood-paneled station wagon labeled #TheDoose that carried a handful of very cool-looking 20-somethings; and three tatted-up members of the Nashville Rollergirls, who whipped in and out of the other groups.

After the parade, I walked back through East Park to the main stage, where the Shelby Bottom String Band was entertaining the crowd, filling time until Bill Purcell stepped onstage to say a few words.

"We're going to play Bill's favorite," the lead singer told the crowd. They started in on a Merle Haggard classic:

Eating rainbow stew with a silver spoon
Underneath that sky of blue

We'll all be drinking that free bubble-up
And eating that rainbow stew

Purcell wasn't ready when they finished the song, so they soldiered on through another couple of numbers.

My guy showed up about the same time Purcell did. We wandered around, looking into our various options. Lines had started forming in front of each of the hot-chicken tents. He told me he lived down the road from the new Hattie B's in the Nations and ate there all the time. I told him the story of Prince's founding.

The line for Prince's stretched the length of the green, past the lines for Hattie B's and Pepperfire and Bolton's. At the end of the green, the queue took a sharp turn, wrapping around Prince's competitors.

A curious thing was happening. Folks at the back of the Prince's line stayed in their groups, chatting with the people they'd come with. But by the time they reached the bend in the queue, they were running out of things to say to their friends. They stood, arms crossed and hips cocked, staring into space.

But after a few more minutes of waiting, they started talking to the others in line around them, telling strangers the story of when they first tried hot chicken and trading insider knowledge of what to order from the other hot-chicken joints. ◊

—

Rachel Louise Martin, Ph.D., is a historian and writer whose work has appeared in outlets like The Atlantic *and* Oxford American. *The author of* Hot, Hot Chicken: A Nashville Story *and* A Most Tolerant Little Town – *the forgotten story of the first school to attempt court-mandated desegregation in the wake of Brown v. Board of Education* – *Martin is especially interested in the politics of memory and in the power of stories to illuminate why injustice persists in America today. She lives in Nashville.*

IMMIGRANT SPAGHETTI

—

by Farhan Mustafa

Illustration by Kristen Solecki
This story was originally published March 28, 2023

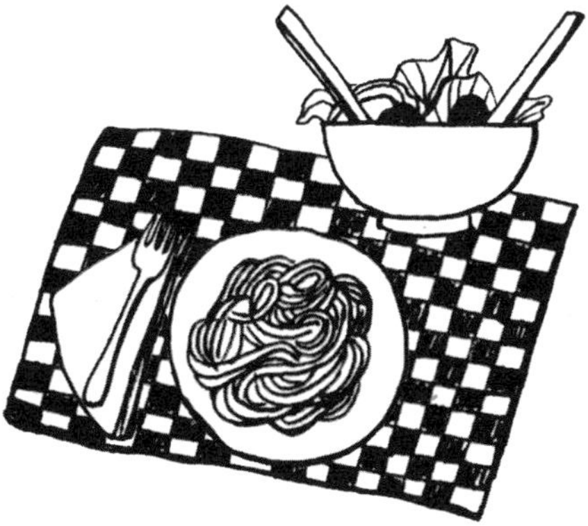

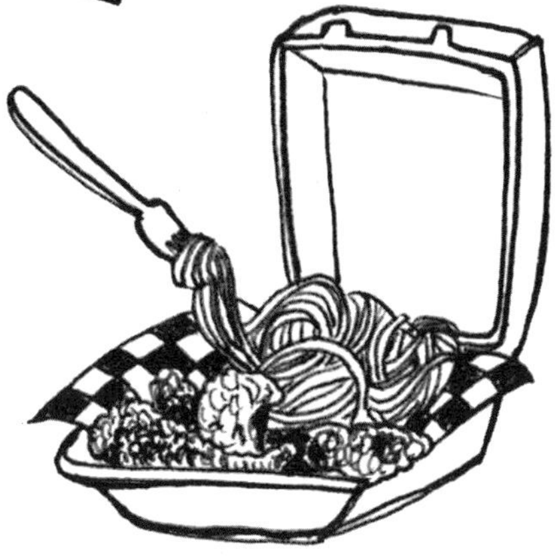

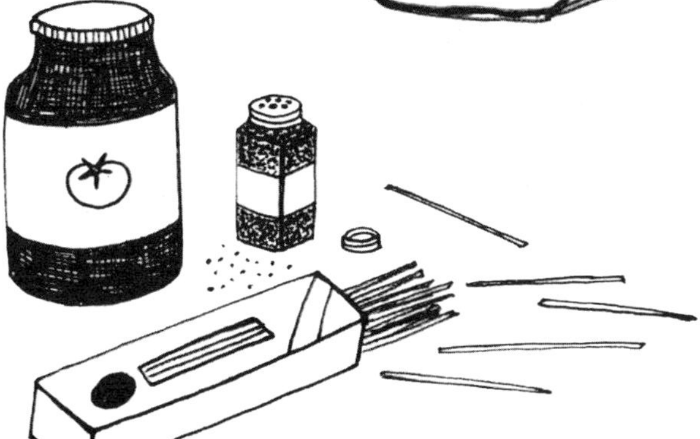

Immigrant Spaghetti

I'll never forget the first time I had a taste of Ethiopian spaghetti. It was a balmy, latespring night in Chapel Hill, North Carolina, in 2011, at the now-closed restaurant Queen of Sheba. Nearing closing time, the crew started dishing out its nightly staff meal. Owner Frieshgenet Dabei sat down at my table with a plate of spaghetti, and I caught a scent of tomato and berbere. I may have actually floated out of my seat like a cartoon character on a carpet of aromatics into the seat across from her. Without my having to ask, she explained that spaghetti is as popular as injera in Ethiopia, and sometimes they'll even eat spaghetti on top of injera. She taught me how spaghetti was introduced by the Italians, who have a long history of violence in Ethiopia, during and following Italy's invasion and occupation of East Africa in the late 1930s and early '40s. That influence now sat on Dabei's plate, noodles swathed in a homemade tomato sauce with onions, garlic, berbere spice, ground beef, and green peppers. She'd incorporated the last ingredient when she moved to the South.

For the rest of the evening, my life in immigrant spaghettis flashed before my eyes. We loved having "Italian night" growing up. On those evenings, my mom, or Ammi as we called her, jacked up storebought Ragu or Prego with Indian spices like coriander, cumin, and a little turmeric, along with fried onions and garlic, green peppers, ground beef and denture-friendly soft noodles. We'd triumphantly carry a massive foil-wrapped loaf of garlic bread from Walmart or Kroger back home and pop it into the oven. Sometimes we'd also toss together an American salad with lettuce and baby carrots and bleu cheese dressing. I say American because otherwise our "salads" were either slices of cucumber,

radishes, and carrots served separately like crudites; or just onions, tomatoes, cilantro, and a few sliced green chiles mixed together. While the garlic bread and bleu cheese-dressed salad sides never changed, my mom made the spaghetti different every time.

At Friday-night mosque potlucks in my hometown of Greenville, North Carolina, there would be even more versions of spaghetti. Our Egyptian friends, who lived down the street, made a dry version with vermicelli noodles redolent with more cinnamon, cardamom, and allspice, as well as finer ground beef, and the noodles way more al dente. Our Palestinian pals made a simple version with tomato puree, tomato paste, sweated onion and garlic, black pepper, parsley, and, of course, ground beef. I'd barely make it back to the tarps spread out on the floor with my sectioned Styrofoam plate (this was 1989) heaving with these international takes, along with rice dishes, curries, and salads, all crashing into each other and obliterating the plate's false borders, the bright red and orange oils soaking through it onto my white kurta. Later, I'd see my Filipino friend slice hot dogs into noodles cloaked in a ketchupbased sauce with a little Maggi Seasoning. Our Nigerian friends' jollof spaghetti might have been the most intense — woody and spicy. And the Southern spaghetti bake made by my best friend's mom broke down to about 30 percent noodle and 70 percent ricotta cheese and sausage.

I've been in Seattle for the last two years, where my little brother Nanu, his wife, and my two amazing nieces live. As we talk about the community experiences my nieces are having, we find ourselves reminiscing about how much we loved those mosque potlucks. For a small college town in the rural South, it felt like a weekly international food festival. Modern community get-togethers these days tend to be catered by local businesses, food trucks, or pop-ups, which makes me feel like they're missing out on tasting as many home kitchens as possible. Inevitably, we always bring it back to the different spaghettis we ate, which we now fondly call "immigrant spaghetti" — one name with infinite expressions. For me, immigrant

Immigrant Spaghetti

spaghetti is a celebration of what makes all American tastes so personal and unique, immigrants or not.

Allow me a Bubba Gump-ish list of spaghettis that I have personally eaten in the U.S.: Jamaican jerk, rasta pasta; Dominican spaghetti called empaguetadas; Nigerian jollof spaghetti; Ethiopian, Eritrean, Somali suugo suqaar; Indian, Pakistani, Bangladeshi, and Nepali spaghetti with tomato sauce, and Chinese-influenced versions based on ketchup; Filipino spaghetti with hot dogs; Egyptian spaghetti with shorter-than-normal vermicelli; Lebanese hashweh spaghetti; Southern AF baked spaghetti; Black spaghetti with lots of ground beef; meatless spaghetti with fried catfish; Korean spaghetti with a healthy kick of garlic and gochujang and cheese; yakamein (it often uses spaghetti, so I'm counting it); Creole spaghetti; Greek spaghetti; Memphis barbecue spaghetti; and Mexican spaghetti as interpreted by Southern white moms in community cookbooks. And let's be clear: I'm not even talking about macaroni and cheese, because that's a whole other dissertation.

No two families, no matter where they're from, make spaghetti that tastes the same — or any dish, for that matter. As much as my mom would mess around with Ragu, my aunt made a textbook-perfect Betty Crocker-adjacent baked rotini or macaroni with jarred sauce, ground beef, and Italian seasoning without ever having read a recipe in her life. In a time when we're all having more nuanced (and necessary) conversations about cultural appropriation, spaghetti seems a safe canvas for everyone to paint on. Our approaches are unabashed and, I'd argue, free from shame or guilt. I'm not saying that we're not offending anyone, just that we don't feel the need to have a Twitter conversation about whether any group of people can have their own version of spaghetti. Maybe it's like rock 'n'roll? We all know where it really came from, but its impact has unspooled across the globe like so many spaghetti noodles twisting into exponentially different styles seasoned by those who play it. And remixed with even more influences and memories as time marches on. Somehow it belongs to everyone. Spaghetti does, too — arguably the most accessible food in the world, and not just because of its physical availability.

In his book *Soul Food*, the food historian Adrian Miller had this to say about that special case, mac and cheese, the first true breakout pasta hit in the United States, typically made with elbow macaroni (although also made with spaghetti in parts of New Orleans and Mississippi): "For soul food cooks, mac 'n' cheese had multiple identities as rich people's food, a special occasion food, a convenient comfort food, a meal-stretcher, and a poverty food."

The same holds true for regular spaghetti with marinara sauce — from authentic Italian versions to the commercially bastardized American ones. It allowed us to express our own evolving American identities, whether families immigrating to the South in the 1980s or Italian, Black, and Creole families in the early 1900s.

• • •

To really understand how spaghetti grew the way it did across the South, I decided to learn where this proverbial melting pot started boiling. I spoke to Liz Williams, author of *Nana's Creole Italian Table: Recipes and Stories From Sicilian New Orleans*, a book packed with historical nuance and family stories of immigration and identity, particularly how southern Italy and the American South share common cultural threads.

New Orleans became home for the majority of Italians immigrating to the South; roughly 64,000 settled here in the late 19th and early 20th centuries. Most came from southern Italy and Sicily. After Giuseppe Garibaldi unified Italy in the early 1860s, southern Italy became an agrarian center meant to feed the factories in the northern part of the country. Southern Italians flocked to the cities and took their dried pastas with them. In his book *Dinner in Rome: A History of the World in One Meal*, Andreas Viestad posits that this migration of pasta across Italy was the real spur to cultural unification, as Italians were finally eating something in common.

After reunification, southern Italy was giving up more food to the effort and didn't have much left over. The region was hungry for sustenance and for opportunity. America was an option for those with relatives or

Immigrant Spaghetti

other connections. New Orleans was a mecca for Italian immigrants, but wherever they settled, New Orleans or New York City, they usually lived side-by-side with the lowest socioeconomic classes that were already there (or recently arrived). In New York City, that meant living near Irish and Chinese immigrants; in the South, that mostly meant living with Black people. After the Civil War, the Louisiana Bureau of Immigration recruited laborers from Sicily to replace formerly enslaved people. Hundreds of Italian men lived in abandoned cabins where enslaved people once lived. Sicilians and Black people worked in sugar cane, cotton, and strawberry fields together.

In New Orleans' storied Tremé neighborhood, they lived, played, and ate together. They shared plates of food and incorporated recipes. Spaghetti was being passed around, replicated and personalized as more tasted it. By the 1930s, in both New Orleans and Harlem, Black patrons became big customers of spaghetti houses. Recipes for spaghetti appeared in Black community cookbooks, and Italian food took off in Black neighborhoods across the country.

Perhaps the most important twist in the tale of immigrant spaghetti is the eventual commodification and mass availability of spaghetti and tomato sauce. In Massimo Montanari's A Short History of Spaghetti With Tomato Sauce, he documents how southern Italy's warmer climate meant that farmers there could grow better varieties of wheat purpose-built for dried pasta. Once it became shelf-stable, dried pasta quickly became ubiquitous. And thanks to advances in safe canning, tomato sauce became widely available, too. Nutritionally, it met many needs cheaply. Those tastes eventually got transferred here, and with economical and plentiful spaghetti, Black folks decided to use spaghetti noodles for things like mac and cheese and, much later, yakamein. Williams makes a clear distinction, however, between Italian tomato sauce and what became distinctly, and still is, a New Orleans thing: Creole red gravy, which begins with a roux plus the holy trinity of celery, green bell pepper, and onion.

In my TV-addled mind, a strong memory of Dom DeLuise lingers. Specifically, his cooking demonstrations along with "Italian night"-themed advertising wars when Prego and Ragu decided to chunk up their sauces in the 1990s. These are the sauces I learned to doctor up with coriander, cumin, turmeric, a lot more garlic, and ground beef that I would then pile on top of spaghetti alongside garlic bread. I was curious how Williams, an Italian-American, felt about the concept of "Italian night." After a thoughtful pause, she said she guessed it felt nice that people cared, but it never felt like cultural appropriation. It meant some sense of acceptance. Personally, she didn't experience the awareness of being an "other" but knows that her mother and grandmother did. Her mother prepared her to avoid that discrimination, as a protective instinct. Ultimately, she said, if your food gets accepted into the canon of American food, then you're a part of it.

I asked Miller the Italian-night question, too. He said his mother often made spaghetti and marinara with beef, and even calzones. And while they were her recipes, it always felt intentionally like they were having Italian food. It didn't feel like soul food in the way macaroni and cheese did. Meanwhile, one of my oldest friends, Mandrill Taylor, said the spaghetti they ate was definitely considered a family recipe, and to him that made it taste like soul food, not something inspired by commercials. He grew up in Fayetteville, North Carolina, but his parents and extended family are from Taylor County, Kentucky. Their fascinating family spaghetti recipe evolution started off as a salad of chopped tomatoes and onions with rice. They eventually replaced the rice with spaghetti. The next stop was just replacing the chopped tomatoes and onions with sauce. His aunt makes a punchy, soupy one with ground beef, but they refer to it as "more like chili with spaghetti." Not for nothing is Taylor County roughly 170 miles from Cincinnati, home of distinct chili parlors where you can get a Greek-influenced sauce served over pasta, and, if you want, onions, cheese, and beans (what's colloquially called a "5-way").

...

After the Southern Foodways Symposium in Oxford, Mississippi, this past October, chef Ricky Moore's fried catfish with gravy and onions alongside jollof spaghetti (more on that dish later) loomed heavily in my mind. It was

Immigrant Spaghetti

the first I'd heard of the combo, which meant, sadly, that I was decades late to the party. Catfish and spaghetti is indeed a thing, as spaghetti is an expected side dish at many Southern barbecues, church suppers, and family potlucks.

I was eager to learn more about catfish and spaghetti but especially that jollof spaghetti. Moore, the 2022 James Beard Best Chef: Southeast, said he first found catfish and spaghetti (also served with corn) while serving as executive chef and instructor at the South Shore Cultural Center in Chicago. His students lived in the surrounding neighborhood, and being new to the area, he'd venture out with them to see what they were eating and cooking. He learned that the catfish spaghetti duo came up with families on the Mississippi River during the Great Migration. He tasted both meat and meatless versions of spaghetti, the common connection being that the pasta was always overcooked and soft. "It occurred to me that people treated spaghetti like rice, and once I thought of that, it was easy to start trying new things with it but also understand why the dish itself existed." He and his students started talking more about the regionality of dishes like spaghetti, and they even practiced a culinary exploration, starting with a "mother" spaghetti recipe and moving into versions like jambalaya spaghetti.

Around the same time, I started my own pasta explorations. I was in my mid-20s, living in Washington, D.C., and going through a rite of passage for many children of immigrants: cooking what your mom did, but with your own variations. I was living with two Pakistani roommates, one of whom would desi-fy any dish, often unnecessarily. I was no purist by any means, just unapologetically more American in my tastes. I insisted we go to a Golden Corral buffet, an hour's drive away, on my birthday every year even though I was the only one who actually enjoyed the food. For my international crew, I began to make spaghetti and meatballs, with the latter more resembling kofta, South Asian meatballs deftly spiced with garlic, ginger, fried onions, hints of clove and black cardamom, and, my own addition, dried mint. I also made chicken tikka masala pasta, already a fairly creamy tomato-based dish, and the best bolognese I've ever had in my life after tweaking a recipe from a 2002 issue of Gourmet and simmering it for over eight hours.

Moore's wife is from the D.C. area, and they lived there after he graduated from the Culinary Institute of America. He worked at

Food Stories

legendary spots like Galileo before opening up Equinox with chefs Todd and Ellen Gray. Living in D.C. myself at the time, I'd unwittingly been tasting his creations all over town. Especially at Le Tarbouche, a Lebanese restaurant where he cooked for a few years and that I'd often visit with friends. There he came up with an all-spaghetti version of a rice dish called hashweh, traditionally a one-pot rice dish made with ground or minced beef (or lamb), toasted nuts, and, very often, broken vermicelli. It can be eaten as a side dish, main dish, or even stuffed into chicken, which is how my Palestinian friend's mom did it. Each bite of Moore's version was layered in flavor thanks to toasted garlic, cinnamon, and allspice, and I could immediately feel the weight of that foam potluck plate in my hand. Looking back, it feels like that scene from

"Interstellar" when (spoiler alert) we find out Anne Hathaway was actually touching Matthew McConaughey's hand from the past as they neared the black hole in the present. It does make sense that if anything can both time-travel and defy circular logic, it's the humble noodle.

As of 2019, the D.C. metro was home to the third-largest African immigrant population in the U.S.; for some time it has been home to one of the largest Ethiopian populations in this country. It's there that Moore explored both East and West African tastes from restaurants and new friends' homes. By the time he presented his jollof spaghetti to the SFA crowd in Oxford in 2022, it had been decades in the making. He wanted to honor that spaghetti tradition, especially down in Mississippi, where it evolved and spread north. He also wanted to bring forward his favorite flavors from the African diaspora. But his most personal inspiration for the dish was something quintessentially American: good ol' Rice-A-Roni. "I remember eating my mom's doctored-up Rice-A-Roni as a kid," Moore said, "but that rice itself ... how the tomato was browned to a deep tomato flavor and how that speckled reddish-brown color coated every grain — I really loved that nutty flavor profile, and it was on my mind." He said that people who love to cook also often love to latch onto things to make their own. It's easy to dress pasta in curiosity and homage.

Immigrant Spaghetti

Doctoring up Rice-A-Roni, macaroni and cheese, instant ramen, and Lipton pasta mixes binds home cooks of all backgrounds. By the age of 5, I was making instant ramen on the stovetop and hacking broccoli and cheese that I'd seen in the school cafeteria. Microwaving frozen crowns and melting orange American slices on top was a "recipe" I learned out of necessity, as my aunt, who had just come from India, was babysitting me at the time and I knew she wouldn't know how to feed a growing American kid like me. At 14, I learned about the existence of pesto after I found an old Knorr "pesto seasoning" packet in the back of our pantry. On instinct, I added it to some Ragu tomato sauce, and my world changed. It was one of those food memories that split the world into what you knew and what was possible.

The restaurant in Chapel Hill where I first tasted Ethiopian spaghetti is long gone, but I did reconnect with the flavors of that first bite with the Desta family in Atlanta. They own Kategna, located off Buford Highway, the city's international hub, where restaurants reflecting every corner of the globe line the seven lanes of traffic. When I spoke with Obinne "Obi" Baker, an employee there, about wanting to learn more about Ethiopian spaghetti and immigrant spaghettis in general, she lit up and offered her own story.

As did Kategna owner Sinidu Desta, endearingly known as Nani, who said it was a no-brainer to put spaghetti on the menu here because of its popularity back home. The chefs at Kategna are all women, born and raised in Ethiopia. Each has her own version of the dish and couldn't imagine a home table, let alone a restaurant one, without it. Baker describes Kategna's spaghetti as tasting like American meat sauce with standout spices like cardamom and cloves. They add sauteed vegetables like cabbage and carrots. They also have a few protein options, including berbere-spiced salmon, chicken, or tibs, which is Ethiopian chopped lean beef. Naturally, spaghetti stands out as familiar to those customers who may be hesitant to jump head-first into the country's complex cuisine — though while we chatted, an Ethiopian customer came in and ordered the spaghetti with chicken.

Baker's mother, a Nigerian immigrant to the U.S., would make jollof spaghetti for her when she was young, but it was too spicy for Baker's taste.

She fondly remembered the first time she had non-Nigerian spaghetti, in the cafeteria in elementary school. It was just tomato sauce and soft noodles and cheese. "It had, like, no spices and was so bland, so great. I loved the simplicity compared to what I ate." I asked Baker for her mom's jollof spaghetti recipe and she said it's different every single time — you make it with what you have. That's how Africans do it. She did offer up her own recipe, though. She, like past generations of immigrants, didn't have any measurements, just instinct. "I know how to gauge it with my eyes because I saw my mom making it and remember how it looks. So I don't measure anything, I just know how it should look and smell at each step."

Baker is continuing the fine tradition of "dump cooking." It's a phrase my little brother and I toss around nearly every time we talk about cooking. Dump cooking is without measurements, using just instincts and memories as your guide. We'll use it to describe when it's clear there's no actual recipe for what we made. For example: "How'd you make the spaghetti this time?" "Oh, just dump, but basically more fennel and less cumin than usual." Nanu and I cook a lot of each other's creations, but I can't remember a single time where we've ever traded a recipe. Just notes on variations, as if it's a piece of music.

• • •

There's a whole branch of immigrant spaghetti recipes that veer off from the "marinara" base to ketchup instead. While you'll see plenty of American recipes that call for adding ketchup to tomato sauce or paste, you'll often find ketchup as the only tomato component in spaghetti recipes across South, Southeast and East Asian families. Think Filipino spaghetti, made with sweet banana ketchup, or Japanese Spaghetti Napolitan, where the stir-fried ketchup takes on a deeper, almost sun-dried profile. While my North Indian family often used Prego, most other South Asian families we knew would go the ketchup-and-soy-sauce route, to replicate the more familiar Indo-Chinese flavors from back home. You might even have seen dishes like "hakka noodles" or "chow mein" on an Indian restaurant menu.

Immigrant Spaghetti

Sumeyya Malik was born and raised in Middletown, Maryland, before moving first to Pakistan and then to North Carolina. Her mom would make a dish known back in Pakistan as "Chinese macaronis" (yes, the plural form is intentional). South Asian noodle dishes in this China-influenced vein are based on ketchup, soy sauce, garlic, ginger, and vegetables like onions, carrots, cabbage, green peppers, and, of course, lots of hot chiles. Thing is, Malik hated it. Much like Baker, she preferred the bland simplicity of jarred sauce and noodles and, for Malik, some cream cheese mixed in, too. In fact, when they'd visit family in Pakistan, they'd take jars of Prego just to meet her desire for a gentler taste. A few years later, they moved there and took as many jars as they could. After her supply ran out, however, Malik was forced to eat Chinese macaronis. "For some reason, eating it there, it was love at first sight. I never touched American pasta sauce again." When Malik moved back to the U.S., she resisted American pasta sauce for years. If she has to have it, she can only enjoy it by adding chili garlic sauce and lots of extra pepper.

Every South Asian family I know has its own version of "Chinese macaronis," mine included. You'll often find it on expanded Indian restaurant menus as hakka noodles, Szechuan noodles, or even just chow mein. By the 1930s, Chinese noodle dishes were appearing in Black cookbooks as well. You can still find yakamein all across New Orleans, made with spaghetti noodles, rice noodles, instant ramen, and more.

...

Spaghetti has offered a box of possibilities for people from nearly every culture across the world. A blank slate that will absorb any flavor you throw at it. So accessible and affordable that everyone has an instinct to make it their own.

In this era of "identity politics," we're all hyper-aware of the cultures and groups we're a part of and how they're evolving. While it seems those fighting the so-called culture wars are doing their best to either amplify or erase identities outside our homes (or even inside them), our kitchens remain intensely personal spaces in which to privately play and express.

Where we're not even cooking so much as practicing instincts. We can access, re-create, and taste decades-old memories in minutes with nothing more than a box of spaghetti and a jar of sauce or a few condiments or spices in the pantry. In between the noodles' bends and curves nestle memories, journeys, learnings, aspirations, personalities, and necessities. And while immigrant spaghetti isn't unique to the South, I don't know if there's another place in the world where it unfurls so many stories so beautifully. ◊

—

Farhan Mustafa has worn many hats as a waiter, a cook, and a freelance food writer. Now a tech founder by day, Mustafa was also an investigative journalist for Al Jazeera during the Arab Spring. His work has been published in Gravy and Serious Eats. He will still defend any Southern buffet, including Golden Corral's, with his life.

Immigrant Spaghetti

BEANS & RICE: MORE THAN A POOR MAN'S MEAL

by Nikesha Elise Williams

—

Photo by Denny Culbert
This story was originally published February 13, 2020

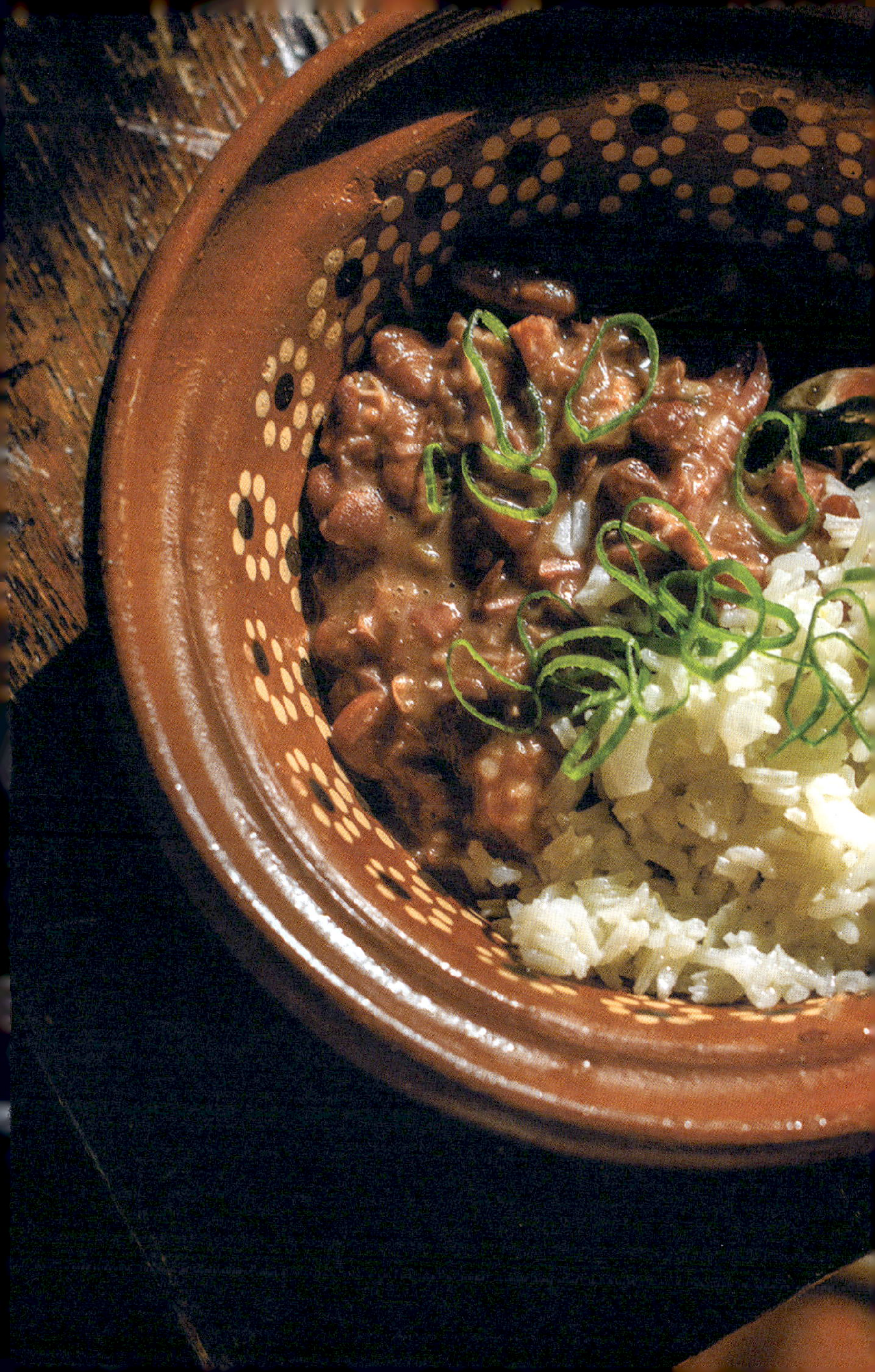

Beans & Rice

I grew up in a family where it was tradition for my parents to eat red beans and rice every Monday. This is a tradition of New Orleans, where my parents are from. The meat left over from Sunday's dinner was thrown in a pot of red beans and set to simmer for hours for dinner Monday evening. My mother, upon moving north to Chicago — where she worked first as a high school gym teacher and then as a dean of students — brought her food traditions with her. While my brother and I may not have had red beans and rice every Monday, it was in the rotation of our meals enough that it became a staple of my diet, my palate, and eventually my cooking repertoire.

When I left Chicago at 18 to attend Florida State University in Tallahassee, I distinctly remember craving red beans and rice on fried chicken day in my dorm's cafeteria. However, that wasn't the side the cooks prepared, and I only had a microwave in my room, which lent itself to reheating fast-food leftovers or warming a bowl of chicken-flavored ramen. I was desperate for a familiar meal, and my grandmother obliged. She sent me a few cans of Blue Runner red beans in the mail; the closest, she said, I could get to what tasted like homemade beans. Upon receiving my gift, I immediately took the bus to the grocery store and picked up some Minute Rice and turkey smoked sausage I could heat in the microwave. With my ingredients stocked in my room, all I had to do was bide my time until the next fried chicken day. When it came around weeks later, I scurried out of the café, ran up to my room on the fourth floor, and got to work. Rice, beans, and meat were all warmed in the microwave, I carried it down to the café, got in line, and heaped a crispy fried leg and thigh on my plate, went to the table where my roommate sat, and ate. The first bite was home. I savored it on my tongue. Even though I was far away from my mother and my grandmother, I had them — albeit underseasoned — on my plate.

My love for red beans and rice has never wavered. I doctored the dish in my dorm, I cooked it for the first time on a stove in my college off-campus apartment, and perfected my technique when I moved to Amarillo, Texas. I worked my first news job and met my husband there. The first meal I ever made for him was red beans and rice. In our 10 years together, I've made them often, not every-Monday often, but often enough that I never miss them, I never crave them.

Then one day he said, "All we have is beans and rice?"

"Yes, what's wrong with that?" I asked.

He calmly responded, "That's, like, poor-people food."

I was taken aback, completely unaware, and hurt. The dish that reminded me of home, of love, of the comfort of my mother and grandmother (and my husband's) had been relegated to a dish for the lowborn, the lowbrow, the impoverished. He explained that beans and rice — no matter how perfectly seasoned, filling, and flavorful — were no different than pork and beans, or beans and weenies. These were dishes he sometimes had no choice but to swallow and stomach in his youth because hunger is a beast that knows no class. I immediately recognized the contrast between my tradition and a socioeconomic tragedy I did not identify with.

In a New York Times review of the 2007 cookbook *Beans: A History* by Ken Albala, Southern Foodways Alliance executive director John T. Edge echoes the sentiment. Beans, red and otherwise, he says, carry a social stigma. Albala writes that the stigma began with the ancient Greeks and has lasted into this century.

In the review, Edge writes, "Because beans are cheap to raise and offer a protein payoff that is comparable to meat's, poor people have traditionally eaten them. The plants that bear beans don't appeal to the aspirational native migrants, and neighborly immigrants. In our own way we have shed our humble beginnings for more: a higher ladder rung and tax bracket, more socioeconomic power and freedom, and a more well-established place in the capitalist hierarchy. But even with our own social climbing and striving, remnants of our genesis are present all around. That includes the bag of black beans and the two bags of dried red beans sitting on a shelf in our pantry, the pot of red beans and rice I cooked and we ate two weeks ago, or the black-eyed peas I made for us on New Year's Day.

Bean dishes have traversed the world with people from early civilization until the present day as markers of poverty and movement. The unwillingness to remain in one spot, to stay in one place — or one's place. In that movement, bean dishes have become popular and trendy, and venerated as much as they are stigmatized. But more than anything, for me, they are a fond reminder of home, of family, and of love. ◊

—

Nikesha Elise Williams is a two-time Emmy Award-winning producer, an award-winning author, and producer and host of the "Black & Published" podcast. Her latest book, Mardi Gras Indians, *was published by LSU Press in October 2022. A Chicago native, Williams is a columnist with JAX Today. Her work has also appeared in The Washington Post, Essence, and VOX. She lives in Florida with her family and is working on her next novel.*

THE LAST OYSTER TONGERS *OF* APALACHICOLA

—

by David Hanson

Photo by David Hanson
This story was originally published February 1, 2022

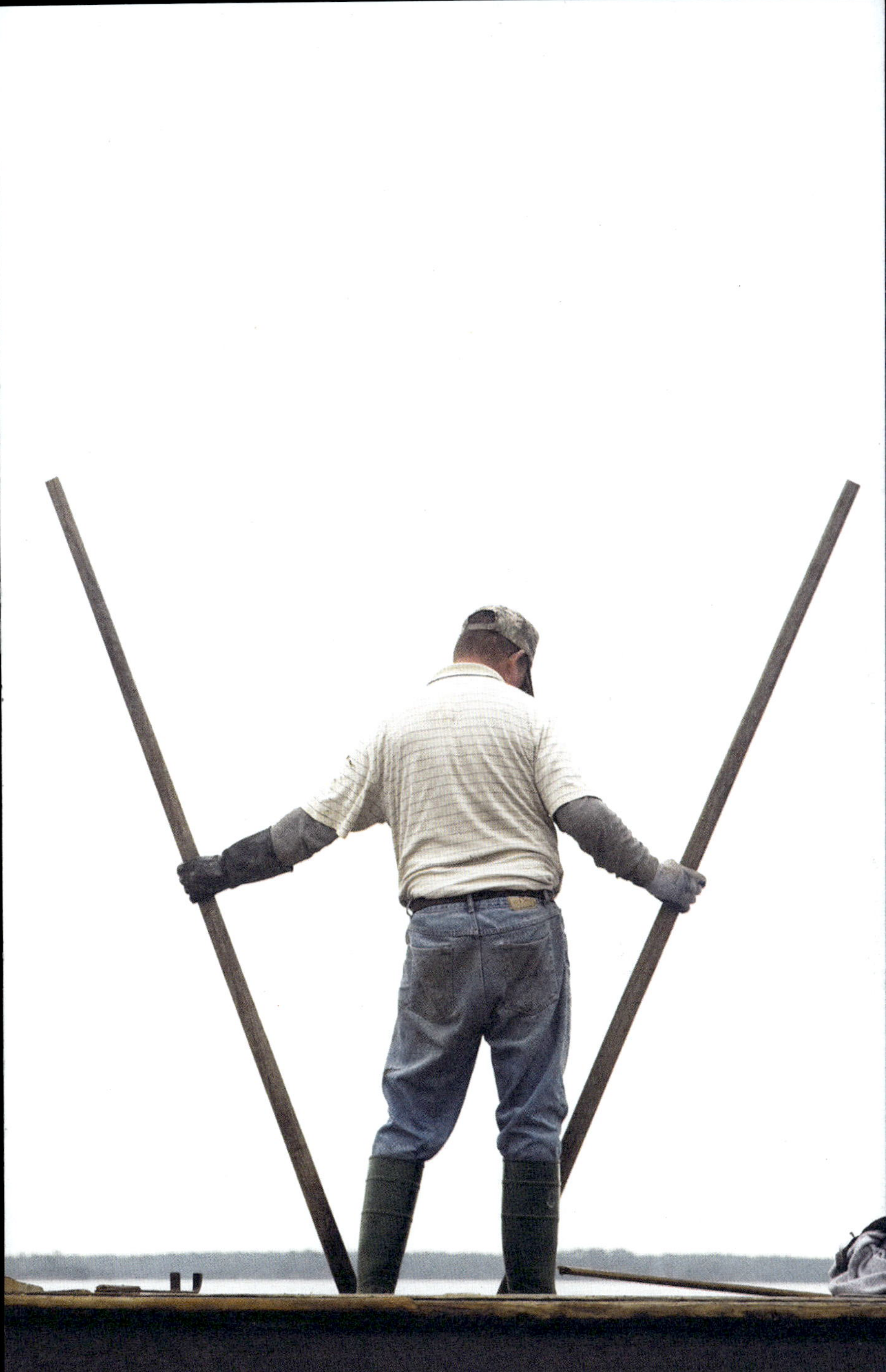

The Last Oyster Tongers of Apalachicola

At 60 years old, Kendall Schoelles, pronounced shell-ess, has never worked a land job. This morning, like most others, he drops his anchor, a rusted engine block, into 5 feet of latte-colored water, grabs a 10-foot-long rake handle made of pine, and steps to the edge of the boat. The rake's handles cut a V against dawn's cobalt sky. Then, as it drops in the water, the teeth clawing for shells make a muffled crunch.

Schoelles harvests oysters from beds his grandfather established in the early 1900s, 11 miles west of Apalachicola, Florida. He's made his living aboard this 22-foot plywood skiff since 1984. Back then, over 400 similar skiffs would be spread across the bay — anchored at Cat Point, Indian Pass Lagoon, Dry Bar, Hagan's Flats, 11 Mile, and Nick's Hole.

Decades of accumulated oyster shells made up the beds (or reefs) sitting a few feet below the water's surface. The oyster tongers would anchor over their favorite beds and literally rake up the oysters growing on top of the reef — with some rake loads yielding a dozen perfect oysters. A few local boat makers were building two to three skiffs per month in open-air backyard shops. Oyster shucking houses dotted the shore and the docks in downtown Apalachicola, neighboring Eastpoint, and down the bay to Tommy Ward's 13 Mile Oyster House. Schoelles and his oyster tonger peers could clear $200-$300 a day.

This year, though, no one is taking oysters. In 2020, the state of Florida, responding to a historic collapse in oyster populations, closed Apalachicola Bay to all wild oyster harvesting for up to five years.

A severe drought that took place from 1955 to 1957, as well as hurricanes Elena and Kate (1985) and Dennis (2005), and tropical storms Fay (2008) and Debbie (2012), led to oyster declines, but the bay always recovered quickly. The state has historically regulated the harvests by closing the bay during some summer seasons and mandating a minimum size for the oysters that can be taken. But now is different.

Schoelles has a rare private lease on his 100-plus acres of beds. Although he's allowed to rake, he won't reap much of a harvest. He's just here to see what he pulls up.

The rake's rusted metal teeth emerge from the water and drop a mess of broken shells on the plywood culling board. They look like the scrapings from the bottom of a cereal bag.

"These are probably 50-, maybe 100-year-old oyster shells," Schoelles says. "My granddad put them here. They should be buried under a mess of oysters."

Schoelles puts the rake down and grabs a 60-pound sack of spent, sun-cured shells, the insides bleached white, smooth and clean as a dinner plate. He dumps them into the bay. It's become an almost daily gesture of science, restoration, and hope.

...

I first saw the oyster tongers in 2009, from a canoe. I'd paddled 500-plus miles on the Chattahoochee and Apalachicola rivers, starting in North Georgia and ending in the Gulf of Mexico at Apalachicola Bay.

In the bay, I paddled past low boats anchored in the west end. On one, a guy raked and culled alone, letters spelling "The Goat" affixed to the skiff's cabin. A few hundred yards away, a man raked while a woman sat beside the broad culling board, tapping oyster clusters with a firm finesse, a pile growing beside her. She'd sweep the small ones and broken shells back into the bay with a mindless brush of her gloved hand. A painted cross and the words "Freedom" decorated the gray hull.

The oyster tonger cuts an independent, rugged shape atop the bay's flat horizon. There's no shelter from a frigid north wind, or from the summer thunderstorms that have killed people on the water. Oyster tongers work on their own schedule, with no boss, getting paid in cash based on their daily harvest. Big business never muscled its way into the scene. In Apalachicola, there's no automated alternative to raking wild beds. The tongs are homemade from pine or fir by locals. Profits are based on market price and how hard you work. There's a cowboy romance to the independent industry.

I met Schoelles in 2013. I had again paddled down the entire watershed, this time with my brother. We were making a film about the Water Wars, the back-and-forth conflict between Alabama, Georgia, and Florida over allocation of fresh water. Historically, the Apalachicola — which is fed by the Chattahoochee and Flint rivers — deposits more water into the Gulf of Mexico than any river aside from the Mississippi. During the prolonged droughts of the late 2000s, Georgia relinquished only minimum flows to Florida. The lack of fresh water is widely recognized as the central culprit of the current oyster collapse.

The oysters themselves lead sedentary lives, attached to other oysters in clusters or reefs. Most spawning occurs in the summer, when the mature oyster releases eggs or sperm into the water column. The fertilized eggs then spend about two weeks floating as larvae, looking for a solid place to settle down, preferring other oyster shells. Once attached, they are officially baby oysters, known as spat, and they do not wander. When the spat develop into mature oysters, they can filter-feed nearly 2 gallons of water per hour, sifting bacteria, minerals, and nutrients brought down by the rivers.

"It takes the right mix of nutrients and salt and fresh water, but also the geography of the bay itself matters," says Bill Walton, the Shellfish Aquaculture Program Coordinator at the Virginia Institute of Marine Sciences. "Part of the success of wild oysters is getting successful years with lots of fresh water to knock back predators and disease."

There is a natural ebb and flow, Walton notes; in years when the rivers run low, populations temporarily decline. "But if you get a bunch of dry years, numbers really go down." The oyster, once affixed to its reef, has to wait for life to come to it. In that way, the oyster is the ultimate downstream user, a keystone species stuck on the bottom, at the mercy of not only Mother Nature but our water power structure, too.

The Apalachicola is routinely dredged to allow boat traffic. One of the bay's barrier islands has been artificially cut to open a new channel. Pumps on the Flint River irrigate cotton, corn, and peanuts. There are 14 dams in the upstream watershed. These rivers have been engineered to serve the demands of modern society. The bay gets whatever is left.

Despite all three states having governors in the same political party, the Republican leaders have never reached a compromise around water. The ACF Stakeholders — a tri-state coalition of industry leaders, municipalities, nuclear power plants, agriculture, scientists, and conservation groups — invested years of collaboration and more than $1 million in a hydrologic study, hoping to prescribe sufficient water to the Apalachicola, Chattahoochee, and Flint watersheds. Consensus was building. Then, in 2013, reacting to the oyster collapse in Apalachicola Bay, Florida Governor Rick Scott sued Georgia, claiming that Georgia overused Chattahoochee and Flint water, leaving an inadequate amount for the Apalachicola and downstream Florida users. The legal jockeying shelved the science and scrambled any budding compromise.

In a 9-0 decision, the U.S. Supreme Court ruled against Florida in 2021. Now that the legal fight is over, the ACF Stakeholders can revisit the possibility of implementing a new water-management regime, one that could ensure more fresh water for Apalachicola Bay.

A decade of natural challenges and legal and political conflict is a mere blip in the timeline of a species. The oysters will likely recover if fresh water returns. But what about the oyster tongers?

...

Perhaps because of its potentially deadly bacteria, raw oysters' sea-to-plate stories were being touted by purveyors long before chalkboards listing food sources became restaurant-standard. The ice machine, first patented in 1851, meant oysters could be packed in barrels and shipped up the Apalachicola River, reaching East Coast cities. When a restaurant received a shipment of oysters, it would make ads promoting the amount on hand along with the oysters' origin.

Otherwise unheralded fishing outposts like Bluffton and Daufuskie Island, South Carolina, and Apalachicola took on outsize culinary status as the sources of this exotic raw delicacy. St. George Island has beautiful beaches, but the oysters put Apalach on the map.

Apalachicola, a dot on Florida's Forgotten Coast, still has the feel of an old, slightly gussied-up fishing village. There are appropriately authentic fishing boats tied up nearby, and it smells of salt and pluff mud. Buddy Ward & Sons Seafood and Trucking processing house and fish market remains prominent, rusty, and salty.

The Forgotten Coast doesn't seem as forgotten these days. It's Memorial Day weekend — with many Americans emerging into a false sense of calm before the Delta variant surge — and Apalachicola is exploding. The last remaining hotel rooms cost over $400. The midafternoon crowd at Oyster City Brewing Company downtown spills off the sidewalk and into the street, where double-parked, lifted golf carts act as impromptu booths. It's a 30-minute wait for a table at Tamara's Café and Tapas Bar. Trays of dozen-raw-half-shell and cheese-crusted oysters cover the flat surfaces.

It hardly seems to matter that the bay is closed. People have come here for oysters, so oysters will be served, even if they are from Louisiana, Texas, and Florida bays farther east. Does anyone know the bay is, for all intents and purposes, dead? That without thick, stubborn oyster reefs anchoring the bay's bottom, the town is more susceptible to powerful hurricane swells?

The iconic Boss Oyster, an oversize rambling wood shack on stilts leaning over the last hundred yards of the Apalachicola River, is closed, damaged in Hurricane Michael. It, along with the adjacent River Inn, Caroline's River Dining, and the Roseate Spoonbill Lounge, was recently bought by a Florida investment firm. Time will tell what that restoration yields.

I order a beer and try to talk with the 50-something-year-olds in the golf carts about the bay closure. They glare at me then turn away, mumbling something about the media.

...

Noah Lockley Jr.'s silhouette is barely visible behind the screen on his front porch. It's midafternoon and hot; a porta-potty sits beside the road, rented

Food Stories

by the neighbor for a high school graduation party. Lockley's small clapboard house is in The Hill, Apalachicola's historically Black neighborhood that begins a few blocks west of downtown and constitutes a "hill" only if viewed through a surveyor's device or during a hurricane swell.

The Hill is Apalach's hot real estate market. Home prices are quickly climbing as retirees, COVID work-from-home escapees, and Airbnb'ers buy up the Craftsman bungalows and clapboard homes.

Lockley grew up here, attending the all-Black Holy Family Catholic School until desegregation offered a chance to attend the town's public school. He bought this house in 1975 at age 24, and he and his wife, Georgia Ann, raised their kids here. Lockley's in his fourth term as the county's District 3 commissioner, but an oyster skiff on a trailer beside the house, its purple paint faded and flaking, gives away his former vocation.

He started on the water in 1972, after a stint in the Army. His father worked at the St. Joe Paper Company — but the mill employed only one family member at a time. So Lockley joined an uncle on the water. Eventually, he bought his own boat and took it to Louisiana and Mississippi to oyster in the summers when Apalachicola Bay would close.

"The bay was a good living," Lockley says. "It was one of the main jobs in town. Everybody did it. Black and white, white and Black. You could take care of your family if you got out there and worked. My kids went out with me when they were in school. They're mostly in law enforcement now."

1985's double whammy of hurricanes Elena and Kate was the worst year Lockley can remember. Tornadoes accompanied the hurricane winds and swells, destroying hundreds of acres of oyster beds. The oyster tongers stayed off the water for two seasons while the beds recovered. Then came what Lockley calls the bonanza years — plenty of oysters and money.

Things had changed radically by the 2010s. It wasn't just the drought. Though oil from the 2010 BP Deepwater Horizon explosion never reached Apalachicola Bay, the fear of oil prompted the state to lift all restrictions on oyster harvests. It was as if during a food shortage, Kroger had opened its doors, removed the cash registers, and said, "Come and get whatever you can carry." Tongers raked the bay to the mud.

"It's so many things," Lockley says. "If Mother Nature wants to come back, it'll come back. But I don't know who's going to work the beds if they do come back. I won't. There won't be any more boats — they'll all rot out. Most of the young guys who were oystering had to go back to get their GEDs and find land jobs. They thought the oystering would last forever. We all did."

Six miles away, across the Apalachicola River, is a no-stoplight town called Eastpoint. Schoelles had told me that a lot of oyster tongers live in this neighborhood; proof was in the skiffs languishing on trailers in many of the yards.

David Gilbert sits on his screened-in porch, an 8-foot-wide chest freezer behind him. He's been here since 1949, back when there weren't many other homes along Wilderness Road. When he was 14, he started oystering with his dad every Sunday. "My education is on the water," he says.

Gilbert stopped oystering in 2014 and started looking for a land job. Since he'd never worked on land before, he feels lucky that he was hired by the state to manage roadside cleanup crews.

"Ninety percent of this neighborhood used to be oystermen," he says. "It was scary when the oysters went down. I'm the breadwinner of the house. A lot of what you see around — rundown places and such — when you could oyster the bay, they had more respect for where they lived. I believe when the bay was working, it was like a machine — all the parts working together. Now it's like a broken wheel. In five years, there aren't going to be any more boats. They'll all rot. No one will be making the tongs. Tourism doesn't do nothing for the people around here."

Gilbert looks out over his neat front yard to the three camellia trees he planted when he built his current house, next to the small sign that bears his family's name. Across the street, short loblolly pines and scruffy, sun-baked shrubs extend to the horizon.

"I loved every minute of it. Actually, I sit out on this porch and think about it a whole lot. I miss it. In your story, you can call me a 'retired, old, wore-out fisherman.'"

• • •

Schoelles can taste a local oyster and tell you what reef it came from. That's one thing that happens when you spend a lifetime raking your granddad's oyster lease. When his grandfather bought the lease in the early 1900s, there were thousands of acres of oyster beds in the bay. The state of Florida sold off some, like leasing land to farmers, for a small, renewable annual fee. The state cultivated the wild public beds that it managed, but the private leases were left to the leaseholder to maintain and harvest.

Schoelles' dad never made a living oystering. He worked in the post office and, later, for the sheriff's office — too lazy, as Schoelles puts it, for oystering. But his granddad passed along the lease, which has been reduced to just under 200 acres, to Schoelles, who has retained it for an annual fee. He lives alone in a small house under a broad canopy of oak trees, the maritime forest intent on overtaking his sheds, house, and truck as soon as he steps away.

Beatles posters, Florida State University football swag, family photos, and one Pearl Jam "Ten" poster adorn the living room walls. Schoelles was married for a while many years ago, but they never had kids. There's one chair at the kitchen table. He brings out a few smooth stones angled into dull ax-like blades by the Native Americans who fished and ate oysters here for millennia. Schoelles' family has been here for over a century.

He regularly drives into town to check on his 92-year-old mother and picks up bags of old shells. At home, he cures them in the sun.

The Florida Fish and Wildlife Conservation Commission plans to "cultch" — deposit shells or other materials to create beds — but not until later this year. For now, state officials are testing materials and construction techniques to restore 1,000 acres of beds. (At one time the bay supported over 10,000 acres of productive wild oyster beds.) They are considering the potential of farming oysters in the bay. Florida State University, with $8 million from Triumph Gulf Coast (a nonprofit established to manage the funds from BP), is also studying the bay, with plans for restoration efforts.

Schoelles can't wait. He pours Quikrete into egg cartons, then uses the concrete eggs to weigh down the baskets and offer a landing spot for passing oyster spat. He has 14 small baskets of live oysters and shells attached to buoys to keep them off the bottom. It's his own version of oyster farming, a way back to productive wild beds: The baskets protect the young oysters from predation by crabs and conch while the spat can attach and develop safely.

"I don't have the money for all the stuff you'd need to really farm them on top of the water," Schoelles says. "Plus, nobody can find seed right now. And thieves would just grab the baskets anyway. But it's something."

In addition to cultching wild oyster beds, another proposed solution for the bay is aquaculture: farming oysters in big floating trays lifted off the ocean floor. But this replaces one challenge with another. Oystering on wild reefs may depend on the whims of nature — and the decisions of upstream humans — but it requires minimal equipment. Natural reefs are a shared public resource. Aquaculture hurtles the industry into privatization: If an oyster farmer invests in equipment and hard-to-find seed, they will want to control that part of the bay.

Virginia Institute of Marine Sciences' Bill Walton has a stake in aquaculture. But, more so, he believes in the human culture that has developed around and helped cultivate wild fisheries. He and his wife had a small oyster farm in Cape Cod and, more recently, managed an oyster farm on Alabama's Dauphin Island. "Shellfish aquaculture has helped a lot of communities, but there are equity issues. It takes money to set up aquaculture. There's some concern that the entire Apalachicola Bay could be privatized, versus the open bay that they have now. I would hate [it] if aquaculture was ever used as a cudgel to say, 'We've solved it if you just do it this way.'"

Nothing in nature exists in a vacuum, especially the bottom of a river. Peanut farms need their Flint River water. Millions of Atlantans need to drink and shower and shave, and the metropolis keeps growing. Alabama's nuclear plants must be cooled with Chattahoochee water. None of that can be left to nature.

The South once had its own cowboys roaming the piney woods. They're gone now; we have the beef, we just don't need the cowboy. Perhaps the oyster tongers will go the same way.

Schoelles holsters a pistol on his hip as we head out for a second morning. I hadn't noticed it, tucked under his shirt, the day before. He started carrying the pistol every day after the Deepwater Horizon spill, when tensions were high on the bay. Today he's just checking his baskets again, hoping to see new growth.

As oyster yields dwindled through the 2010s, fewer oyster tongers ventured onto the bay. Thirty dollars in gas money for $60 worth of oysters didn't add up. Schoelles, adhering to his strict practice of harvesting only full-grown oysters, kept his beds going longer than most, but that just made them more appealing for theft.

Amid the Wild West mentality following Deepwater Horizon, Schoelles chased poachers off his lease in his boat. During that tense time, about a dozen poachers were arrested for stealing from his lease; four did jail time. In more recent years, with the oysters almost gone, he's seen boats out, illegally, at night, poachers raking in a few dozen oysters here and there.

Schoelles wishes the state had closed the bay in the early 2010s as the numbers fell off a cliff. It crushed him when the state opened the bay up after the oil spill. He heard people were coming in with 50 to 60 bags of oysters at dawn, having been out all night. The contraband was bought by oyster houses to be packaged raw or shucked and shipped to restaurants. His friends in the oyster houses told Schoelles they knew the oysters were from his beds because no one grows them like he does.

"I checked my number 9 basket last week, and someone got my big oysters I put in there as cultch," he tells me as we bob on the gentle bay just after dawn. "Probably some rich old bastard in a sport fishing boat just getting him a mess to eat for lunch."

Before we motor back to shore, Schoelles checks his baskets, meticulously counting the predators: stone crab, blue crab, oyster drills (conch). He jots the tallies in his journal, along with daily notes on tides, weather, money earned.

He's kept the journals for years, initially as a way to keep track of his oyster harvests, income, and expenses. Since 2020, however, the journals' columns of predators and prey have become a hand-written witness to what could happen if we leave the bay alone.

"People said the bottom's dead and it ain't never growing back," he says. "I say bullshit. I want to show that the bottom ain't dead."

He fills each journal in a matter of months, then places it with the others on a shelf in his house. The obvious question is why. The writerly answer is almost too easy: An oyster bed's future relies on its past. The discarded shells are a potential home for the next passing spat. If you rake clean the past, you imperil the future. The journaling notches the past, daily layers made up of predator and prey, of money made and money lost, tides in, tides out.

I ask Schoelles why he keeps the journals and what will become of them. "Just for the hell of it, really," he says. "They'll probably get thrown in the trash when I'm gone." ◊

—

David Hanson is a writer and filmmaker based in Oregon. His 2011 book Breaking Through Concrete *chronicles the American urban farm movement, and his 2014 documentary film "Who Owns Water" tells the story of the water conflict between Georgia, Florida, and Alabama. He's currently working with the USDA to document the impact of invasive feral swine on the American landscape.*

THE MAN BEHIND THE COUNTER

—

by Sayaka Matsuoka

Photo by Jack Moebes/News & Record
This story was originally published February 11, 2020

15¢
Coca-Cola
LEMON
MERINQUE
PIE
15¢
CHICKEN
POT PIE
55¢
HOT
COFFEE 10¢
Pepsi-Cola
HOT
CHOCOLATE
10¢

The Man Behind the Counter

Charles Bess walks hastily, arms pumping at his sides, through downtown Greensboro, North Carolina, weaving between the couples and parents with small children who crowd the sidewalk. He's running late, and he's left his jacket in the car.

Sprightly even at 82, with two tufts of bright white hair he likes to fluff and shape gently with his hands every now and again, Bess soon arrives at the International Civil Rights Center & Museum and blends into the crowd.

It's the 60th anniversary of the Greensboro sit-ins, and the museum is packed. A few employees glance up from the ticket desk to smile warmly and welcome Bess into the building as they hurriedly admit a long line of college students at the counter. Other than that, Bess goes largely unnoticed by the dozens of people who fill the space.

As he makes his way past the groups of people, Bess pulls out his new cellphone (he lost his old one about a week ago) and pulls up a black-and-white image. It's a familiar one, especially today. Four young African American men sit at a lunch counter and glance back over their shoulders at the cameraman. Three look directly into the lens. The fourth, the closest to the viewer, either ignores the shooter or has missed the invitation.

Many have written about the four men who sat defiantly on February 1, 1960, at the Woolworth lunch counter in Greensboro. But on the other side of the counter stands a fifth person — another young African

American man, this one in a white paper hat and a busboy uniform. His eyes are downcast, as if he, too, missed the cameraman's cue — or, more than likely, looked deliberately away, not wanting to get too caught up in the moment. The photo of Bess behind the counter was taken on February 2, 1960, on the second day of the sit-ins, with two of the original members of the sit-ins.

"That's me!" Bess exclaims as he points to the man behind the counter. He laughs and emits a high-pitched giggle, one that resounds through the space and somehow makes Bess seem both aged and youthful at the same time.

Bess was 23 years old when he began working at Woolworth in Greensboro. He had come to the city in 1957 from Kings Mountain, about 130 miles away, to live with his sister, Virginia. It wasn't long before he got a job at Woolworth, first as a dishwasher.

"It was hard work," Bess says. "I would take the dishes off the elevator and put them in a tray and send the tray through the machine — the dishwasher. And then it would come out on the other side and I would leave [the dishes] in the tray and they would dry. Then I would stack the dishes up and put them on the little elevator and send them down to the lunch counter."

Upstairs in the dish room, he worked with just one other employee — an African American woman. They cleaned and rotated dishes throughout the day to keep up with demand.

"All the ones working up in the kitchen was Blacks," Bess says.

The waitresses were all white. The counter manager, whom Bess knew as Mrs. Holt, was also a white woman.

"Woolworth was kind of a hard place to work because sometimes the manager would get on you a lot, but she didn't bother me too much because I did my job," Bess says with pride.

About a year later, in 1958, Bess was promoted to busboy. The previous busboy had quit to attend college in Charlotte, and by then Bess had won the approval of Mrs. Holt and was deemed worthy of working in front of the white customers. Downstairs, he sent dishes up to the dishwashers and made sure the waitresses had the plates they needed. He also served cakes and pies if needed.

The Man Behind the Counter

It wasn't a glamorous job, but Bess took pride in it.

"If you were going to be a busboy at Woolworth at that time, you had to be fast," Bess says. "Oh yeah, I was fast. I think that's why Mrs. Holt kept me there, 'cause she saw that I could keep up."

FEBRUARY 1, 1960

Bess was working as a busboy on the day that Joseph McNeil, Franklin McCain, Ezell Blair Jr., and David Richmond walked into the store. He says that before making their way to the counter, the young men bought some school supplies. Bess says he had seen other Black people try to sit at the counter before the A&T Four, but none had attempted to stay after being asked to leave. After doing just that, the men kept calmly asking the waitresses for a cup of coffee each time one of them passed by.

"I remember it was kind of a cold day," Bess says. "I guess that's why they wanted the coffee."

He remembers how one of them asked why he couldn't be served if his money was just as good as anyone else's. After being ignored by the waitresses, they stayed for about an hour until closing time.

"Here's the thing," Bess says. "They didn't move. Nobody could understand that. They were just teenagers. It really took the younger guys to get it to boost off because at the time, the older people were afraid to do that. The older folks were set in their own ways. These four guys, they were not hungry for just food, they were hungry for a change."

He was so surprised by their actions that he stopped working for a while and just watched the four students as they protested.

"I really wanted to see what was going to happen," Bess says. "I was looking at 'em. I didn't say nothing to them."

And while the now-famous photograph shows Bess as reserved and a bit distant, Bess says, he was ecstatic on the inside.

"I was excited about it," Bess says. "I was really excited to see it happen. I felt like whites and Blacks and any other race should be able to sit down and eat together."

After his shift was over, the four had gone, and he had finished his closing duties, Bess caught a cab home and remembers telling the driver all about the young men who came into the store that day. As soon as he got home, he told his sister, and then his brother-in-law.

"I felt like I wanted to tell everybody," he says as he waves his arms up and down. "I was excited about it. It was a very exciting week."

Bess says that working for a company that kept white and Black people separated — not only behind the scenes, but publicly — felt complicated at times.

"I did have to wrestle with it," he says. "I was on the other side, being paid by a company that was keeping me going, but [at] the same time, I was kind of on their side. I was on this side, but I was rejoiced by the people on the other side. I felt like there needed to be a change."

Bess says he experienced segregation in his hometown of Kings Mountain as a child. Segregated water fountains, movie theaters, restrooms, and more dot his memories. And yet, he says, he didn't think it was all that strange at the time, because that's just how it was.

"It didn't bother me too much, because my parents and people older than me was going along with that and I felt like that was the way to go," Bess admits. "That's what it was like for years. We were set in our own way. We had gotten comfortable in our own way. Like, we go in this bathroom, and the whites go in that bathroom."

It wasn't until he saw the A&T Four that it dawned on him that things could be different, Bess says.

"I just felt like that a change had to come when these four guys were sitting there," he says.

JULY 25, 1960

A few months after the sit-ins on July 25, 1960, the Woolworth counter in Greensboro was quietly desegregated.

Bess and three of his coworkers had been told by Mrs. Holt and upper management the day before that they would eat at the lunch counter the next day.

"She came to me and said, 'Charles, we are going to start serving colored folks here, but I want my employees to be the first ones to sit down and eat first,'" Bess says. "I had a good feeling about it. I knew that things were gonna change."

Mrs. Holt asked Bess and his coworkers to change out of their work clothes and into their regular outfits and sit at the counter in the middle of their shift. Bess says he wore jeans and his "regular old clothes" and sat down to eat Woolworth's signature meatloaf.

"I love meatloaf," Bess says. "I also had some green beans, maybe a potato salad with it."

It took a total of about 10 minutes.

Then they just went back to work.

"After that, that's when other Blacks started sitting at the counter," Bess says. "I didn't realize that it would be a big deal. I didn't realize that I would be talking to you about it 60 years later."

In 1961, Bess left Woolworth to go work at Odell Mill Supply Co.

He had just gotten married and was looking to make more money. In the years that followed, Bess says Mrs. Holt reached out to him to ask if he could cover some shifts here and there, but he never went back as a customer.

"It just didn't cross my mind to go back," he says.

BACK AT WOOLWORTH

It wasn't until decades later that Bess reconnected with Woolworth and his time there. He had been invited to the 20th anniversary, which took place at a motel downtown. There, he read a poem that he had written about the sit-ins. During the anniversary, the A&T Four also reunited and sat once more at the historic counter at Woolworth, which is now on permanent display at the Civil Rights museum in Greensboro. Portions of the counter that were added during the store's expansion after integration were donated to the National Museum of African-American History in Washington D.C., the Smithsonian National Museum of American History, and the Greensboro History Museum. The lunch counter at the

Greensboro museum is as it was during segregation and includes the original seats where the A&T Four sat.

Bess says that of the four, he became closest with David Richmond because he had remained in Greensboro.

Richmond passed away at 49 in 1990. McCain passed away in 2014 at 73. Blair and McNeil are still alive.

Bess says Richmond told him he was scared the day of the sit-ins.

"At the time he was getting ready to sit, he said that he was getting kind of scared," Bess says. "He was the last person to sit. He really didn't know what was gonna happen."

Today, Bess lives just a few miles up the road from the museum and says he "drops in" every couple of months. Most of the employees know him by name, and sometimes he gives his firsthand account during public tours.

A trio of college women from Chicago approach Bess and ask for a picture. Bess excitedly accepts, but not before fluffing his hair just so. Later, he struts behind the counters, the same ones he once worked behind 60 years ago. He finds what looks like an original metal bus bin, the kind he used every day.

"I'm excited to see that it's still here," Bess says. "I would never forget Woolworth, the hard work I put in here, the good friends I made. I didn't have a big position at Woolworth like cooking or baking cakes. I was just a plain busboy working with dirty dishes all day, but I praise God that I can still be here talking about Woolworth." ◊

—

Sayaka Matsuoka is a writer with Japanese roots who was born in New York City but raised in Greensboro, North Carolina. Her favorite foods – sushi and fried chicken – are a representation of who she is.

The Man Behind the Counter

THE ELUSIVE ROOTS *OF* ROSIN POTATOES

—

by Caroline Hatchett

Photo by Rinne Allen
This story was originally published November 22, 2023

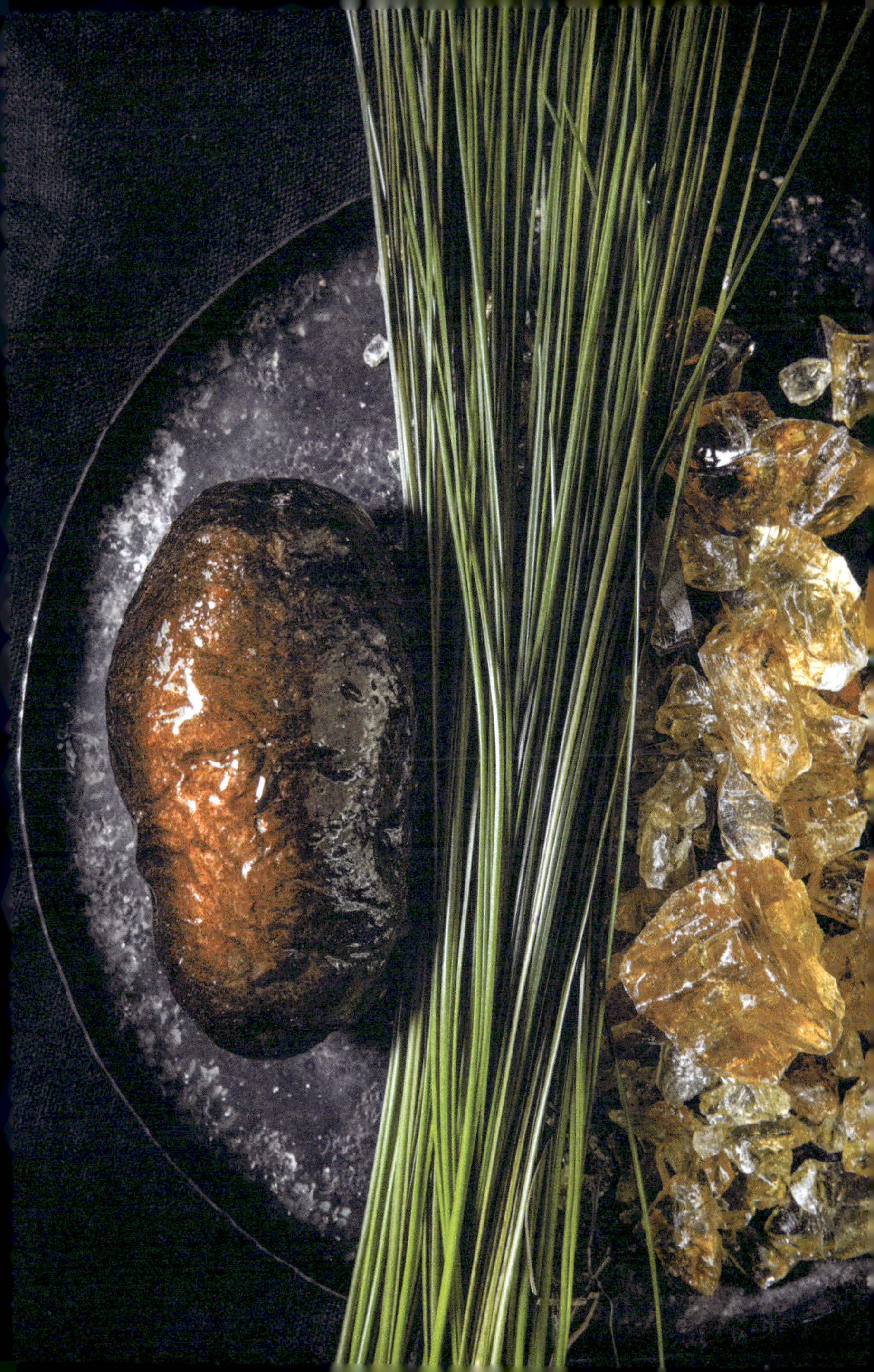

The Elusive Roots of Rosin Potatoes

During the decades my hometown of Baxley, Georgia, hosted Tree Fest, men from Akzo Nobel, a chemical manufacturer with a local plant, would gather around a 6-foot-tall pot filled with 200 pounds of rosin. Led by Bo Herndon — a plant supervisor, former police chief, and father to my catechism classmate Heather — the team would bring the rosin to a vigorous simmer over a high-powered propane burner, and then drop in potatoes, 50 or so at a time. After 30 minutes, the potatoes would bob to the surface and Bo and Co. would pluck them out with tongs, wrap the potatoes — perilously sticky with molten rosin — in newspaper, and sell one of America's great culinary oddities for a buck or two.

I was oblivious to this culinary display. Tree Fest had other diversions: an early-morning fun run, funnel cake, vendors selling scented candles and Kiss My Grits T-shirts. My sister's Labrador, Dixie, won the pet costume contest three years in a row. I tapped with a troupe from the Gail Hursey School of Dance, and, one year, as a junior chamber of commerce volunteer, I roamed the fairgrounds dressed as Woody, the festival's pine tree mascot.

Pines meant something in Appling County. I grew up with slash pines towering over me and wheelbarrows' worth of pine cones in the yard. The trees would paint our driveway yellow with pollen in spring. Lightning would occasionally strike their crowns, and, with the immediate boom of thunder, every wall and window of our house would rattle.

My dad, Tom Hatchett, managed timberland for Union Camp and, later on, International Paper. My best friend Lindsay's dad worked at Rayonier, a plant just east of downtown with stacks of denuded pine trunks piled high in its yard. Pine trees brought our families to this part of rural South Georgia. And I couldn't wait to leave it.

Neither could Thurnell Alston, the protagonist in *Praying for Sheetrock*, Melissa Fay Greene's nonfiction account of McIntosh County's late-to-arrive Civil Rights Movement. Along with his father and a pickup truck full of men, Alston rode from the Georgia coast to inland piney woods to clear paths for other turpentine workers and deposit gum collected from the trees into barrels; they toiled from early morning until nightfall for monthlong stretches and slept in windowless shanties on the floor.

After six years of grueling, low-paid work, Alston literally walked off the job, trekking 60 miles on foot from Baxley to Brunswick. I read *Praying for Sheetrock* in late 2019 and mentioned Baxley's cameo to my dad. Sensing a rare connection in our work, he posed a question, some version of which I've since asked the living and the dead across 10 states and two countries: What do you know about rosin potatoes?

It's widely accepted that rosin potatoes hail from the South's turpentine camps, where workers chipped and slashed and scraped pine trees to collect oleoresin (aka resin or gum), the trees' natural defense mechanism. When a tree's bark is breached — by a beetle, fungus, or a woodsman's hack — it oozes gum, not sap, from the wound. When fossilized, oleoresin transforms into amber. When distilled, it yields turpentine and rosin, whose uses range from paint thinner and Vicks VapoRub to rubber cement and chewing gum, respectively.

The rosin potato origin story goes one of two ways. A hapless worker dropped a potato into hot rosin as it was coming off the still, and when the potato came to the surface, he pulled it out and found a perfectly cooked spud. Alternately, an industrious worker saw in molten rosin an efficient method for making a hot lunch.

Outside the context of the woods, cooking potatoes in rosin is a wholly impractical preparation.

Rosin is highly flammable, and its fumes are noxious. It requires a dedicated pot and tongs; there's no easy cleaning of hardened rosin. Oh — and you can't eat the potato's skin.

Despite those odds, the technique went mainstream in the 1950s and merited inclusion in James Beard's 1960 *Treasury of Outdoor Cooking* and in the 1975 edition of *The Joy of Cooking*. In 1976, rosin potatoes were on the table the night my parents got engaged at Art's Steakhouse in Gainesville, Florida, and Cracker Barrel served the potatoes from 1983 through 1991.

Rosin potato loyalists say the preparation yields a superior potato with a flaky texture. Just as oleoresin seals a tree's wounds, rosin traps a potato's flavor and aroma, according to chef Sean Brock, who included rosin potatoes on the debut menu at Audrey, his fine-dining restaurant in Nashville. "Because none of the potato's flavor or aroma compounds can escape, you get the most intense potato flavor you've ever experienced," Brock says. "And they're steaming in their own water, which is why you get a totally unique texture."

Outside of Audrey, you won't find rosin potatoes in many restaurants these days. Except in vintage cookbooks, Reddit forums, and a smattering of rural festivals, rosin potatoes all but disappeared from the American culinary canon.

In the summer of 2020, Dad drove to Patterson, Georgia, to pick up 25 pounds of rosin from Diamond G Forest Products, a boutique producer of gum rosin and turpentine. I drove from New York to Baxley. In his garage, with the door rolled open, we fired up a propane cooker, melted rosin, and dropped in potatoes. The fumes coming off the pot were piney and potent, enough to make you dizzy in the heat, so I stood back, bare feet on smooth concrete, watching as a fury of bubbles rose from the swampy liquid. A half-hour into the boil, the potatoes began to emerge one by one.

But it would take another year for their origins to surface. Turpentiners did not record the grand discovery that is rosin potatoes, or from where, exactly, they hail.

They left that up to me.

In the history of humanity, rosin is a relatively modern product. Before it came tar and pitch, derived from European birch and pine at least 10,000 years ago. Ancient Greeks and Vikings used pine tar to waterproof their ships. In Genesis, God tells Noah, "Make yourself an ark out of resinous wood. Make it of reeds, and caulk it with pitch inside and out."

By the 17th century, England needed a new source of tar, pitch, and turpentine — a trinity of supplies known as naval stores that would coat, seal, and preserve the Royal Navy's ropes and ships. The world superpower had produced the stuff on an industrial scale since at least the Middle Ages, but as its forest resources thinned, England turned to Prussia and Sweden, and eventually to the American Colonies, for its naval stores.

The Carolinas had seemingly endless stretches of longleaf pine and soil ill-suited for cash crops and by 1725 produced a net surplus of tar, pitch, and turpentine. By the mid-19th century, North Carolina's naval stores industry was booming, with the state boasting nearly 800 stills and operators producing more than $5 million ($185 million today) of gum and turpentine. That wealth and labor, of course, were derived at the expense of enslaved workers, of whom we know little aside from their impact on plantation balance sheets.

Plantations hired out enslaved people to turpentine operations for up to $250 a year at the industry's height. Swinging giant axes, these men would box 75 to 100 trees a day, or around 10,000 trees each winter, and chip 1,000-2,000 faces a day. (Faces, or catfaces, are the areas from which bark has been hacked off and rosin flows.) They were housed in dirt-floor lean-tos and issued daily rations of salt pork, cornmeal, and, yes, potatoes. One of the few advantages these men had over enslaved plantation farm workers was their ability to supplement their diets with wild foods like fish, turtle, raccoon, and possum.

If these workers ate rosin potatoes, we do not know it. Rosin, at this point, had little commercial value. Rather than paying to ship it, producers let it run off the still onto the land and into waterways. When Frederick Law Olmsted toured North Carolina turpentine operations in the early 1850s,

The Elusive Roots of Rosin Potatoes

he observed "a congealed pool of rosin, estimated to contain over three thousand barrels," according to his *A Journey in the Seaboard Slave States*.

I looked to historical accounts like Olmsted's and expected, at any moment, for rosin potatoes to leap off the pages.

In the seminal *Tapping the Pines*, Robert Outland introduces Sarah Hicks Williams, the wife of a North Carolina turpentiner, whose letters detail meals of cornbread, biscuits, sweet potatoes, peaches, apples, and vinegar-dressed pork barbecue — but no rosin potatoes.

I hoped to find them on plantation menus and checked with folks at the Bellamy Mansion in Wilmington, North Carolina. The 10,000-square-foot home was built by John D. Bellamy, a merchant, farmer, and turpentine operator, who owned 115 enslaved workers, 24 of whom labored at his turpentine camp in Columbus County. The family's elaborate Christmas menus included duck, roast pig, rutabagas hashed with Irish potatoes, brandy peaches, coconut pie, and syllabub (sweetened curdled milk), but there's no rosin on the menu, nor records of what Bellamy's enslaved workers ate at camp.

"No one was keeping good records," Outland told me. "It's hard to write about a life when they were considered unimportant people."

Outland, who lives in North Carolina, spent the summer of 1996 driving across the southeastern United States, researching the dissertation that would become *Tapping the Pines*. He combed archives, knocked on doors, and held rosin in his hands for the first time. Nowhere in his fieldwork did he encounter rosin potatoes.

"There was fire everywhere around backwoods processing facilities. Why not roast potatoes? People really were struggling out there in the woods," Outland says. "I don't know who got it in their head, but it seems to be human nature, looking back with rosy glasses at the past. They imagined an old-time turpentine lifestyle and invented a way to celebrate it."

...

After its mid-19th-century boom, the Tar Heel State (named after a slur associated with turpentine workers) saw its naval stores industry decline rapidly. Between 1840 and 1893, more than 90 percent of North Carolina's longleaf pine forest had been boxed, destroyed, and abandoned. In turn, operators moved to the virgin forests of South Carolina, Alabama, Mississippi, Georgia, and Florida.

But it was South Georgia — in particular, on land between the Savannah and Chattahoochee rivers — that would supplant North Carolina as the nation's naval stores capital.

In the decades leading up to the Civil War, turpentiners transplanted entire plantation populations to Georgia's piney woods, and migration continued at an even more rapid pace after the war. Newly emancipated Black workers followed the industry, having few other choices, and by the late 19th century the average Georgia turpentine worker was a "young, single, illiterate, Black man from North Carolina," Outland wrote in *Tapping the Pines.*

Baxley was transformed by turpentine into a rural engine of the South's economy, and in ways I could not comprehend, turpentine wealth, power, and culture steeped themselves into my upbringing.

Abandoned turpentine shacks, unpainted and with tin roofs and front porches caving in, dotted county roads. In downtown Baxley, there's a four-columned white mansion off U.S. 1 with a tennis court in the backyard; it always looked too fancy for the town and was owned by Edgar Dyal, a turpentine magnate. The tracks that slice Baxley in two were part of the Macon and Brunswick Railroad, built to haul naval stores and lumber to the coast. Lewis Parker, Appling County's sheriff for 20 years, hailed from the Veal family, one of the county's biggest naval stores producers. And when the last bucket of American pine gum was dipped for commercial use by Major Phillips, he delivered it from Soperton, Georgia, to Baxley for distillation at Akzo Nobel, the last U.S. processor of gum rosin.

Early in my potato hunt, my dad introduced me to Bill Baker, a retired Akzo Nobel engineer and plant manager. Baker's grandaddy had timber stands and a fire still out near the Veals', and though he expected to leave town for good, rosin cemented Baker in place. He started working at Filtered Rosin Products in the mid-'60s and stuck around as the plant was sold to Akzo Nobel in the '80s and, eventually, to two investment groups.

The Elusive Roots of Rosin Potatoes

"We made products from rosin from living pine trees. There are other rosins made from paper mills, where they grind pulp and extract it with sulphuric acid. That rosin, you don't want to use for potatoes," explains Baker, who over the years entertained visiting businesspeople with steak and rosin potato dinners.

He doesn't remember where he first learned about the dish, but the story Baker has heard and told for decades rings true: "Turpentine workers would be collecting rosin from the fire still. They'd have hot rosin in barrels, and around noon, they'd throw potatoes in the barrel and let them cook."

In 1981, the Georgia Museum of Agriculture built a turpentine still complete with an antique copper kettle, and every April, David King, the museum's superintendent of restoration and maintenance, fires the still. Just off I-75 in Tifton, the living history museum is one of the few places in the country where you can see pine gum transformed into turpentine and rosin and eat potatoes cooked in hot-off-the-still rosin.

My dad and I met King, a little sunburned and with graying hair tucked under a camouflage cap, in a giant, shadeless parking lot, and he led us back to the nine-barrel still, encased in red brick and sheltered under a rustic two-story wooden structure. Workers would roll barrels of gum to the top and tip the contents into the still. The steam, containing water and spirits of turpentine, would rise through a pipe and then wind through copper tubing set inside a cypress water tank. Once condensed, the solution would flow into a barrel and turpentine would rise to the top. At the end of distillation, workers opened a chute at the bottom of the still and rosin gushed out through screens and cotton batting and into a trough. Men with long-handled dippers would then transfer the filtered rosin into barrels.

Standing next to the still — the ground in front of it puddled with semi-firm rosin — was like going to church. It made me want to believe. Just as Baker knows the rosin business, King has mastered the mechanics of 19th-century production, working with old-timers and historians and firing stills five or so times a year. He sent me home with hunks of rosin, new leads to call, and a glimmer of hope that I'd find the potatoes in South Georgia.

Food Stories

• • •

At the end of "A Longleaf Legacy," a 2018 documentary about the industry, Buster Cole, a still worker and interpreter for the Georgia Museum of Agriculture, extemporaneously calls out varied rosin uses: "gunpowder, glass, fiberglass, acrylics, polyester, chewing gum, costume jewelry, tile, carpet, Elmer's glue, shellac, shoe polish, soap, sprinkle it on your dance floor to make it slick, they make nine cosmetics out of it and three perfumes out of it. Gymnastics you got a rosin bag, bowling you got a rosin bag, tennis you got a rosin bag. Baseball pitcher, he use a rosin bag, fiddler put rosin on his bow, ballet dancer put it on their shoes. ... "

Having visited the still and watching the video, I hoped Cole would blurt out, "And you can even cook a potato in it." But he didn't.

Folklorist Laurie Sommers founded the South Georgia Folklife Project at Valdosta State University and, with Tim Prizer, interviewed dozens of turpentine workers with multigenerational ties to the industry, such as George "G.W." Harrington, a man born into the business. Harrington's father managed 16,000 acres of forest, and his mother helped run the camp commissary. "Mama believed in a hot meal," he told Sommers in 2004, recalling Friday-night fish fries and the scent of greens, sweet potatoes, and homemade biscuits wafting through the camp.

According to Harrington, a typical day's menu in the 1940s and '50s consisted of grits, fried eggs, bacon, and oatmeal for breakfast; dinner (aka lunch) meant "something that would stick with you" like fried chicken, rice, speckled butter beans, cornbread, corn, okra, new potatoes, sliced tomatoes, biscuits, and some kind of dessert; for supper, the family ate leftovers or country sausage.

Most workers' lunches were more humble affairs, according to Sommers, like cornbread or canned salmon with rice and beans, carried in cane syrup cans and hung from trees.

"There is no way something as unusual and fascinating as rosin potato would be something that flew under the radar and was forgotten," says Prizer, who went on to write his master's thesis on nostalgia and memory in the waning days of the industry.

But none of Sommers' or Prizer's subjects mentioned the potatoes. They're similarly omitted from Carroll Butler's *Treasures of the Longleaf Pines*, notable for being the only scholarly book on the industry produced by a former turpentiner, and Pete Gerrell's *The Illustrated History of the Naval Stores (Turpentine) Industry*.

Both works are a feast of food details. Butler describes lunches of hoe cakes and doobie (a savory cobbler relative), as well as workers hunting for rabbit, squirrel, raccoon, and gopher tortoise. He also describes backwoods booze, including "alcohol strained from Sterno and then mixed with sugar water and spirits of niter [ethyl nitrite]." Gerrell shares recipes for cottage beer, pigs feet, and Spanish moss jelly. "You know that times are bad when there is nothing left to eat but Spanish moss seasoned with fish bladder," he wrote.

Gerrell and Butler are both deceased, as are all but one or two of the folks interviewed by Sommers and Prizer. But as a daughter of one of the last important turpentine cities, I hoped I might find living workers — and rosin potato camp stories — in Baxley.

James Copeland tapped trees in Appling Country until 1960, and his family line extends back to North Carolina. His father farmed tobacco and cotton and collected gum on his own land, in addition to working faces for another operator. "There was a man he worked for, probably 25 or 35 years. My grandfather worked for that man's daddy doing turpentine. The first work I did, as far back as I can remember, was farm work and turpentine," Copeland says.

Copeland is married to Pearl Copeland, who was raised on the Veals' turpentine farm and whose brother and father worked in the business. Pearl is an accomplished country cook. She was making a jelly cake the last time we spoke and promised a feast of fried chicken, lima beans, cornbread, blackberry pie, peach pie, and pear pie the next time I come home.

The Copelands had never heard of rosin potatoes.

Pearl recalls folks cooking sweet potatoes under a pile of sand with a fire built on top. James took cold potatoes into the forest and field, but more often lunch was a biscuit sandwich with bacon, peanut butter and homemade jelly, or a smear of preserved pear, packed in a syrup can.

"You didn't heat no food up. Whatever you left home with, by the time you eat it, it's cold," he says. "When you ate, there wasn't nothing like ... take an hour for lunch."

They were incredulous that the technique would even work. "I don't know nobody in Appling County who could tell you about that," Pearl told me. "That somebody who was telling you the way they did it, they were saying something that was untrue."

• • •

The Copelands' experience working family land and trees represents the zenith of the industry for Black workers, who sold gum to central distilleries as supplemental income. But before Civil Rights legislation passed in the 1960s, the Jim Crow South held a significant number of Black turpentine workers in bondage through debt peonage, most often by forcing them to buy marked-up goods at camp commissaries. Though the practice was illegal at the federal level, Southern states enacted laws that forbade workers from leaving jobs while indebted to their bosses.

The industry also leased convicts — a majority being Black men — from the state. Though it had been outlawed elsewhere, Georgia and Florida practiced convict leasing until 1908 and 1923, respectively.

Though Prizer found relationships between some owners and Black workers were warm, respectful, and often nuanced, anyone poking through turpentine's past will find, in abundance, brutality, kidnapping, coercion, paternalism, and searing racism.

The more I poked and dug and read, I could not understand why a Black worker in the Jim Crow South would cook his lunch in rosin, a commodity product whose value was determined by its clarity. Were workers really dropping dirty potatoes into rosin that had been distilled and filtered through cotton batting and screens? It sounded like a punishable offense.

• • •

The Elusive Roots of Rosin Potatoes

By this point, I had grown mighty suspicious — like, rosin-potatogate conspiracy theory suspicious. With no collective memory — written, recorded, or alive — of rosin potatoes in turpentine camps, I turned my attention away from workers and toward the industry, the bigwigs, moneymakers, and political influencers who might have something to gain from rosin potatoes.

At the University of Florida's Smathers Libraries, I hunched over volumes of the Naval Stores Review, following two-plus decades of industry exploits. Published weekly from 1890 to 1953 (and later monthly and bimonthly), the Review provides a play-by-play of the industry's swings, technological advances, best practices, politics, labor woes, and evolving culture. Its pages instructed producers how to convert from harmful box cutting to installing metal gutters and ceramic Herty cups, a method that prolonged trees' viability and allowed the once mobile industry to put down roots. It documented the move from backwoods distilling to central stills in towns like Baxley, the rise of acid sprays to increase gum production, and every possible use for turpentine and rosin — from soap production in Peru to home insulation, cough syrup, and a depilatory for pigs.

The Naval Stores Review also chronicled the American Turpentine Farmers Association, or AT-FA, formed in 1936 and led by Judge Harley Langdale, a powerful naval stores producer and politician from Valdosta, Georgia.

AT-FA loomed large over the industry's fading years. Members funded successful national ad campaigns and an effort to get gum turpentine onto retail shelves. The organization supported research and lobbied to classify turpentiners as agricultural workers, exempting producers from minimum wage laws and Social Security taxes. AT-FA administered a federal loan program that sought to limit naval stores production and stabilize market prices. They also threw one helluva party.

Each April, more than a thousand producers and their families would gather in Valdosta for the annual AT-FA Convention. Langdale would rally turpentiners behind the cause of the moment and conjure the industry's demise if action was not taken, and then get voted in as president for another term.

Food Stories

"The gum industry faces able, aggressive, and intelligent competition from many new spirits companies. This competition must be met by the gum industry or the industry will be swallowed up by it," he told attendees in 1947.

They'd host a stag-night fish fry for the men, along with a beauty contest in which women dressed in longleaf pine needle bikinis. The weekend would conclude with a picnic featuring 700 barbecued chickens (and ham in later years), peas, grits, potato salad, beer, and Coca-Cola. In 1949, they switched up the menu and harvested Florida sabal palms to make swamp cabbage.

Had the rosin potato existed in naval stores culture, it should've been at that barbecue. Just as Langdale wrapped his arm around each Miss Spirits of Turpentine, he would have been pulling a potato out of the rosin pot for a photo op. Rosin potatoes were also absent from Swainsboro's Pine Tree Festival, from industry conferences, and from field trips to the Naval Stores Research Station in Olustee, Florida, a hub of scientific advancement for the industry.

Starting with the year 1933, I flipped page by page, year by year, through the Naval Stores Review, expecting to meet the potato at any moment. And there was nothing — until June 1956.

The year before, N.J. "Jack" Stallworth, whose brother was an AT-FA director, had demonstrated rosin baked potatoes at the Alabama State Fair. Stallworth served the potatoes in his Mobile, Alabama, restaurant, Stafills, and advertised direct-to-consumer rosin in pamphlets, as well as in Gourmet, Living, and House Beautiful. Naval Stores Review did not credit Stallworth or anyone in particular with the invention, but noted, "Rosin baked potatoes is not an entirely new idea, having been initiated some two years ago."

In other words, folks in the industry had not eaten rosin potatoes, a "Southern delicacy" as they called them, until 1954. They didn't associate the newfangled technique with turpentine camp culture, nor did they know when or where the potatoes had been invented.

...

Rosin potatoes first appeared in print in April 1939 in a syndicated dispatch from Damon Runyon, a journalist best known for writing "Guys and Dolls." "We recently came across a brand new way of cooking white potatoes. You boil them in resin — the same kind of resin that violinists rub on their bowstrings and also the very same kind of resin prizefighters shuffle the soles of their shoes in," wrote Runyon, attributing the dish to Black Caesar's Forge, a restaurant in Miami. "The Dade County folks love to introduce their Yankee friends to the ceremony."

Later that year, Charles H. Baker, a Florida-born bon vivant and writer, published The Gentleman's Companion: Exotic Cookery Book, a collection of recipes of "manly dishes for men" according to The Miami Herald. In it, he shared a recipe for "Rosin Potatoes in the Manner of J. Marquette Phillips as Done at Black Caesar's Forge for Various Friends & Guests, at Various Times." Those guests, according to Baker, included senators, poet Robert Frost, and actor Errol Flynn.

Black Caesar's Forge opened in 1938, 15 miles south of downtown Miami in Palmetto Bay. Named for a legendary pirate rumored to have buried treasure on the Miami coast, the restaurant's sunken dining room was carved into coral rock and lined with wine bins. In the early years, guests brought their own steaks, salad fixings, and potatoes, which Phillips charged a fee to grill, toss with a house vinaigrette, and drop in a rosin pot, respectively. "The problem in World War II was you couldn't get steak," says David Phillips, J. Marquette's grandson. "These were people with connections."

Phillips had moved from Detroit to Miami in 1925 at the height of a south Florida real estate boom. The place was warm, notoriously wet despite Prohibition, and accessible by rail line, and wealthy snowbirds built mansions and flocked to newly minted hotels on South Beach. Phillips established himself as a furniture importer and decorative iron worker, and you can still see his handiwork at mansions built by Harvey S. Firestone and William K. Vanderbilt II.

Phillips' business survived a series of devastating hurricanes and the 1929 stock market crash, and he built a South Beach home with a storefront and studio — and likely a speakeasy. After Prohibition's repeal, and with the support of wealthy patrons, Phillips transformed the space into The

Forge Club, a nightclub, casino, and steakhouse decorated with intricate iron grilles and palm trees. He sold the club in 1942, and it operated as The Forge, an iconic Miami steakhouse, until closing in 2019.

By the time Black Caesar's Forge came around, Phillips had considerable social capital, and his potatoes were a local hit. Miamians added rosin potato hearths to their outdoor terraces. Snowbirds transported the potatoes back to their home states. Francis Kinney and Alberta Paskvan both served as World War II pilots, and, in the years after the war, met and married in Miami, where they frequented Black Caesar's Forge. After moving to Michigan and, later, Montana, they continued to cook rosin potatoes over a wood fire in the backyard, and often for a crowd of bewildered neighbors. "For my whole life, they were part of our family's cuisine," says their son Will Kinney, a theoretical cosmologist at the University of Buffalo and avid rosin potato maker. (Kinney cooks his potatoes for 20 additional minutes after they rise to the surface of the pot, for optimal texture.)

Rosin potatoes' popularity surged as families like the Kinneys moved to the suburbs and America's backyard barbecue culture took root. Hamilton and Abercrombie & Fitch, among other manufacturers, started selling rosin potato kits complete with a pot, an aluminum stand, and rosin.

With wartime rations lifted and celebrations in order, steakhouses flourished, and plenty of them added rosin potatoes to their menus. My grandparents ate them in Palm Beach in the '50s, when rosin potatoes had gourmet connotations. At a 1953 gathering of Les Amis d'Escoffier, "a band of real gourmets" ate rosin potatoes alongside bouillon, clams casino, oysters Rockefeller, caviar, crawfish quenelles, wild mallard, and Champagne.

There was no turpentine camp narrative at this point. Just as AT-FA promoted the newness and novelty of the preparation, so did the national press. But that started to change as rosin potatoes established themselves in the South and in turpentine strongholds. Soon they were on menus at the Mayflower Hotel in Jacksonville; Heritage Inn in Columbia, South Carolina; the Pirates' House in Savannah; and Coyner's in Macon, Georgia. Rosin potatoes were also a specialty of notoriously racist Aunt Fanny's Cabin in Smyrna, Georgia. By the '70s, the rosin potato myth had

The Elusive Roots of Rosin Potatoes

cemented and Planters Back Porch Seafood Restaurant in Myrtle Beach, South Carolina, told the tall tale on its menu:

"Many years ago a worker in a turpentine plant dropped a raw potato into an iron vat of bubbling hot rosin. The potato sank out of sight ... but some 20 minutes later suddenly reappeared floating on the surface of the heavy rosin. The worker took a large ladle and scooped the potato out of the rosin and after curiosity got the better of him, he cut the potato open and proceeded to enjoy the most delicious potato ever before baked. Word of this culinary find circulated throughout the pine belt of the South and soon practically every plantation in the land had its own rosin pot out back for cooking the famous 'rosin-taters.'"

The rosin potato had outgrown Black Caesar's Forge and taken on a whole new identity, but Phillips had already moved on. He sold the restaurant in 1946 and settled in Cuba, where he ran a 35,000-acre fruit, mining, and timber plantation. Fidel Castro's government seized the land in 1960, and Phillips died six years later.

Phillips never claimed to have invented the potato. He told friends and reporters he had seen it elsewhere but never revealed his source. There's a chance he witnessed the potato cookery in central or northern Florida, where his wife Edna Valentine Paul's family operated a lumber business. But there's not a lick of proof rosin potatoes existed in the deep woods, and if they did, I can't believe J. Marquette Phillips was the sole person to have brought them to the public's attention.

On the contrary, I think he was concealing the potato's backstory.

...

Outside the industry, resin and pitch — the latter made by cooking down oleoresin until thick and sticky — often are used interchangeably. At a certain point last summer, and on a desperate whim, I typed "pitch potatoes" into a newspaper archive. The first dozen or so hits were commodity lists; pitch and potatoes follow each other alphabetically. But then I found exactly what I was looking for: rosin potatoes' predecessor boiling in the pots of Cincinnati's pre-Prohibition German-American breweries.

Food Stories

By the mid-19th century, Cincinnati was home to a thriving beer industry whose German brewers were no strangers to pitch. In his 1829 *The Art of Brewing*, writer David Booth details the distinctly German practice of lining barrels with pitch to prevent contamination, leakage, and the transference of wood's flavor and color into beer.

The 1850s and '60s also coincided with the rise of pale lagers, a style of beer invented just a few years earlier at Pilsner Urquell in the Czech Republic. Lager means "storeroom" in German, and requires brewing and conditioning at cold temperatures. Modern light lagers are brewed year-round and age in refrigerated storage tanks, typically for 10 days to a month, but before commercial refrigeration, Cincinnati breweries made lager in the winter months, placed the barrels in deep cellars, dropped in ice harvested from frozen lakes and rivers, added straw or sawdust for insulation, and sealed it all with pitch. That way, crisp, fresh lagers flowed all summer long.

"Breweries were going through radical changes in the lager era," says Mike Morgan, a Cincinnati beer historian and author of *Over-the-Rhine: When Beer Was King*. "You have to have these big lagering cellars. So brewing goes from something you can start on a small scale to digging a four-story hole and building over the top of it this brewery that would cost tens of millions of dollars today. Capital gets shifted, the spaces are a lot larger, and brewers are more concerned with politics."

It's in this environment that pitch potatoes, cooked in the same manner as rosin potatoes, have their moment in Cincinnati. The oldest reference I've found to pitch potatoes is from 1892 at a lunch hosted at a social club associated with the Christian Moerlein Brewing Co. According to a note in The Cincinnati Enquirer, "John Moerlein gave a 'pitch' potato lunch at the Elm Street Club rooms yesterday afternoon to a party of friends. It was quite a novel affair, and was heartily enjoyed."

The Enquirer's casual mention of the dish, with no elaboration on the cooking method, suggests readers were already familiar with the potatoes, and Morgan believes they could date back as far as the 1870s. But it was at late-19th-century beefsteak dinners — a raucous style of dining and political campaigning that originated in New York City — that pitch potatoes flourished. To court votes and favors, raise campaign funds, and reward political donors, boosters and clubs would throw hours-long, all-you-can-eat steak dinners. In Cincinnati, breweries often played host, hanging chandeliers, setting up white-linened tables, and letting amber fluid flow freely, according to Morgan.

While bread was the carbohydrate of choice in New York, Cincinnati embraced the pitch potato. In addition to the John Kauffman Brewing Company, where "steaks were broiled over the coke fires in the malt dryers, and were served with 'pitch' potatoes and other vegetables," the potatoes were a fixture at the Bellevue, Mohawk, Windisch-Muhlhauser, Lackman, Buckeye, Jackson, Wiedmann's, and Bruckmann breweries.

Beefsteak dinners didn't have an exclusive hold on pitch potatoes. They were served in the city's beer gardens. In its 1904/1905 Sigma Chi Quarterly, frat boys visiting Chester Park, an amusement complex, recorded "an open-air dinner, spread upon the longest tables I have ever seen — one hundred yards if an inch: a dinner consisting of potatoes cooked in tar and served in round balls of paper, and many other strange and awful edibles and things."

Turn-of-the-century Cincinnati was also a major hub for conferences and conventions, of which pitch potatoes were a feature. At the 1898 gathering of the Master Horseshoers' National Protective Association, 350 members, representing 130 cities, ate a pitch potato supper. The Iron and Steel Workers' Convention of 1906 featured a beefsteak and pitch potato dinner, as did a 1909 gathering of 2,000 Knights of Pythias, a post-Civil War fraternal organization. In 1913, the National Association of Trunk Manufacturers ate pitch potatoes at Wiedmann's. In 1910, the Cincinnati Elks chapter threw a "beefsteak and pitch potato feast" for Elks en route to a convention in Detroit.

The preparation also emerged in cities like Buffalo and Pittsburgh. But almost as suddenly as pitch potatoes rose from the newspaper archives, they vanished again.

· · ·

When World War I broke out in 1914, so did anti-German hysteria. Ohio, once a bilingual state, declared English its official language and banned German language classes in schools before eighth grade. German street names changed. The press renamed sauerkraut "liberty cabbage" and hamburger "liberty steak." The Espionage Act of 1917 explicitly outlawed interfering with military operations and recruitment and essentially outlawed anything un-American, aka German.

"That was the death blow," Morgan says. Cincinnati's German clubs, almost infinite in number, disbanded. Prohibition finished the job. Shifting to near-beer production, Bruckmann Brewery was the only Cincinnati brewery that operated from 1920 to 1933, and only six breweries reopened after states repealed the 18th Amendment. Pitch potatoes did not survive the upheaval.

By the time rosin potatoes made a national splash in the 1950s, most — but not all — Cincinnatians had forgotten pitch potatoes. I found one article, from 1955, in which a Cincinnati journalist connects zeitgeist-y rosin potatoes with "brewery days when kegs were lined with rosin," and at least one enterprising Cincinnati family continued to make the potatoes at home.

David Hackman, whose father, Arnold, was head brewer at Hudepohl Brewing Company, remembers eating the potatoes, along with steak and corn on the cob, as far back as 1947. He and his father built a brick structure in the backyard so they could melt pitch in a kettle over wood. Hackman eventually upgraded to propane, which provided a heat so intense it scarred a nearby magnolia tree. Still, something got lost in translation. Hackman cooks his potatoes in petroleum-based pitch, a substance that scares away skeptical friends and children. "This is my tar thing," says Hackman, insisting, "the worst thing to happen is you get black shit between your teeth."

Hackman, who's now 84, can claim something that no one else his age in the turpentine belt can: he grew up with pitch potatoes and can trace the dish's provenance. At least up to a point.

Pitch potatoes were bobbing around so many Cincinnati breweries, it's not clear where they originated. There's a single blog post on the internet linking the potatoes back to Germany, but it's a fuzzy connection at best.

I sent queries to a German-American beer scholar, a German food historian, and the Berlin-based Society for the History of Brewing, a collective of more than 300 members who research and publish German beer histories and maintain an archive and library. None had ever come across pitch potatoes in their research, nor had a beer museum in Thuringia, a region once known for producing exceptional brewers pitch.

There's perhaps one clue in a 1912 article in Tägliches Cincinnatier Volksblatt. Though the article is written in old German, the words "pitch potatoes" appear in English, as if there's no direct translation. The piece concerns the visit of Gustav Stresemann from Dresden to Cincinnati. Stresemann would go on to serve as Germany's chancellor and win the Nobel Peace Prize, but at the time he served as executive director of Germany's Federation of Industrialists. The son of a beer distributor, Stresemann, who wrote his Ph.D. on beer bottling, wanted to visit a brewery while he was in town, and Windisch-Muhlhauser extended an invitation.

"Yet this was on such short notice that they could not offer pitch potatoes and steak but only bread, sausage, and ham, along with beer. They thought pitch potatoes were a delicious thing they should serve this grand dignitary," explained Jana Weiss, a beer historian at the University of Münster, who translated the article for me. "They would almost surely have used a German term if there was one."

...

I doubt I'll ever know for sure, but I believe pitch potatoes originated in Cincinnati breweries, where pitch was abundant and brewers found creative ways to cook with what they had on-site. At some point, J. Marquette Phillips came in contact with the dish, perhaps while traveling through Cincinnati or Pittsburgh, serving with Cincinnati men during World War I, or hobnobbing with Cincinnati snowbirds in Miami. But because his rosin potatoes debuted during World War II, Phillips chose not to disclose their German origins.

There's the possibility of parallel development, sure — the idea that the potato could have arisen independently in Cincinnati and the South. But I don't buy it. We know what turpentiners ate. It was recorded and passed down over centuries, and their foodways are alive today in homes like the Copelands'. What's quite clear is that while the early naval stores industry greedily consumed longleaf pines, German-American breweries were buying Southern-made pitch, feasting on potatoes cooked in it, and sharing it broadly with the public.

The rosin potato is weird. It's wild. It's captivating. It's also a pain in the ass. At both points in history when the rosin (née pitch) potato emerges, it hitches onto bigger cultural phenomena and explodes in popularity, only to recede into obscurity. German-Americans had more potent traditions and symbols. They gave us Budweiser! Phillips thought of himself on a grand scale; after he was ejected from Cuba, he sent a letter to President Kennedy asking to be installed as an ambassador to a small Central or South American nation. Rosin potatoes were a mere side note in a colorful life.

Rosin potatoes never merited serious thought in the South precisely because they did not matter in the culture. They had little commercial value to the AT-FA crowd. Akzo Nobel sold 20,000 pounds of rosin a month to Cracker Barrel, according to Baker, but shipped out millions of pounds more of its rosin-based products to other buyers. Only when the naval stores industry cratered and its real traditions — the songs, camps, catfaces, and stills of the piney woods — started to disappear did folks latch onto rosin potatoes.

...

In May, I flew to Nashville to eat Sean Brock's pine rosin potato at Audrey. As part of the snack course on a tasting menu that was upwards of a C-note, servers presented (for visual devouring only) gorgeous, lacquered Appalachian Gold potatoes that had been boiled in rosin and set in a ceramic bowl atop pine needles. After those were whisked away, diners got a tiny bowl filled with rosin-cooked potato flesh mixed with local Cruze Farm buttermilk and topped with fresh trout roe and freeze-dried buttermilk.

The Elusive Roots of Rosin Potatoes

Brock told me rosin, and its pine aroma, reminds him of growing up in Appalachia, and on Instagram he had called the potatoes an "old mountain tradition." That night at dinner, I told him I would be setting the record straight. These potatoes don't hail from Appalachia; they're not even from the South.

But in a bite, with pure potato flavor lit through with buttermilk tang, I recognized an unmistakable Southern accent.

Rosin potatoes may not hail from the South, but potatoes, when boiled in Southern-made rosin, are a portal that can both flatten and complicate the history of the naval stores industry — an industry that transformed whole regions, extracted wealth at the expense of Black workers, replaced longleaf ecosystems with slash pine farms, and, especially in later years, put groceries on the table and gave men purposeful work.

The faith folks have in rosin potatoes isn't just an act of blind, unquestioning nostalgia. In Tim Prizer's work with turpentiners, he writes, "It is clear that nostalgia is often productive, insightful, critical — even progressive. ... From turpentine's material remains, former workers are able to extract profound experiential meaning, evaluate the current state of their communities, and determine which aspects of the past are worth transmitting into the future, which virtues of history should be upheld for posterity."

The rosin potato myth, as rosy as it is, imagines a world in which there was greater parity between white and Black turpentiners, that men working at the stills would break to share a hot lunch, a potato cooked in the literal fruits of their labor. And this potato would have been so exceptional that it would be replicated in restaurants and backyards across the country.

"The rosin potato fortifies [turpentiners'] own history," Prizer tells me, confessing that he, too, hadn't thought twice about the turpentine-camp origin story. "It makes their own past and the region's past more interesting, more alive, through this unusual food tradition, a food made from this thing that was their livelihood."

The first time I spoke with Bill Baker, he told me he felt proud every time he drove by Akzo Nobel. In it, he saw a lifetime of honest work with the living pine. Likewise, what the rest of the world sees as a truly strange potato preparation, turpentiners recognize and taste as the work of their hands.

What is Southern cuisine, Brock asked me at dinner, if not a combination of cultural influences, geography, and ingredients? "I'm mostly interested in what Southern food can become," he says. "Because it's about discovery. And what if everything hasn't been discovered?"

In 1991, the year Cracker Barrel discontinued the rosin potato, the restaurant chain offered a free dinner to anyone with "written proof of the use of recipes for rosin-baked potatoes before 1958." They didn't include a deadline for submissions, and I expect to collect on my comped plate of chicken and dumplings soon. In the same spirit, I'd love to buy a beer or dinner at Audrey for the first person with written proof of rosin, or pitch, potatoes before 1892. ◊

—

Caroline Hatchett is a freelance writer and senior editor at Plate, a restaurant industry magazine. She lives in New York City but was born and raised in Baxley, Georgia, and graduated from the University of Georgia's Grady College of Journalism. Her work has appeared in The Washington Post, Garden & Gun, CNN, Wine Enthusiast, Robb Report, and Eater, among other publications. She also serves on the board of Restaurant Workers' Community Foundation, a workers' advocacy nonprofit.

The Elusive Roots of Rosin Potatoes

THIS LAST EARTHY SWEETNESS

—

by Chelsey Mae Johnson

Photo by Chelsey Mae Johnson
This story was originally published September 22, 2020

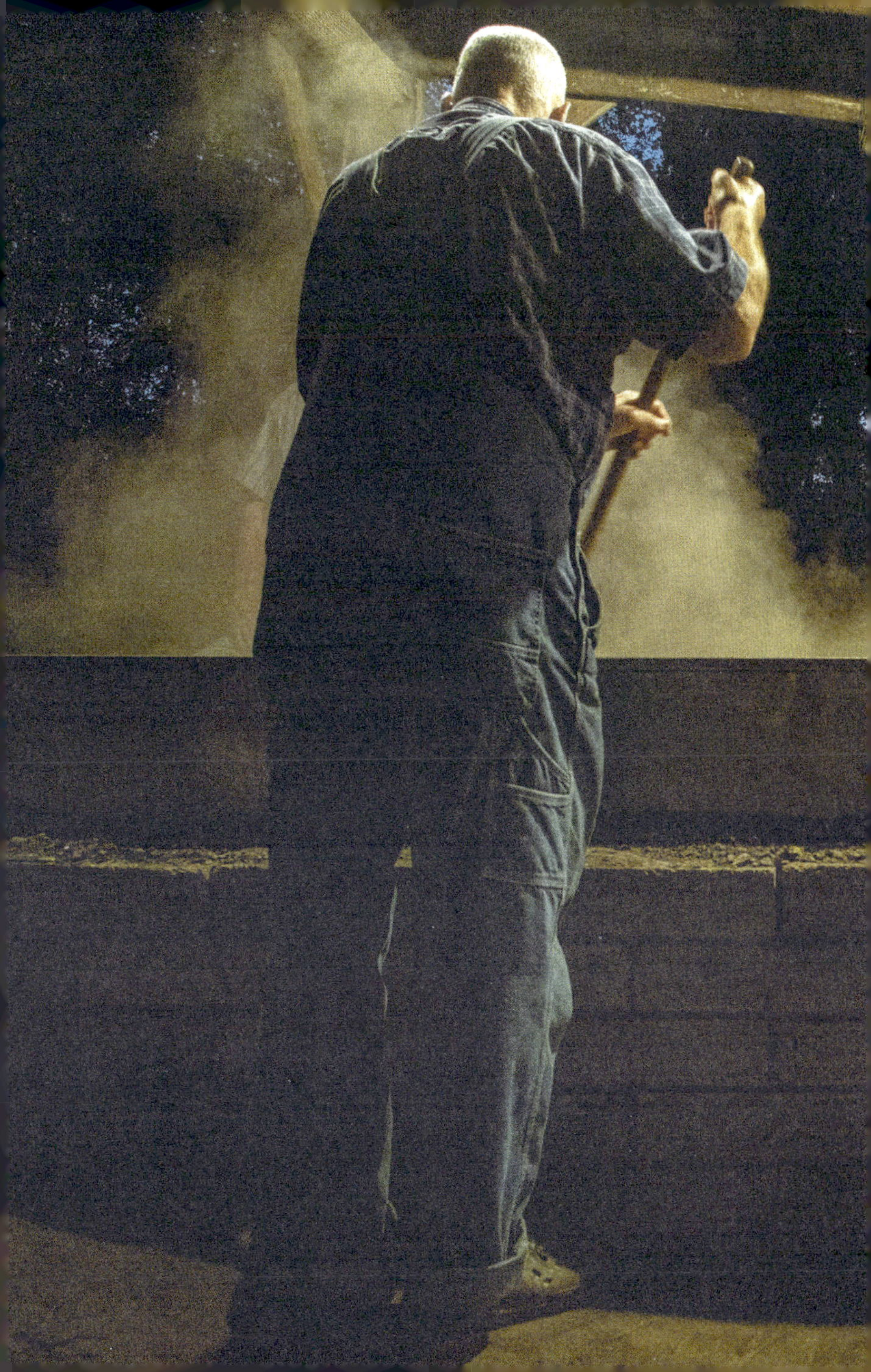

This Last Earthy Sweetness

HOW TO MAKE MOLASSES

First, realize you are not making molasses.

Not unless you're in the tropics — maybe Louisiana, Georgia, or Florida — and you're at a near-commercial level of production with sugar cane, genus *Saccharum*. You cannot miss true sugar cane; it grows up to 20 feet tall and each stalk is obscured by a dense tangle of leaves that will slice bare skin right open.

If you're anywhere else in the United States, and especially if you're in the Appalachian Mountains, you're dealing with sweet sorghum cane. *Sorghum bicolor*. Somebody driving by a sorghum patch might miss it, because from a little ways back, it looks a lot like corn. You're going to work a few hundred hours in that patch to raise cane and make it into a syrup you might eventually pour on a biscuit, and you're going to call it molasses, too.

You will haul the 5-gallon buckets rustling with last year's seedheads out of the shed in the early summer, and you will get the seeds into the ground at just the right time. You will know when it is the right time because you have done this for 50 years; 50 batches of buckets; 50 early summer days. You may hitch up a mule and till the patch before planting, or you may use a tractor. It depends on how you're feeling this year — depends on your knees, your back, your knuckles.

Watch as the cane stalks grow taller than your hounds, then your horses. Watch your bees help this patch through June, July, August. Rob the honey. Whelp the puppies. Bring in the scuppernongs for jelly; and when the apples start to come, watch the seedheads. As long as they sway green atop the cane, your attention is welcome elsewhere. When they start to flush garnet, put out the call to your friends and neighbors. Once they've dried to a burnished oxblood, you've got a few long weekends ahead of you.

The first days will be spent with however many of those friends you can wrangle, stripping cane in the patch on the crest of the hill. They will come decked in ball caps and straw hats and strong gardening gloves, those available to help in the daylight hours but not yet too old to work in the midday sun. Together you'll peel the floppy leaves away, leaving a field full of swaying green stalks about as big around as a broom handle. On a second pass, you'll chop the tops and the bottoms, tossing the seedpods aside to fill next year's buckets, piling the now-smooth sticks into the bed of the truck. To prep a quarter acre, allow about a week.

Haul out the ancient mill, scrub the boiling pan, get the tractor and loaded truck beds into position. You need to be grinding by 7 a.m. if you aim to sleep at all the night of the first run.

In the morning, have coffee, have some pancakes, too. Gather the eggs, feed the dogs. Shuck your jacket knowing the late September day will soon swelter. Wait for whoever will show up first to help; you need at least one other to run the mill efficiently. Tamp down your impatience as your watch hand slides past 7. Greet your buddy's truck with a wave, fire up the tractor before the dust of the driveway has settled.

Stand in the sun. Stand there as it climbs over the poplar tops right into your eyes, making you squint while you feed 70 cubic feet of stalks through, a couple at a time. Chat easy over the comfortable rumble of the tractor and let those with younger backs pitchfork the papery piles of spent cane stalks into a trailer. Be realistic about the convenience of the tractor, geared just so to run these antique steel rollers, but wish it were horses snorting slow circles around you to turn the mill — that you still had the time and the help and the knuckles and knees to use horses.

Check that the trickle of juice is steady, joggle the hose that runs down the hill to the pan. Squeeze the bloated filter bag when the sediment buildup overpowers the gravity flow and juice starts to create tiny fountains through pinprick holes in the linen. Watch the murky green waterline climb the stainless sides, smelling like cut grass and corn sweetness, and do not think of it as looking like pond scum, or kale juice, or anything except exactly what it is.

Break for lunch. Share what everyone has brought: casseroles and dips and layered desserts, a basket of apples and a cut crystal bowl of foxy grapes, cold cornbread and chow-chow and Yoo-hoos, all spread on card tables under a tent set out for the occasion.

Start the fire while everyone else is still eating. Push and pile wood all the way to the back of the 6-foot pit under the boiling pan. Stoke the blaze while they grind the last stalks, waste no time waiting when it isn't necessary.

Cut the tractor engine, spray away all the stickiness, tidy up the grinding gear enough to last till tomorrow morning. Pull up a chair next to somebody you've been meaning to catch up with. Wait.

Skim the junk as the juice begins to bubble, scooping froth with a small shovel that looks like it's been blasted with buckshot. You ought to skim, but you really don't have to skim all the time, not like they say. You just have to watch it, keep it pretty clean. Keep the fire hot. Keep the conversation flowing. Expect to keep on skimming, stoking, and telling old jokes for eight or 10 hours.

You will not smoke or chew or drink anything but the coffee your daughter brings from the upscale market she manages. She grinds it for you right there in the store, and you perk it on the stove, and your son passes around Styrofoam cups in the darkening hours and everybody has some. The last of the jar flies whine loud. The air cools, finally.

Dip the scoop into the simmer, then swing it back and forth in a slow arc to cool the layer of syrup that's stuck. Let it form little drips, see how thick they are. See if it tastes right. When it's ready — when the green has gone gold then caramel then the color of rich peat, shining and beading up strings of bubbles like frog eggs — assemble four to lift the steaming pan like pallbearers, shuffling over to the bare soft dirt by the driveway and setting it there to cool. Let some younger person ladle the syrup into a clean sack to be filtered so you can spend the time tracing your finger through film left coating the pan, licking up this last earthy sweetness of the season.

If you had good weather this year and the juice got to the right sugariness and your luck in general is running high, today's 120 gallons of thick green juice will yield 10 gallons of molasses.

When someone asks you what advice you might give to someone younger who wants to be like you, to try their hand at raising sorghum cane, say, "It's work." Say, "If you charged $50 a quart, you wouldn't make 5 cents an hour for the work you put in." Maybe just laugh, and say, "Good luck."

HOW TO LEARN HOW TO MAKE MOLASSES

Chat up an older man selling honey in his overalls at a fiddlers convention in Western North Carolina. Pay attention when he says he's been raising cane and coon hounds on a piece of family land a few miles down the valley, just about as long as he can remember. Give him a call around molasses-making time, be curious and sweet, get an invite to his family boil.

Spend your birthday weekend watching syrup boil, even though your boyfriend's come to visit for only the second time this year, even though you had plans, even though you're hungover. It's ready when it's ready.

Get lost the first, third, and fourth visits. Gag helplessly at the smell of the chicken farm a few miles up the road. Worry that your car won't make it back up the steep driveway. Worry that your accent isn't strong enough. Wear the right boots, but bring the wrong thing to the potluck.

Stand in the sun. Sweat through your black V-neck, know that the mirrored sunglasses are ostentatious but know that without them you'll get a headache.

Recall that even though you grew up here, in these mountains, you did not taste sorghum until you worked in a very expensive restaurant for a chef obsessed with the food of Appalachia. No one in your family romanticizes this bitter, salty sweetener. After a lifetime of working graveyard shifts at the plant, your grandparents retired loving Charms

Blow Pops and Reese's Puffs, loving to watch you stuff your tiny-toothed mouth full of their store-bought sweets.

Break for lunch. Assume this means you should make an exit; realize that is impossible and rude, besides. That even toting your own water bottle instead of accepting a cold drink comes across as borderline impolite.

Want to be involved, do work, get your hands sticky. Worry too much about being in the way. Hang back.

Coo and pet the puppies. Call them cute then wonder if this is offensive, these being serious and expensive working dogs. Feel better when you're told nobody's ever seen a redbone puppy that wasn't cute.

Wait around. Sit and talk. Listen to stories not told for you, watch it get dark. Watch everything.

Think, damn, this is a long day. This is work. ◊

* *In memory of Stanley "Cotton" Marley (1950-2020), who loved to share his knowledge of mountain traditions.*

—

Chelsey Mae Johnson earned a master's degree in Appalachian Studies and Public History from Appalachian State University in Boone, North Carolina. She researches and writes about food traditions, folk artists, and kitsch culture.

THE WOMAN WHO ATE ATLANTA

—

by Wendell Brock

Winner of the James Beard Media Award in 2016 for Best Profile

—

Photo by Troy Stains
This story was originally published April 7, 2015

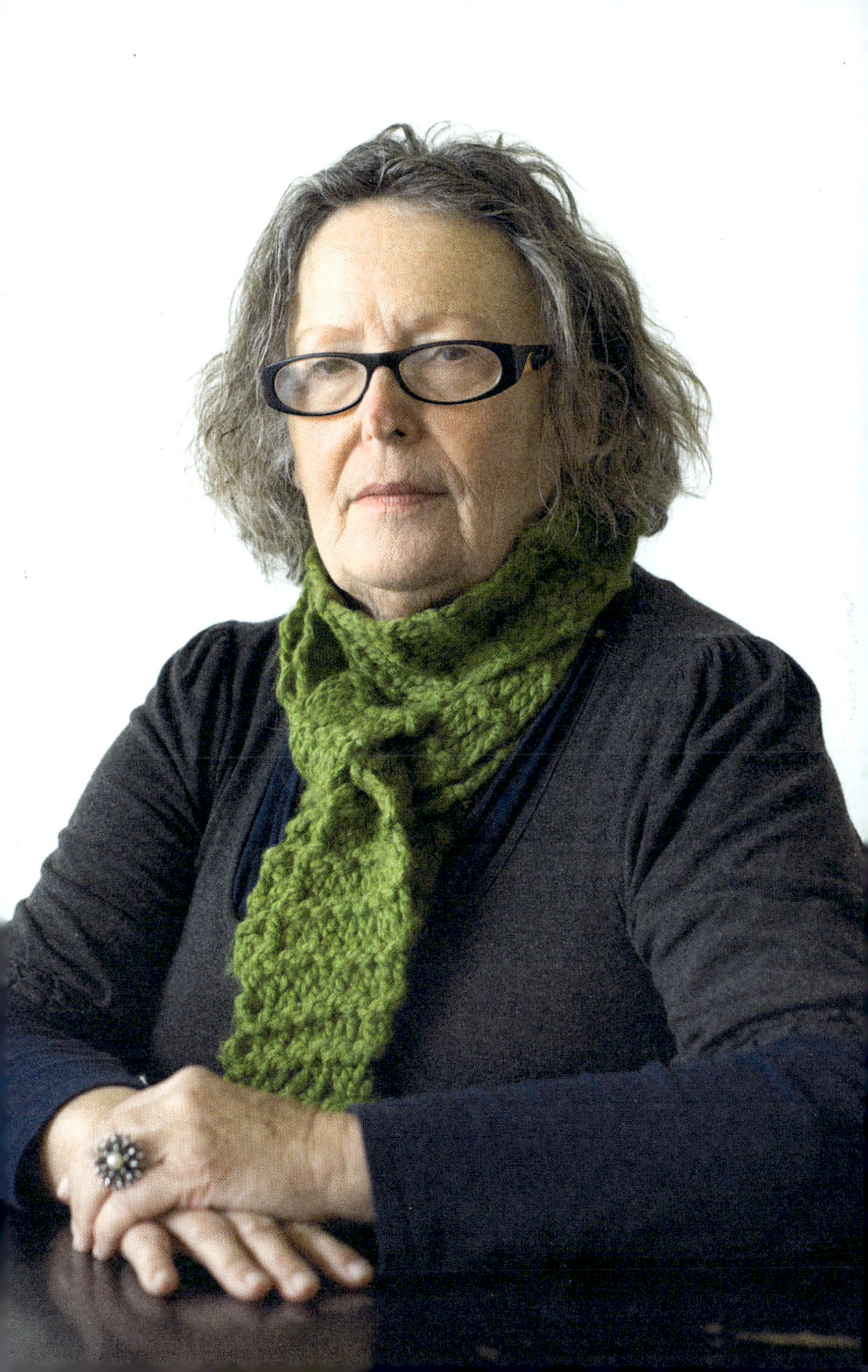

The Woman Who Ate Atlanta

Her mother left her when she was a baby, and the grandmother who ended up raising her could be mean and difficult. This paternal *grand-mère* was a terrific cook, though, and a gardener. So when she wasn't bossing her granddaughter or tending to her fruit trees, chickens and rabbits, she fed her sumptuous food.

We should probably mention that this was the Paris of the 1950s, a moment in time when the cuisine was as rich as the culture. At her grandmother's table, the lonely little girl might stuff herself on duck eggs, lamb brains sautéed in black butter, apricot pies, and freshly fried beignets. Then, with nothing more than a Paris Metro card tucked in her pocket, she could escape her grandma's smothering presence to wander the City of Light, looking for delicious things to fill her belly.

So while Edith Piaf trilled songs of love and sorrow, and the existentialists contemplated the meaning of being and nothingness, little Christiane Françoise Luc would save her coins to buy a can of pâté de foie gras — or shyly approach the counter of a gourmet deli and ask for a scoop of hearts of palm salad.

• • •

When the great Atlanta food writer Christiane Lauterbach describes the Paris childhood that shaped her palate, there is a fairy tale, rags-to-riches quality to her story — a touch of Cinderella.

Food Stories

"If you have seen the movie 'The 400 Blows,' it's a little bit of my background," she tells me as she sips a cup of cortado at Little Tart Bakeshop in the Krog Street Market in Atlanta's Inman Park neighborhood on a cool winter morning. She's referring to François Truffaut's New Wave classic about a troubled young boy who eventually finds freedom by running off to the seashore.

"I had a pretty fierce grandmother, but otherwise, it was pretty loosey-goosey, and not wealthy, for sure," says Lauterbach, who was born in the 6th Arrondissement of Paris and later moved to suburban Colombes, which she describes as "about as glamorous as living in Queens."

Her mother, a schoolteacher, ran off with another man when she was 2. Her father worked in a factory that made X-ray tubes.

"We were a weird family," she says, punctuating her heavily accented English with girlish giggles, nervous hiccups of laughter, and, every once in a while, an unapologetic little snort. "We were definitely a weird family. At the time, it was very unusual. I didn't know anybody whose parents were divorced; who had been abandoned by their mother."

· · ·

When The Bitter Southerner asked me to profile the fearlessly opinionated Lauterbach — a longtime restaurant columnist for Atlanta magazine and the publisher of the indispensable, 32-year-old "Knife & Fork: The Insider's Guide to Atlanta Restaurants" — I immediately agreed.

Over the years, my interactions with Lauterbach had been brief but pleasurable. I met her in the late '90s, when I first began to write about food for The Atlanta Journal-Constitution. Later, when I became the paper's theater critic, our paths rarely crossed.

Many will tell you that Lauterbach is intimidating. But from the get-go, I found this short woman with spiky red hair, cat-woman glasses, and fishnet hose to be a fabulously fascinating feline.

A bit of a performer, a purring sensualist, a delightfully dishy conversationalist, Lauterbach was sexy in a bookish kind of way: a great person to sit by when you found yourself dateless at the wedding of a mutual friend, a raconteur who responded to tedious questions about her work with dismissive, coquettish jokes.

On the occasion of her 20th anniversary as dining critic of Atlanta magazine, Rebecca Burns, then editor-in-chief of the publication, recalls the scene at which she introduced herself to Lauterbach.

This was 1995. At that time, Burns was a bit of a reticent freelancer, while Lauterbach was the resident diva and exotic. When Burns asked the preening glamor-puss her favorite thing to eat — a question that nearly every critic loathes — Lauterbach responded: "My favorite thing to do when I get home is to get naked, crawl between the sheets of my bed, and eat a big bowl of thick, plain yogurt."

In 2010, the Southern Foodways Alliance gave Lauterbach the Craig Claiborne Lifetime Achievement Award. Around that time, John T. Edge, the director of that organization, quoted Lauterbach in the Oxford American as saying: "In my declining years, I'd like to run a dominatrix training school for waiters and waitresses. I'll wear fishnets and carry a whip. I will help them see it my way."

These are the kind of glib comments Lauterbach, who is cagey about revealing her age, tosses off when she doesn't want to give serious answers. They are part of a highly crafted public persona that has been called punk and futurist, difficult and demanding, snobby and unfathomable, quirky and just plain weird.

It's the armor a vulnerable, intensely private woman puts on to protect herself from the prying interlopers who dare to put her in a box. What I was eager to discover, and what I pursued over the course of a half dozen meetings and meals with her, was the complex personality within.

I wanted to see what was behind the mask.

...

Here are some things you should know about Lauterbach, who has been eating her way around Atlanta since moving to the city in 1974:

She forms opinions quickly and sticks to them, even when the consequences are costly.

Food Stories

She likes to eat alone, often sitting at the bar of a restaurant. That way she can gather her thoughts and concentrate without interruption. Naturally, it doesn't always work out that way. Sometimes she needs company so she can try as much food as possible in a single sitting. In that case she prefers men with large appetites. She lets them take home the leftovers, so that she's not tempted to indulge.

She has an ego. "Sometimes I want to tell people: 'Don't tell me what you think, because you are just a prop. You are there so I don't look like an idiot ordering five meals. But your opinion" — she pauses for a second, and makes the sound of a whining cat — "it really doesn't matter."

She wears Prada glasses. She hates cats.

English is her third language, after French and German. She also speaks Spanish and gets by in Italian and Dutch. She has studied ancient Greek and Latin, Russian, and Arabic.

She is fastidious about cleanliness. Servers whom she sees playing with their hair or otherwise touching their bodies are unacceptable to her.

She has been terrorized by restaurant owners. "One time I moved out of my house because I got death threats and they sounded pretty serious. ... I reported it to the police, and I moved out for a few days because I was freaked out about that. It hasn't happened in a while, but people used to scream at me and carry on. 'Oh, how could you say my chandeliers are vulgar?' Because they are."

Once, after a particularly withering review of an Atlanta establishment that shall go unnamed, she was told never to return to any of the restaurant group's locations. She defied the ban, appearing at the company's next new place with two well-known restaurant reviewers. No one got thrown out. She told me that she didn't care what the restaurant owners thought of her: She refused to be intimidated. "I know I am a fat French fuck," she says.

At this point in her career, she is frequently recognized. Not by her appearance. But by her voice. I have witnessed this.

She does not own a TV, but she does stream video via the internet. She loves "The Wire" and the Korean TV series "Boys Over Flowers." She's up to date on Netflix's "Unbreakable Kimmy Schmidt."

She is a Pisces. She likes to knit.

The Woman Who Ate Atlanta

She is not interested in social media. No Facebook, no Twitter, no Instagram. "If I had wanted to take pictures of cheeseburgers, I would have made a different career. I'm not supervisual." For the record: For a short time during the rise of the Atlanta food-truck scene, she kept a blog, Atlanta Food Carts. The last post is dated September 10, 2010. "Knife & Fork" has no online presence — and never has in its 32 years of existence. "I don't follow anybody, and I don't want anybody to follow me," she says. "I don't want to be followed!"

She prefers not to drive on interstates. She is likely to find more surprising places to eat on the back roads.

She adores thrift stores.

She has two grown daughters and three grandchildren. She is a doting grandma who uses Skype to communicate with her 2-year-old grandson in Washington state. In her home, there is a tiny menagerie of miniature animals that she plays with during these conversations. Apparently, the kid has picked up grandma's favorite word: "Bleh!"

She has survived things that would send other souls clamoring for psychotherapy, yet I have never seen her play the victim. For example: Her second husband abandoned her with two small children. Simply didn't show for an Easter brunch, where they were waiting. As a result, Lauterbach and her two daughters don't care much for Easter. I learn this when I take her with me to research a piece for the AJC on the Blue Willow Inn, an iconic Southern restaurant in Social Circle, Georgia. We happen to stop by the Blue Willow gift shop, which is laden with toy bunnies, eggs, and candy, and she opens up about her divorce. By all accounts, she was devastated when her husband left her. "I was crazy about Jeffrey," she tells me. "He may have been a monster. But he was my monster."

Since starting "Knife & Fork" in 1983, she has chronicled the ethnic cuisines of Atlanta, from Buford Highway to the Korean boroughs of Duluth. In this way, she can indulge her curiosity for new discoveries, just as she did as a little girl wandering the streets of Paris. "The thing is," she tells me, "very few people go to a restaurant they have never heard of. Me, I'll be driving around and I'll just be going in and out, in and out, and I make up my own mind. If you don't go to the bad places, you shouldn't be able to talk about the good places, because you don't really know the gap, the difference. So that's very much the way I conduct my life."

This endless pursuit of the city's changing dining demographic is part of her remarkable legacy and one of the reasons she is Atlanta's most essential omnivore.

...

How did Christiane Lauterbach evolve into the person she is today?

As a young woman, Lauterbach says, she wanted to become a librarian. But her grandmother told her she'd never get married if she did. She later considered archaeology. "Then I thought: No. Creepy. Bleh! Digging in real places!"

This is how Lauterbach talks, how she entertains me during our first interview at Little Tart. She ended up being a preschool teacher in the Paris public school system. This was partly for mercenary reasons. She wanted to be independent, and by attending teachers college, she could draw a small salary. So she left home at 17.

"I was very impatient as a teacher," she says.

"You terrorized the children?" I ask her teasingly.

"A little bit. I'm a disciplinarian in many ways," she answers. "So being a teacher, it satisfied my desire to perform. But I was way too impatient. Forty kids in a small Paris [classroom]. Bah! Insane!"

...

In her early 20s, Lauterbach met Volker Süssmann, a man almost eight years her senior, the son of General Wilhelm Süssmann, a German air force officer who was killed in the Battle of Crete. They married, lived in Munich, and ate well.

"He taught me how to travel in style," Lauterbach wrote in the 2004 issue of Atlanta magazine celebrating her 20th year as the publication's restaurant critic.

Süssmann was a corporate lawyer for a subsidiary of an American pharmaceutical corporation, and the two moved to New York in the early '70s. She was excited and invigorated to be back in a big city, but soon her world changed again.

Süssmann introduced her to a paralegal named Jeffrey Lauterbach. "I fell in love with Jeffrey, who was five years younger than me," she tells me later in an email.

When I asked her if she was not in love with Süssmann, she replied, "I was a confused and ambitious chick on the make, more than anything else. ... I was also seduced by the New York lifestyle — so free, so exciting."

To stay with Süssmann would have meant returning to Germany. Instead, she and Lauterbach married and moved to Atlanta in 1974 so he could study law at Emory University.

As a European who didn't drive, Lauterbach was shocked by Atlanta, which was then a rather provincial black-and-white town.

"I loved the city and the trees kind of thing," she says in her curious English. "But it was not enough city for me. I was not able to do what I normally do, which was walk constantly — explore. It was very difficult just to even conceive of that in Atlanta, but I was charmed by the vegetation and a new culture. I mean, for me, invading a new culture is incredibly interesting."

Forty years later, she is still investigating this strange city, where she has maintained the tricky duality of being both an outsider and an insider. That is the great contradiction that is Christiane Lauterbach. But is it a gift, or a limitation?

• • •

When somebody gave Jeffrey Lauterbach an Atlanta guidebook featuring restaurants to visit, his wife picked it up and thought: "Gee, I could do that." After all, she had always been an adventurous eater. "For me, comparing food experiences has always been part of what I have done — subconsciously."

Soon they were reviewing restaurants as a couple, and in February 1983, they formed "Knife & Fork" with three friends: Bill Cutler, now deceased, and Sue and Steve Kreitzman, with whom Lauterbach has since lost touch.

The Lauterbachs' daughter, Hillary Lauterbach Brown, can't remember a time when the family wasn't reviewing restaurants.

"I remember them doing the paste-up for the layout on the floor or the kitchen table every week," says Brown, who has been proofreading the newsletter since she was a kid and has been the designer since she was a high schooler at The Paideia School, a private academy in Atlanta.

According to Lauterbach, the original group met to assign reviews. The couples often paired up to write; at the end, everybody got together again for a group edit.

From the get-go, "Knife & Fork" had a slightly stilted, rather dandified Old World tone that Lauterbach attributes to Cutler. "We used the 'royal we' from The New Yorker, which we all read," she says.

Visually, "Knife & Fork" hasn't changed much in its three decades; it has retained its eight-page, three-hole-punch format so that it can be filed in a folder.

"Every once in a while, a subscriber will call me and say: 'I have 25 years of "Knife & Fork." My wife wants to throw it away. Can I give it back to you?'" says Lauterbach, doing a very good imitation of a creaky-voiced elderly person.

"That's exactly what we wanted, what I wanted," Lauterbach says. "So it's just like a blog, but better digested than most blogs."

One by one, the original writers died or left town. The Lauterbachs divorced in 1989. Since then, Lauterbach has maintained the ship solo, writing in a tone that is consistent with the earliest issues.

Today "Knife & Fork" remains the single most comprehensive record of Atlanta dining history — an encyclopedic, 30-year database that exists in written form and in the brain trust that is Lauterbach.

"She is the holder of our collective culinary knowledge in Atlanta," says Bill Addison, who replaced her as Atlanta magazine's chief dining critic in 2009. "At a time when criticism is transitioning in Atlanta, she is more vital than ever, and her voice remains not just authoritative but enlightening."

John Kessler, the AJC dining critic who befriended Lauterbach after he moved to Atlanta from Denver in 1997, agrees.

"'Knife & Fork' is such a living document of where Atlanta was, the way nothing else has really been," he says. "It's not prettied up and presented at all. It's not marketed. It is a snapshot of a month in the life of Atlanta's restaurant scene."

According to Lauterbach, "Knife & Fork" has 1,500 subscribers. They pay $28 per year or $46 for two years.

"We virtually never go out to eat without consulting 'Knife & Fork' and make a practice of giving it to new colleagues when they arrive in Atlanta," Bill Amis, a subscriber since the beginning, told me in an email. "We currently give 'Knife & Fork' to 11 friends."

And yet Lauterbach is so fiercely competitive that she has been known to ignore subscription requests from some Atlanta food writers and news outlets. Some get around that by subscribing anonymously.

"She does not make it easy to subscribe to 'Knife & Fork'," says Brown, who has followed in her mother's footsteps and reviews restaurants for the Athens publication Flagpole. "It's like a speakeasy. You have to know the number."

Apparently that strategy is working. Even in the digital age, when news updates are just a click away, "Knife & Fork" consistently scoops competing publications like the AJC and Atlanta magazine.

Brown told me that her father, now a Philadelphia-based financial planner, still subscribes.

• • •

Lauterbach may not have the name recognition of Kessler or the national readership of Addison, who left Atlanta magazine last year and is now the national dining critic for Eater.

But in the circle of American dining critics, she cuts a formidable figure. Since 1997, she has been a member of the James Beard Foundation's Restaurant and Chef Awards Committee.

Back in the '80s, when Atlanta magazine hired Lauterbach to review restaurants, the trend in Atlanta fine dining was "continental." Her European background was an obvious plus. In her early days at the magazine, she shared a byline with then-husband Jeffrey Lauterbach.

"For Atlanta magazine, we were fascinated with her European savoir faire at the beginning," Addison says, "while she herself found a devotion to Buford Highway and the cuisines that were much more far-flung. I feel like over the years she has tried to blend the two in the publications that she's written for." Now, he says, "the rest of the population has caught up with Christiane's curiosity."

Lauterbach has never been shy about talking to restaurateurs — unlike reviewers for American newspapers, who generally try to dine out anonymously. "I think there is no conflict in that in her mind," Kessler says. "And there isn't in her copy."

Says Lauterbach: "Anonymity is very overrated. ... I'm sure I know the 20 most important food critics in the nation, and they are not very anonymous, believe me." According to Lauterbach and every restaurant critic I know, there is only so much a chef can do to alter a restaurant experience once a reviewer has been spotted in the place.

Lauterbach never makes a reservation in her own name, and she always pays her own way. If she doesn't like a dish, she will ask that it be removed from the bill.

"I have been with her," Kessler says, "when the waitress, the sweet little hi-my-name-is-Kimberly, comes over and says: 'Is it fantastic?' And she goes, 'No, I wouldn't say it's fantastic. This is inedible.' And you'll just see this girl going, 'I'm sorry???'

'This is inedible. I can't eat it. I don't want it sitting here. And you have to take it away.' And [the server] goes: 'Oh, my goodness! I'm so sorry! Everyone else loves that dish.' And then she'll go: 'I don't care what everyone else says. I hate it. It's inedible. Take it away.'"

In her words: "If you are a restaurateur and I say something bad about you, you should seriously consider that it was bad. And fix it. I am giving you the benefit of my opinion. You could be paying dearly a consultant to find out why this or that aspect of your business sucks."

If that sounds harsh, Lauterbach can be insanely funny, too.

Kessler quotes her as saying the best advice she could give him was this:

"If they bring the wrong dish to your table, if it was meant for the neighboring table, take a bite quick so you can try it."

For free.

. . .

While I was researching this article, Lauterbach invited me to Watershed on Peachtree, a restaurant she has followed since its founding in 1999 by Emily Saliers of the rock band Indigo Girls and restaurateur Ross Jones.

Lauterbach championed the Southern restaurant during its heady early days, when Alabama-born chef Scott Peacock ran the kitchen. A protege of Southern-food doyenne Edna Lewis, Peacock won a James Beard Award while at Watershed. He and Lauterbach became friends. (Once, while driving them back from an event in South Georgia in the middle of the night, he hit a deer with his red Volvo, she told me, remembering the moment with some horror.)

But when Peacock passed the toque to chef Joe Truex and the restaurant moved to Buckhead, Lauterbach lost interest. She panned Truex's cooking and wasn't so crazy about designer Smith Hanes' gray decor, either.

Recently, Zeb Stevenson replaced Truex, who moved to Dubai late last year to operate a pizza joint, and Lauterbach wanted to sample the new executive chef's menu.

I make a reservation under an assumed name. We arrive. We blend in.

But when Lauterbach begins to order, her demeanor changes. She tells the server she wants to try Stevenson's new menu items and that's all she cares about. She grows stern and professorial.

Not long after that, Stevenson arrives at our table to say hello. The server has told him about this rapt woman who is interested only in his food. When he asks if the lady has a French accent and the staffer tells him yes, it's a giveaway.

Soon, co-owner Jones and her girlfriend, Susan Owens, stop by with a bottle of rosé. The meal is impeccable.

When Stevenson swings by again, Lauterbach tells him the half-pint portion size of his chicken liver mousse is too large, that it could give somebody a heart attack.

"She said the portion size was 'immoral,'" Stevenson recalls on the day I call him to ask about the experience. "That is a verbatim quote. I laughed my ass off."

But he listened to her advice. Instead of serving it in a chubby jar, "I now make it in a terrine mold and cut a slice for service," Stevenson says. "It's quite a bit more moral."

...

"Knife & Fork" may have a small readership, but Lauterbach's words, good and bad, are wildly influential.

"In the community of chefs in this city, a kind word from Christiane is equivalent to bragging rights," Stevenson says. "When I am fortunate enough to have her say something nice about me in 'Knife & Fork,' you better bet that I get text messages from other chefs in the city saying, 'Hey, I read that. Nice job.'"

Apparently, getting too close to Lauterbach can be a slippery slope.

"It's live by the sword, die by the sword," she told me. "If you want to know me a little better, be aware that it doesn't buy you a better opinion. On the contrary, I may be harder on you because I know you."

"She pulls no punches," Addison says. "A chef being charming and speaking to her at the table for a few minutes does not sway her judgment. She will say what she feels needs to be said about a restaurant."

During the course of our meal at Watershed, I ask Lauterbach if she considers herself Southern after living in the region for so long. She responds with an unequivocal "Noooooooooo."

She's a Parisian. First, last, always.

...

Lauterbach lives in a beautiful modern space in Atlanta's Candler Park neighborhood. Except for the office where she keeps her files and papers, it is sparsely furnished, with a calm, minimalist aesthetic that reminds me a bit of the house of Alvar Aalto in Helsinki.

The kitchen has an industrial-size stainless steel refrigerator and sink, and a movable work table with a white marble top. Stacks of white china, of the sort you might find at a Parisian café, are stacked neatly beside the sink.

A central skylight illuminates a small collection of tall, lush-looking plants. Her dining table originally came from a school, and has the markings to prove it.

A pair of white slippers is on the floor next to her bed — Japanese style — and when I comment on the TV, she reminds me that it is a computer monitor, not a television.

Lauterbach rarely lets strangers into her home. But she takes obvious pride in the clean, well-lighted space and in showing me and a photographer around a garden where she grows tomatoes, lettuces, herbs, and other edible things.

Like her grandma, who loved her lilacs, ferns and hydrangeas, she is a devoted gardener. But she only grows edible plants. Once, I arrive to find her with a reference book on weeds in her hands: She is trying to find the name of a particularly invasive specimen — using the approach of a librarian.

But there is one thing beside the door she will not allow us to photograph, even though she points it out with her usual chattiness.

It's a bloodstain.

Last July, while her daughter and grandchild were sleeping in a bedroom, Lauterbach awoke to find an invader prowling through her home. He punched her over the eye, and took her car and her iPad.

She later found the car herself, doing the job of the police.

It was, as her daughter Hillary recalls, a horrific moment. When they went for takeout at Taqueria del Sol in Decatur, Lauterbach was so spooked that she only ordered one fish taco instead of her usual two.

That became the family's little joke.

Even though her face was bruised, she didn't stop eating out.

Nor is she likely to.

Food Stories

• • •

So this is what I learned about Christiane Lauterbach over the two months I spent following her around: She's been abandoned. She's been demoted. She's been bullied, and she's been bludgeoned.

But she is a survivor. And she refuses to stop doing what she loves.

When I ask her if she is tired of reviewing restaurants, she seems to have trouble understanding the concept. Burned out? Au contraire.

This feisty, indefatigable Parisian intellectual with the rapier wit and ravenous curiosity is nowhere near pushing back from the table.

She was born hungry — always ready for her next great bite. ◊

—

Wendell Brock is an Atlanta-based food and culture writer. During a long and varied career with The Atlanta Journal-Constitution, he held many positions, including theater critic and restaurant reviewer. His "lost interview" with Truman Capote's Aunt Marie Rudisill is a Bitter Southerner classic, and this portrait of Christiane Lauterbach won the 2016 James Beard Award for Profile Writing.

The Woman Who Ate Atlanta

A HUNGER FOR TOMATOES

by Shane Mitchell

Winner of the James Beard Media Award in 2019 for Foodways
—
Photo by Fernando Decillis
This story was originally published September 25, 2018

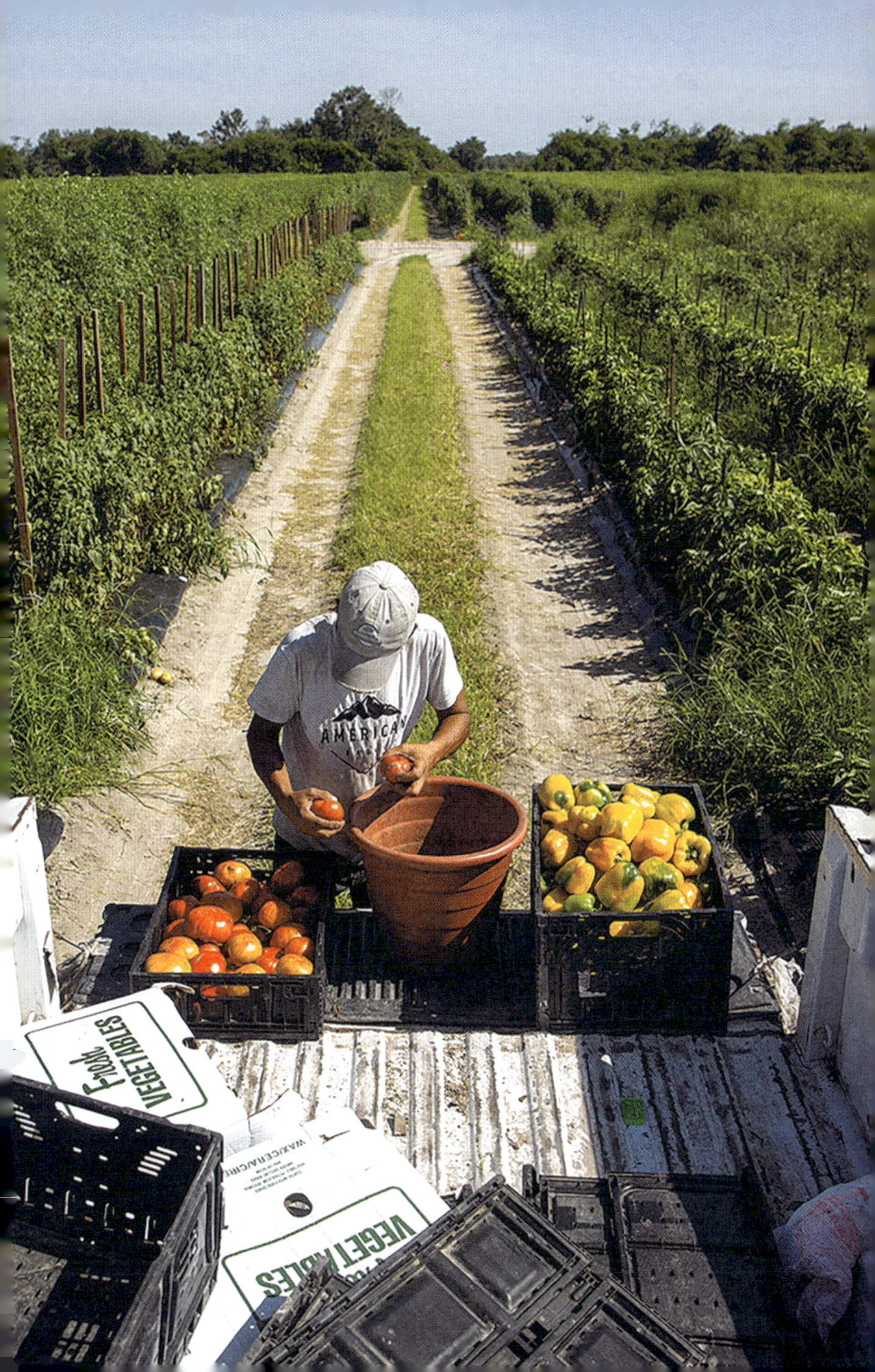
Fresh VEGETABLES
VEGETABLES

A Hunger for Tomatoes

"It's difficult to think anything but pleasant thoughts while eating a homegrown tomato."

—

Lewis Grizzard

My cousin Edward Mitchell Seabrook Jr. was a shy man with two passions. The first was science fiction. He would read it in his office on Broad Street in Charleston, South Carolina, where he ostensibly sold real estate and insurance. The pulp-novel overflow crowded the bookshelves in the second-floor bedroom I shared with one of my sisters during a grossly hot summer vacation at Edward's beach house on Folly Island. Edward's mother was sister to my Nana, his father cousin to my grandfather. (Our family's bloodlines are tangled; don't anyone crack *Deliverance* jokes.) As a teenager, lying next to a box fan with a damp washrag on my forehead, I devoured paperbacks with lurid cover art by Roy G. Krenkel and Frank Frazetta: *Tanar of Pellucidar*, *Pirates of Venus*, *The Cave Girl*.

His other passion was tomatoes.

Because Edward's front yard on the Folly River was a sandy coastal mess of prickly crabgrass and spartina, he positioned 50-gallon industrial drums, sawed in half, outside the kitchen door. He basically grew tomatoes in tin cans but was a member of the Agricultural Society of South Carolina. His seedlings raced up poles in a mysterious soil mix about which he was tight-lipped. As the sun burned off dew and the hour for lunch approached, Edward lumbered down the rows checking ripeness until he found a few about to crack with juice, and twisted the warm fruit from its vine. The smell of tomato leaves fell somewhere on the spectrum between scorched tobacco and a mechanic's grease rag. The flavor of the tomatoes themselves, an excruciating alchemy of acidity and sugar, only he knew how to achieve. In the kitchen, one of my great-aunts or Edward's wife, Lucy, made sandwiches. I can't recall if the mayonnaise was Duke's, but the bread was squishy and white. I ate mine, bare feet dangling at the end of the dock, or in a rope hammock on the porch, with one of Edward's fantasies about mutant aliens inches from my nose.

Where would Southern culture be without the tomato?

One of the earliest references in American cookery appears in the private journals of Harriott Pinckney Horry of Hampton Plantation. By 1770, she was collecting receipts in a journal that became an invaluable household document about colonial life in the Santee Delta of South Carolina, especially during the Revolution, when she managed the property. Her house served as a refuge for women and children fleeing the British occupation, and it was in her fields where Brigadier General Francis Marion, known as the Swamp Fox, hid when enemy troops arrived at her door to search for him. Horry's instructions "To Keep Tomatoos [sic] for Winter Use" by stewing and storing in pint pots with melted butter as a sealant seems labor intensive to those of us equipped with modern refrigeration and access to hothouse varieties at the nearest Publix. Not only was it a hedge against a season of want, but also a pragmatic embrace of what the New World offered.

Since that early recipe, the tomato's appeal for Southerners has become universal. Tomato aspic at church suppers. Tomato pie for picnics. Tomato gravy with cat-head biscuits. Tomatoes in succotash, chutney, puddings, and perloo. Fried green tomatoes did not originate in the South, but we do them best and can thank novelist Fannie Flagg for indelibly mythologizing those golden-crusted disks in *Fried Green Tomatoes* at the Whistle Stop Café. One of the first soul-food versions appears in Helen Mendes' *The African Heritage Cookbook* (1971).

But no one in the culinary canon of the South has ever rivaled Ernest Matthew Mickler. In his seminal *White Trash Cooking*, he wrote this about the Kitchen Sink Tomato Sandwich:

A Hunger for Tomatoes

In the peak of the tomato season, chill 1 very large or 2 medium tomatoes that have been vine-ripened and have a good acidy bite to their taste. Take two slices of bread. Coat them with ¼ inch of good mayonnaise. On one piece of bread, slice the tomato ¼ inch thick. Salt and pepper that layer. Add another layer of sliced tomato, and again salt and pepper. Place the other piece of bread on top of this, roll up your sleeves, and commence to eat over the kitchen sink while the juice runs down your elbows.

Finding my way back to that sandwich took up most of my year.

• • •

The primary job requirements for a tomato picker are to have fast hands, a back that can withstand being bent double in ninety-degree heat for up to twelve hours a day, and legs that can run over loose sand when carrying a thirty-two-pound bucket called a cubeta on one shoulder.

—

Barry Estabrook, *Tomatoland*

"Que es el trabajo?" asked Julia Perkins. "What's the job?"

A group of women facing her at the bulletin board repeated the English lesson in unison. On a Sunday afternoon in late April at the Coalition of Immokalee Workers (CIW) headquarters, female members gathered for their weekly coffee klatch to learn a few handy phrases, trade daycare schedules, and discuss the cost of groceries. Boxes of Polvorones and Canelitas cookies lay scattered on the folding table. A banda tune by Los Jefes de la Sierra Grande leaked from the sound booth of Radio Conciencia La Tuya next door. Murals depicting tomato workers in the field covered butter-yellow walls. Hand-painted slogans — "No Mas Abusos," "Comida Justa" and "Justice for Farmworkers" — hung above a cluster of desks.

"What kind of work is it?" said Perkins. "What do I need to apply?"

Perkins, a CIW education coordinator born in North Carolina, ended her lesson, and the women rose to rearrange the folding chairs and put away the snacks. All dressed neatly in jeans, cotton tops, clean sneakers. Gold necklaces, pierced ears. Long hair pulled back in sensible ponytails or braids. Cellphones tucked back into purses. Many still worked in the fields; others were field agents for the Coalition. Nice ladies, all.

Bet you'd never guess they're expert hunger strikers.

Immokalee (pronounced Im-MOCK-a-lee) is ground zero for Florida's commercial tomato crop. Broad, flat fields line the main road into town from the Gulf Coast, and on certain stretches, high chain-link fences prevent panthers from crossing the asphalt that cuts across their swampy western Everglades habitat. Loaded tractor-trailers rumble out of packinghouses. A pinhooker market in an open lot sells produce too ripe for long-distance shipping. A party store advertises piñatas, and bottles of Mexican Coca-Cola fill the cold drink case at Mr. Taco. Waitresses in bustiers and fishnet stockings circle gamblers hunched over slots at the Seminole casino. Street roosters wage turf wars in grassy ditches. Blue tarps still patch damaged roofs long after Hurricane Irma pummeled Florida last year. In an improvised courtyard between ramshackle mobile homes with boarded-up windows, little girls build sand castles in the dirt, pretending it's the beach. One of their parents, who pays $60 a week to share the single-wide with up to 11 other occupants, mentioned that after the 2016 election, a few babies were named Melania.

Across the street from CIW headquarters, the parking lot at La Fiesta #3 grocery store serves as a depot for the battered school buses that transport agricultural workers. The workers buy warm tortillas inside at crack of dawn each morning. When the buses return at end of day, water coolers are dumped on the asphalt to evaporate in the still torrid heat. Many town residents commute on bicycles, not due to a quaint civic ordinance but because they can't obtain a legal driver's license or afford car payments on a harvester's wage. In 1960, Edward R. Murrow reported from Immokalee on the harsh lives of African American migrant workers in the CBS documentary "Harvest of Shame"; now, the town's population has largely shifted to Latino and Haitian. Whatever change has taken place in the fields since — as basic as access to shade and water, as critical as exposing wage theft and sexual harassment — is in great part due to Coalition activists.

A Hunger for Tomatoes

Members of the CIW are fantastic at nonviolent resistance. One of their cornerstone initiatives is the Fair Food Program, a humane-workplace monitoring collaboration with big ag companies including Gargiulo, Pacific Tomato, and Lipman Family Farms, and fast food giants McDonald's, Subway, Chipotle, and Taco Bell. Walk through the produce aisle at Whole Foods or Trader Joe's and inspect the tiny green Fair Food seal on those packets of glossy grape tomatoes and genetically engineered slicers. It represents decades of toil and deprivation.

But the Fair Food seal can't be found at Publix or Wendy's.

Not yet.

The next day, Nely Rodriguez, a robust woman in her mid-50s, walked into the CIW offices and shook my hand. She wore a caramel-colored knit sweater over a tank top and capris. Rodriguez, originally from Tamaulipas, Mexico, spoke in a low alto.

"When I first came here, I picked apples and asparagus in Michigan," she said. "Then, in Florida, tomatoes, squash, and eggplant; and since 2007, my work at the Coalition is organizing in the community, with the Sunday women's group, the radio, and labor-abuse investigations outside the Fair Food Program."

She also takes part in hunger strikes. Her first fast was in 2012 — a weeklong protest at Publix headquarters in Lakeland, Florida. Founded in 1930 by George R. Jenkins, Publix is the largest closely held regional supermarket chain in the South, with 1,191 stores and gross revenues of $34 billion, so if you shop for groceries anywhere between Alabama and Virginia, chances are good you've bought tomatoes at a Publix, or Publix Sabor, themed stores catering to Hispanic Americans. The company's official position for not taking part in the Fair Food Program maintains that the CIW campaign is a labor dispute between workers and suppliers, rather than a human-rights issue. More recently, Rodriguez traveled up to New York in late winter for a chilly "Freedom Fast" strike outside the Park Avenue offices of Wendy's billionaire board chairman Nelson Peltz.

We sat at a picnic table under a pergola behind the cinder-block building. Doves cooed on a tin rooftop. Breezes rustled the sabal palms.

"I've never fasted. How did you feel at the end?" I asked.

"To be honest, I thought it would be more difficult than it was," she said. "For the first or second day, I had headaches, was tired, but by the third day, I felt more full of energy, lighter, and wasn't hungry anymore. Taking on a fast like this, you know you're doing it for a just cause, and you've seen abuses in the community and you want them to stop."

"Was there a time in your past when you were hungry?" I asked.

"Sometimes, working in the fields back in Mexico, because you had to finish a job and you can't stop, you get hungry. But for days and days because food wasn't available, like the Freedom Fast? No. There were days when food was just tortillas and beans, but there always was something to eat."

"So the strike was a different kind of hunger?"

"During the fast, I found myself reflecting on the things I've seen, like the mothers here who have to get up extremely early to drop their kids off at daycare or school, but under the Fair Food Program, that is no longer the case. If we can make this program expand, those things will change. Those things come into your mind and you can power through. After five or six days, you want to continue. The feedback you get, the support from the community, that encouragement helps you get through the more difficult parts, urges you on."

"What was the first thing you ate after?"

"To break the fast, we ate bread all together. Then we celebrated at the Cathedral of Saint John the Divine. The bishop was there, they had mariachis, and an enormous spread. I served myself salad, rice with vegetables, butternut squash soup. And at the end tres leches cake with whipped cream on top. That tasted so good."

Rodriguez smiled.

"That tasted so good."

Angela Navarette bought the maroon lace curtains shading windows of a modest tan ranch in a subdivision known as Farm Workers Village — company housing owned by Lipman Family Farms, one of North America's largest field-tomato growers, beyond Immokalee town center where sidewalks end.

"They make it look nice. More like home," she said.

A Hunger for Tomatoes

Her husband, Ignacio Lopez, rested in an armchair, a straw cowboy hat tipped back on his head. The room was stuffy in late afternoon. Julia Perkins and I sat at the dining table covered with a floral-pattern vinyl cloth while her colleague, Gerardo Reyes, examined the faulty settings on the air conditioning unit. On the stove, a pot of *pollo con mole* bubbled. Lopez, 76, grew up in Veracruz; Navarette, 61, was born in Guerrero. Both were members of the Coalition. They met in Immokalee; each had children from other marriages living on both sides of the border. She got here first, to harvest lettuce in Belle Glade and corn in Indiana. A coyote dropped him off in Tennessee. They share the house in Immokalee with six more workers during the winter growing season, then follow the crop in summer to South Carolina and Virginia.

"We came because of necessity," Navarette said, her face darkening. "In Mexico, I was taking care of all the kids of my daughters and sons. One was studying to become a nurse, and so I tried to think of ways to support her, and coming here became an idea."

I asked Angela her full name.

"Hernandez-Navarette," she said. "But not the bad Navarettes. When I first got here, people at the company looked at me funny when I said my name, then I learned the story, but it still took a while to clear it up."

She referred to a notorious family of crew bosses that brutalized and enslaved 12 Latino tomato pickers, holding them captive and chained inside a box truck for almost 2½ years.

Navarette got up to stir the *mole*.

"Is there a special technique to working tomatoes?" I asked.

"It took me a month to learn," she said. "The crew leader told me it's really heavy work, and I felt uncomfortable taking a break all the time because everyone was looking at me, but Ignacio works really quickly, picking up the slack. He's a *matado*."

Reyes explained *matado* is slang for killer or badass, the fastest one who makes everyone else look bad.

"Even with my age, I love working in the fields," said Lopez. "I'm fast, they don't beat me. When I get tired, I am limping, my feet hurt, but I'm still out there. I'm fresh like lettuce."

Food Stories

"Do you concentrate on a tomato variety?"

"We pick *tintos*," said Lopez. "It's a little bit easier than picking greens, because with the greens, everyone moves so quickly, but with these, it's easier to spot because they're a little red."

A bucket of *tintos* sat on the kitchen floor, next to a five-gallon pickle tub and six-packs of Grape Crush. Navarette brought one to the table. It was about as ripe as a snow globe.

"How many buckets a day?" I asked.

"Around 75," said Lopez. "Sometimes only 25 or 30 when there's not many left, but the piece rate for the reds is higher."

Each full bucket, or "piece," weighs 32 pounds. On a great day, that adds up to 2,400 pounds hauled by hand to a field truck by a bow-legged septuagenarian shorter than me.

Reyes, passing around a plate of microwaved tortillas, remarked that harvesting the *tinto* used to be a niche market of pinteros, or pinhookers, who hired day labor not affiliated with an established crew and paid them cash under the table.

Navarette served her *pollo con mole* next to generous scoops of rice mixed with dried green pigeon peas and stewed *tintos*. (She doesn't eat raw tomatoes.) Her sauce covering the chicken legs was nutty, mildly fiery, and had an elusive sweetness — indigenous Nahuatl speakers called it *molli* or *chilmolli*. I wanted to bathe in it.

"If we see you in South Carolina, I will teach you how to make this," she said.

We get the word "tomato" from the Nahuatl language. The root word *tomatl* was adapted to *tomate* by the Spanish, and then the "e" distorted to "o" for English speakers. That subtle shift from consonant to vowel is a history of conquest, colonialism, and migration. Nahuatl is the Aztec language spoken in central Mexico (including the Navarette-Lopezes' home states of Guerrero and Veracruz) and was considered the prestige language of pre-Hispanic Mesoamerica.

The wild ancestor of all tomatoes is *Solanum pimpinellifolium*, a resilient perennial with pea-sized fruit originating in northern Peru and southern Ecuador, with cultivar cousins appearing in climates as varied as the Atacama

Desert and on the lower slopes of the Andes. The modern tomato, *Solanum lycopersicum*, took another 10,000 years to evolve, and while the date of domestication is unknown, it was apparently being cultivated by the Aztecs around 500 B.C. The tomato then dispersed on Spanish trade routes to Europe and Asia, Africa and the Caribbean, but unlike other New World botanical discoveries such as peanuts or corn, it was greeted with far deeper prejudice because it belongs to the *Solanacaea* or poisonous nightshade family.

The earliest account of tomatoes grown in North America is found in herbalist William Salmon's *Botanologia* (1710), although Spanish settlers likely introduced the plant to their colonies and missions on the southeast coast centuries earlier. Seeds may also have arrived through the Jamaica slave trade. In Louisiana, emerging Cajun and Creole culinary traditions adopted the tomato for their gumbos and jambalayas. Elsewhere, bias continued into the 19th century. In 1836, S.D. Wilcox, editor of the *Florida Agriculturalist*, wrote after eating his first: "The tomato is an arrogant humbug and deserves forthwith to be consigned to the tomb of the Capulets." At the end of the century, the father of the modern commercial tomato, seedsman Alexander W. Livingston, achieved the varieties he named "Paragon" and "Acme" through generations of selective breeding. One hundred years more, too much hybridization — for shape, durability, color, and disease and drought resistance — had a singular unintended consequence. Tomatoes started tasting downright boring.

And that brings us to the flavorless globe, picked by migrant workers and reddened by ethylene gas in packinghouses before landing in supermarkets with callous public relations positions on labor practices.

I wouldn't grace that between two slices of bread.

Angela and Ignacio left in the night.

...

Apu: Quickly tell me. What is your favorite movie, book, and food?
Manjula: The answer to all three is Fried Green Tomatoes.

—

"The Two Mrs. Nahasapeemapetilons," Episode 7, Season 9, *The Simpsons*

"Let's take the golf cart," said Richard "Bubba" Crosby.

On a cloudless morning in late June, he climbed aboard a sky-blue Ford 3000 tractor and set out for his three-acre vegetable patch, a few hundred feet off the back porch of his house in Hardeeville, South Carolina. A tall man with thinning white hair and gnarled hands, the 91-year-old retired tomato farmer descends from Charles Cotesworth Pinckney, a signer of the Declaration of Independence, and is a distant cousin to Harriott Pinckney Horry, too. At one time, Crosby farmed 300 acres in rented fields strung on the Carolina Lowcountry coast between Hilton Head and Beaufort, before bridges connected the barrier islands on Port Royal Sound.

"I started farming when I got out the Army in '47," he said in a gravelly drawl. "I used my daddy's tractor and planted watermelons. We had to use a horse to side it up close, to work the crop itself, because tractors weren't too good then."

He also grew cotton, daffodils, rice, corn, soy, and velvet beans. Raised beef cattle. By the 1960s, he'd shifted into tomatoes, and for a year contracted to grow for the same company that currently employs Angela Navarette and Ignacio Lopez. That arrangement didn't work out.

"I learned how from nothing, started growing tomatoes because they was growing in Beaufort," Crosby said, shutting off the vintage 1965 tractor inside the electric deer fence. "Planted 20 acres the first time."

His property wraps around a bend of the New River, not far north of Savannah on Oaktie Highway, between alligators in the marsh and rattlesnakes in the piney woods. Crosby and I strolled down three neat rows of staked vines, about 100 feet long, heavy with fruit.

He bent down and moved leaves aside with his walking cane.

"You want to know how we plant those tomatoes to make 'em? Is that important? I fixed the ground like a month before time to plant, put a plow down about that deep right where the row is going, and it brings some clay up a little bit, softens the dirt, and I put fertilizer, 5-10-15 heavy potash, the length of those rows, a 10-quart bucket, there, one time. I put bagged lime down like the fertilizer, because the garden gets blossom-end rot, then wait a couple of weeks before planting the crop. They susceptible to everything, you know."

"What kind of tomatoes?" I asked.

He chuckled.

"The tomatoes that I plant, they come with a number on them, I get a few from a friend of mine who is in charge of the planting operation at 6Ls."

"So you're planting the same kind as Lipman?"

"They owe me plenty."

Southern farmers like Crosby can no longer compete against agricultural conglomerates with million-dollar tractors, acreage in multiple states, proprietary cultivars, and experimental field-trial stations. Independent packinghouses, which once serviced smaller growers, have also shuttered or merged.

We left the tractor in the field and returned to his cement porch, where he showed me a flat of scrawny seedlings reserved for fall. Red orbs, stem side down, ripened on a picnic table. Crosby settled himself in a rocking chair as his wife Joyce, 86, came outside to offer bottles of cold water. They have been married for 64 years. A petite woman with downy hair, she still preserves broccoli, cabbage, collards, and corn from their garden, and had just finished canning 60 quarts of snap beans. We sat, rocking, to catch the breeze and recover from the direct sun.

"We old but we good," she said, smiling at her husband.

A mosquito hawk droned the porch.

"How many tomatoes do you get in a season?" I asked.

"We picked nine gallon buckets so far, but I've given away a bunch, and sell enough off the table to pay for the garden."

Joyce chimed in.

"Bubba just gave up Farm Bureau. He was on the school board, done a lot of community stuff, played softball until he was 79.

"When we got married in '54, there was local Blacks around here didn't have any work," she said. "And they all worked in his fields. We had a boy that started as a teenager, he was an alcoholic, and I fed him a big plate of dinner, ate everything we did."

"There was no welfare then," said Crosby. "Nobody had anything."

"How many workers on the farm?"

"I had two, sometimes three," he said.

"And when picking?"

"Two, three hundred."

"And where did all the pickers come from?"

"They were transit, same as they got in Beaufort now. We had a labor camp. When the season was over, they'd go up the road."

The Crosbys' youngest daughter, Cheryl, pulled into the yard. A horse trainer and wild animal rehabber, she had a baby raccoon in a mesh pet carrier. She used to pick tomatoes for fun as a child and sold them out of the field.

"If we picked a bucket of tomatoes, that was our money. I'd spend it on junk food at the Nickel Pump gas station," said Cheryl, as the raccoon crawled into her arms and perched on her neck. "We'd go to the movies. He didn't pay us, but we went to private school."

She confessed a dislike for raw tomatoes.

"But I like salsa and ketchup and tomato sauce," she said, selecting unripe slicers from the table. "I'm getting these for someone who wants to make fried green tomatoes. Fresh out of the garden taste, it's a lot sweeter."

"Bubba, what's the best way to eat them?" I asked.

Crosby laughed.

"I eat them a little bit green. It don't have quite as much juice running down your arm."

"But what about a tomato sandwich?"

"I use Miracle Whip," said Joyce. "My mother used Hellmann's. You have to do what you want with the mayonnaise, and I peel the tomato and slice it regular. Salt, pepper would be good. We buy that Nature's Butter Bread. That's what he likes."

"Ugh," said Cheryl.

• • •

the tomato offers
its gift
of fiery color
and cool completeness
— Pablo Neruda

A Hunger for Tomatoes

"The migrants are here."

I heard that at gas stations and convenience stores along Highway 21 when, at the height of tomato-picking season in South Carolina, the population balloons on Port Royal Sound. (In the late 16th century, the settlement of Santa Elena, on Parris Island, was capital for the entire Spanish colony of La Florida.) As in Immokalee, trucks hauled loads to packinghouses on the main road. Low-profile bodegas offered check cashing and international call services. Scarecrows in white hazmat suits and bilingual trespassing signs were posted at the entrance to the fields, intentionally shielded from view by high scrub. Outside the antebellum port town of Beaufort and the Marine Corps Recruit Depot, this region also remains rural. Here, the predominant culture is Gullah, with the community of Frogmore on Saint Helena Island a place of historic significance for African Americans; all it takes is a turn onto Dr. Martin Luther King Jr. Drive to pass by the Penn School, where emancipated slaves first received a formal education in 1862 on a campus of whitewashed clapboard buildings.

Early on the morning of the summer solstice, the forecast for Saint Helena included a heat-index warning of 110 degrees.

It remained cool enough under the shade trees as buses dropped off pickers at a labor camp belonging to one of the major tomato conglomerates. Laundry dried on lines outside one of the row houses, portable toilets sat under a carport shed, flatbed trucks stacked with empty dumpster bins parked in the yard. The pickers headed first to a hand-washing station, and then jostled for seats at picnic tables. Most of them young men, wearing baseball caps, back braces, bandanas, work boots, cut-off stretchable sleeves to protect forearms, their jeans stained muddy green on the knees. A few women were scattered among the crews.

Crew bosses and ag company representatives also arrived.

"Hola, muchachos," said Gerardo Reyes.

The response was muted, polite.

The Coalition of Immokalee Workers conducts field sessions at farms that have signed the Fair Food Program agreement, and during the season they travel north along the same route as the migrants. Saint Helena is a regular stop. The session addresses rights and responsibilities of both workers and farmers: standard safety practices, tracking hours, and how to report discrimination or abuse. It takes about an hour. That morning, the CIW activists worked through three sessions, with about 200 workers in all. As Reyes talked, Julia Perkins and Nely Rodriguez handed out brochures. Other staff held up murals painted on plastic tarps to illustrate key points. One had an outsize cartoon sun burning above a row of vines, and Reyes commented that on really hot days, all you see is that big yellow orb. The crews laughed.

The mood shifted when Rodriguez took her turn to talk about sexual harassment, standing next to a mural of two workers commenting on a female picker's appearance as she bent over in a field. Some men snickered, looking nervously at each other for support.

"What if this was your mother or sister?" she asked.

That same morning, Melania Trump left the White House for Andrews Air Force Base, en route to an unannounced humanitarian visit with detained immigrant children and unaccompanied minors at a shelter in a Texas border town. She wore a $39 olive green Zara jacket with the words "I REALLY DON'T CARE, DO U?" printed in faux graffiti on the back.

Neither do many tomato producers. According to Farmworker Justice, a nonprofit advocacy group in Washington, D.C., that addresses immigration policy for migrant and seasonal workers, more than half of America's 2 million farmworkers are undocumented and marginalized. And despite the CIW's outreach, this still engenders an environment where unscrupulous employers, from crew bosses in the field on up to white collars in corporate offices, need to be held accountable for illegal or deficient practices that get their crops to market.

When tomato pickers migrate with the crop, their crew bosses send a truck ahead to transport bare necessities. Personal microwaves and wall-unit air conditioners. Chairs. Storage tubs filled with clothing, linens, pots and pans. Angela Navarette packs chiles because she can't find the right variety for her *mole* in South Carolina. For the season in the Lowcountry, she and Ignacio Lopez were assigned to a rented house with seven other workers, a prefab double-wide set back from the road leading toward

A Hunger for Tomatoes

Land's End on Saint Helena. Cots for the bachelors crammed the living room, but the kitchen made Navarette happy as she preferred it to more basic quarters in the labor camps.

We stood at the sink as she cut up two chickens. She fried plantains in a pan. Then garlic and onion, peanuts, raw pumpkin seeds, raisins, and sesame. Ground-together cloves, cumin, cinnamon. She chopped two large field tomatoes in a blender with toasted chiles and broth from the stewing chickens.

"My secret ingredient," she said, her dark eyes brightening. "I thought this one up myself. *Galleta de animalito.*"

Animal crackers.

Certainly not traditional for *mole*, but the smashed cookies made the sauce intensely personal.

She stopped stirring the pot to check laundry soaking in a bucket outside on a porch next to a dead refrigerator. It's an all-day job to get tomato stains out of her clothes.

"Old house, old bath, old clothes. But it's all going to be clean."

"What do you wear?" I asked.

"A long sleeve blouse, shirt over that. Some people use lots of bandanas, but I put one under my baseball cap. Any other hat gets in the way of the bucket. In Mexico, all the *campesinos* would use a *sombrero*."

Cicadas buzzed in the woods.

"When you're picking tomatoes, your hands get stained and dirty," said Navarette.

"How do you get it off?"

"You take a tomato and break it open and rub on like soap, and then the stain comes out when you wash your hands."

The chicken took three hours to cook down, and despite air conditioning on full blast, the kitchen grew uncomfortably steamy. I asked Navarette how she abided in the summer weather. She dug around in the refrigerator and pulled out a liter bottle of pineapple-flavored Suero Oral electrolyte solution. (*Suero* means serum in Spanish.) The caution label recommended use for severe dehydration caused by diarrhea, vomiting, or excessive perspiration.

"Nobody trusts the water on the truck. Who knows where it comes from? I drink this instead."

Lopez parked a pickup in the yard and came inside. He sat down and pulled up his pants legs to show me his knees, the joints swollen, inflamed, possibly arthritic. He kept rubbing them. Lopez explained he'd been to a free clinic for medicine and X-rays, but the doctors thought he might need an operation. Two months before, when I met him in Florida, he was still in the fields. Now, he cleaned crew quarters.

A *matado* no longer.

"Not a lot of tomatoes right now," he said. "It's not a good year. The cold impacted the crop here, and the rain, too. We used to get checks of $400 a week. There have been seasons when Angela was paid $1,000 in a single check. But now, every week we've been here, it's about $140."

"How do you live on that amount? How can you afford groceries?"

They looked at each other.

"We are worried about what will come next."

"After 18 years, I'm tired," said Navarette, her lined face sadder. "I want to go home. Ignacio wants to go back to Veracruz, but I would like to be in Guerrero again."

"We are living in a country that's not ours," said Lopez. "We struggle with that. We think about how one day to the next everything could change, and how many people have been taken away. You have to be resilient. We need to not let our passions get the best of us. Just endure."

Earlier that same week, while dining at a Mexican restaurant in Washington, D.C., Homeland Security Secretary Kirstjen Nielsen was heckled by protesters shouting "shame" for her role enforcing the administration's zero-tolerance immigration policy and the separation of children from their parents at the U.S.-Mexico border.

Navarette served lunch, the *mole* even better than last time.

"If we see you in Virginia, I will teach you tamales," she said.

・・・

A Hunger for Tomatoes

"You say tomato, I say tomahto, let's call the whole thing off."

—

George and Ira Gershwin

The next day, Howard Chaplin pumped gas opposite me at the Sunoco on Sea Island Parkway. A slim man with wire-rim glasses and curly white sideburns, he politely wished me a good morning in a singsong Gullah accent. I looked closer at his pickup truck, with a jumble of empty crates in the cab.

"Are those crab traps, sir?"

"Vegetable bins. Been up to the food bank in Yemassee with a load of my tomatoes."

I stepped over the median to shake his hand.

Those born and bred on the Sea Islands have reason to be wary of people from off, especially real estate developers. This leads to the misconception that Gullah culture is dying. Far from true. Without the rich heritage of language, music, and cooking of the Gullah Geechee, descendants of the first Africans to toil here, the Lowcountry would be a poorer place altogether. Harriott Pinckney Horry owned slaves who worked in her fields and kitchen; she certainly wasn't out there growing or preserving the tomatoes that appeared in her journals. We wouldn't have most of the dishes that came after, either.

Before retirement, Chaplin, 73, was a civilian employee of the U.S. Marine Corps on Parris Island, and then brick mason at Hunting Air Force Base. With his wife, Harriet, a nurse and daycare operator, Chaplin now owns a country store on Storyteller Road, a byway between the leased fields and labor camps on Saint Helena. They sell mostly dry goods and snacks to the Frogmore community, although later in the afternoon when I turned up there, a sign in the window advertised live crabs, and bushel baskets of fresh-picked okra sat on the floor near the refrigerator case. His T-shirt and glasses splattered with pluff mud, Chaplin had returned with shrimp in his cast nets from the creeks feeding Port Royal Sound. Unflustered, he took me out back to look at his own fields, 20 acres surrounded by mature pecan trees. He also grows squash, broccoli, collard greens, and corn. What doesn't sell in the store gets donated for hunger relief. Yemassee is the nearest distribution center for the Lowcountry Food Bank network.

"How many rows of tomatoes?" I asked.

"I don't got too much, about 16 rows here and 10 rows there," he said. "Nothing big, just to keep me active."

"Have you been farming long?"

"I been doing this since knee high."

"How long has your family been here?"

"Oh, hoo! Quite a few years. About a hundred years back. Most of my folks, grandparents, from Cedar Grove. That's right on the island, too. The rest of them I don't know. We go back, we don't know where. We say 'longa go wit all that.'"

Chaplin had a limp, so we took our time between the rows of tomatoes, a few here and there on the ground rotting, weeds taking over the sandy soil. Chaplin explained he tested every other year, taking samples to Clemson Coastal Research and Education Center for advice on pesticides and fungicides. He let me pick a few red ones off the vines to take away. Chaplin pulled out a handkerchief and wiped his forehead.

"See those greens, that brown ring on it? I got to get them before they start ripening up. I done pick them twice this week, haven't watered in about two days. So hot."

Clouds piled up on the horizon as the sun dipped below the palmettos.

"Most of the time you see rain all around in a circle, not a drop here. I ain't going to complain, we still have it good compared to other places."

"That's for sure," I said. "How do you eat a tomato?"

"I eat it natural, put a little ranch on it, slices of cucumber, that make a meal right there."

We headed back to his truck.

"I don't know why we grew so much this year, golly. I'm waiting for the kids to decide they want to take over. Had six, four still living. I probably give it up next year. Time bring on changes, right."

Chaplin gestured toward the distant rumble of tractors.

"I'm a peanut, just a little peanut to what they plant."

A Hunger for Tomatoes

On leaving Saint Helena, I stopped at a stand closer to Beaufort owned by another Gullah farmer and bought extra tomatoes — pretty good slicers as it turned out — for dinner with cousins up in Charleston. Behind the bins holding cabbages and peaches was an acre-long hoop shed where a Latino worker sorted seedlings. He looked up and waved. Then, as I hesitated over a display of canary melons, face flushed to near heatstroke, he took the tomatoes out of my arms and handed me a slice of the cooling melon.

"Es mejor, muy delicioso."

My car smelled of rind and kindness and tears.

• • •

"The girl of my dreams is a vegetable!"

—

Return of the Killer Tomatoes

"I guess we kinda like to grow the funky stuff," said Matthew Horry.

A husky man with unruly brown hair, he leaned over a dog crate topped with propagation trays holding lumpy, wrinkled, oddball tomatoes in the Chaparral RV camper he and his fiancée, Ashley Loponte, temporarily occupied on a rural lot outside Walterboro, South Carolina. Horry, 31, is a biological science technician who specializes in landrace and heirloom seed increase for the U.S. Vegetable Laboratory at the Clemson Coastal Research and Education Center. His personal pursuit is a half-acre organic plot of experimental cultivars. The couple calls it Kindlewood Farms, their expansion dream after selling a starter home and backyard garden of two raised beds.

Their hothouse is a repurposed trampoline. A wine cooler serves as a storage unit for ripe produce. They favor compost and fish emulsion over pesticides and fungicides. Their dog Gordon, a bouncy Labrador-pit bull mix, deters critters as much as the electric fencing.

Ashley Loponte opened the camper door, letting in the heat and light of early July. Her car keys hung from cotton-knit jalapeños with googly eyes.

"I like your key chain."

"That's her passion," said Horry. "Mine's tomatoes, and hers is peppers. We're a Solanaceae family."

"Before we closed on the land, we were at my mom's house, so I started a whole bunch of things without Matt's consent in the garage," said Loponte. "That's why everything is super-early this year. We're the first to bring heirlooms to the market because I had to get motivated."

"It's a shared passion," said Horry. "A consuming passion."

On weekends, they sell at farm markets in the greater Charleston area. Horry obsesses over the catalog from Southern Exposure Seed Exchange, which preserves the South's rarest varieties, including "Aunt Lou's Underground Railroad Tomato," from original seed stock reportedly carried by an unnamed Black man who crossed to freedom from Kentucky.

"The heirlooms we have are Martha Washington, Amish Paste, Radiator Charlie's Mortgage Lifter, Striped German, Red Zebra, Black Cherry, Valencia, Solar Flare," Horry said, sorting through the flats. "We fought about this a lot. Tried to scale it down this year, keep only a few varieties."

He shrugged, acknowledging his inability to resist planting weirdos. "The homegrown tomato is something that piqued my interest. It's one of those vegetables, if you're fortunate to grow up eating them from the garden, you'll not be satisfied with the supermarket kind." He picked up a mottled yellow and purple tomato and handed it to me.

"We have a whole row from breeder Bradley Gates. These are called Blue Berry. They're not heirloom, but they are open pollinated. It's a little bitter when not fully ripe, but still gorgeous. The word heirloom, that's been overused. What I'm looking for is flavor and character."

I took a bite.

Like tomato pop rocks blowing up in my mouth.

Sadly, not sized for a sandwich.

Horry cut a juicy slice of Cherokee Purple. Only a devoted gardener could love this ugly bruise cultivar from Tennessee, also saved from extinction by happenstance and amateur breeders. Right then, I stopped looking for a slicer that would do justice to Ernest Matthew Mickler's kitchen sink recipe. It had a tingly balance of sweetness and acidity, a flavor that made me want to shout, "Roll up your sleeves, Southerners."

He sold me one for $2.

"So, hey, wait a minute. Are you related to the Santee Delta Horrys?" I asked.

He nodded.

"I'm a descendant."

"OK, that's crazy. I'm related to Francis Marion."

Loponte looked bewildered at the two of us, grinning ancestry geeks.

"Our ancestors fought together in the Revolution," I said.

They included the husband of Harriott Pinckney Horry, early tomato adopter.

...

Homegrown tomatoes, homegrown tomatoes
What'd life be without homegrown tomatoes
Only two things that money can't buy
And that's true love and homegrown tomatoes
— Guy Clarke

Not long ago, I bumped into my cousin Edward Seabrook's widow, Lucy, on the street in Charleston. Folly was no longer a sleepy buffer island. She still owned the beach house but was deeding it to one of her nieces.

"What happened to Edward's books?" I asked.

She winced, and then shrugged, apologetically.

"Oh, we threw them out."

At the end of that childhood vacation, I snitched *The Prince of Peril* and *Thuvia, Maid of Mars* and stuffed them in my suitcase hoping Edward wouldn't miss a few paperbacks from his science fiction collection. (He probably did.) They still sit on shelves in a spare bedroom in my house. Edward Seabrook's formula for a great tomato has also been lost to the ages.

While we now have so many other fanciers, seed savers, scientists, and botanists working on reviving the flavor of the slicer, we remain deeply compromised in our hunger for a fair — and fairly decent tasting — tomato. The Coalition for Immokalee Workers is collaborating with the Student/Farmworker Alliance on another action to boycott Wendy's. Publix is still a Fair Food Program holdout.

Before Edward Seabrook went to the garden beyond, I began to take serious interest in Southern food traditions, and it occurred to me to ask about his mystery soil mix. He could transform my abrupt, gender-bending name into a soft, elegant crescendo, resonating on the scale between Howard Chaplin and Bubba Crosby. I loved hearing Edward talk. Few people alive still have that accent. It also meant I didn't always catch everything he said. He mumbled a series of numbers, some mutant formula, and thinking about it now, I wonder if it was the heavy phosphate favored by Crosby.

Then again, Edward could have been speaking Martian, for all I know.

...

Angela Navarette and Ignacio Lopez (whose names have been changed to protect their identities) are currently in Virginia and will be there until November, when they return to Immokalee, where the planting cycle will start all over again. The *matado*'s knees are a little better. ◊

—

Shane Mitchell is the author of the Crop Cycle series for The Bitter Southerner. Her stories often focus on the intersection of community, culture, and culinary history. While her family has deep roots in the Carolina Lowcountry, she was born in New York, and is grateful for the perspective that adds to her work. Also, she unapologetically hates grits.

A Hunger for Tomatoes

THE SHORT & BRILLIANT LIFE *OF* ERNEST MATTHEW MICKLER

—

by Michael Adno

—

Winner of the James Beard Media Award in 2019 for Best Profile

—

Photo by Michael Adno
This story was originally published January 9, 2018

WHITE TRASH COOKING

Ernest Matthew Mickler

The Short & Brilliant Life of Ernest Matthew Mickler

I n spring of 1986, Ernest "Ernie" Matthew Mickler's *White Trash Cooking* landed on bookshelves across America — a 160-page, spiral-bound anthology of Southern recipes, stories, and photographs.

Oddly enough, damn near everyone loved it. It was immediately revered by literary snobs, Southern aristocrats, Yankees, folklorists, down-home folk, and people on either side of the Mason-Dixon.

The book stirred a firestorm of publicity — partly serious, partly tongue-in-cheek — landing Ernie on "Late Night With David Letterman" and National Public Radio, in magazines like Vogue and People, and in a litany of newspapers. In The New York Times, critic Bryan Miller deemed *White Trash Cooking* the "most intriguing book of the 1986 spring cookbook season." Even the grande dame of Southern literature, Harper Lee, claimed she had "never seen a sociological document of such beauty — the photographs alone are shattering." She called the book "a beautiful testament to a stubborn people of proud and poignant heritage."

White Trash Cooking was a staple on The New York Times Best Seller list for weeks as a gift for Southern kin, an eloquent medley of camp and honesty. It was Ernie's reclamation of the South, as he knew it. And he knew it from a distinctly rural view. Ernie was born on August 23, 1940, in Palm Valley, Florida. Today, the TPC Sawgrass golf resort crowds Palm Valley from the north, but in Ernie's youth, it was a backwoods haunt on a thumb of land along the Atlantic, about 10 miles south of Jacksonville Beach.

Food Stories

In *White Trash Cooking* Ernie provided a thorough account of recipes and conventions many grew up with, some had forgotten, and others couldn't imagine. Broiled Squirrel. Betty Sue's Sister-in-Law's Fried Eggplant. He built a simultaneously endearing and tempestuous catalog of archetypes — vestiges of the South, sets of beliefs and traditions that would otherwise dissolve into lore. Cool Whip, once prosaic, became profound in Ernie's books.

No more than a month after *White Trash Cooking* hit bookstores, its original publisher, The Jargon Society, decided it couldn't meet the demand and sold the rights to Ten Speed Press for $90,000 and a 15 percent royalties clause. Jargon had received 30,000 orders; it had printed only 5,000 copies. Ernie's dear friend Calvin "Cal" Yeomans once said the publication of *White Trash Cooking* was "one fuck-up after another."

Two years later, Ernie published a second book, *Sinkin' Spells, Hot Flashes, Fits and Cravins*. It followed the first's form, but went further. Its sections and stories were built around certain gatherings he grew up with in North Florida: hog killings, cemetery cleanings, wakes. Ernie put the recipes in those contexts and colored them with prose that edged toward writers like Padgett Powell or Zora Neale Hurston in its ability to pin down regional dialect. Ernie himself said he was good at "writing cracker." And as in the first book, you could easily mistake Ernie's photographs for William Eggleston's or William Christenberry's.

It's safe to call *Sinkin' Spells* a more mature, carefully crafted project — more idiosyncratic, regionally specific, and intimate. It was bound to do well after the warm reception of *White Trash Cooking*.

On November 14, 1988, *Sinkin' Spells* arrived at bookstores across the country. The following day, as readers dove in, Ernie died at his home in Moccasin Branch, Florida, of AIDS. He was 48.

• • •

Sixteen years earlier, Ernie Mickler accepted his master of fine arts degree as one of only eight men graduating from Mills College, historically a school for women, in Oakland, California. On May 31, 1972, the San

Francisco Chronicle devoted 10 inches of column space to a photograph of Ernie at the ceremony, under the headline "The Art of Graduation."

Clad in aviator sunglasses, long hair, and a set of butterfly wings on his back, he traipsed out onto the stage — and the previously taciturn crowd hollered and laughed.

"It scared the shit out of me," he later told a friend. "I just became this magnetic thing." Helen "Petie" Pickette, one of his closest friends, told me, "I used to say he glows in the dark, and he may have."

I visited Pickette at the apex of summer in Jacksonville Beach. Cicadas whirred and the temperature spiked as my vehicle snaked toward her house on a Saturday morning. When I knocked, I heard music, a voice with a texture akin to Townes Van Zandt's, spilling onto the porch. When Pickette opened the door, she looked me up and down. She wore a burgundy T-shirt, thin-rimmed glasses, and an ear-to-ear grin.

"Mike, you look like one of mine," she said. "Get in here!"

The seemingly familiar voice I heard from the porch was still playing, and it nagged at me. Pickette told me it belonged to Ernie. That's when I noticed an image of Ernie and Pickette straddling a guitar, framed on the wall, next to an image of Joan Baez. Half of the songs playing, she told me, were tracks Ernie recorded in New Orleans, and the other half belonged to their duo, Ernie and Petie. Ernie sang, and Pickette played guitar. In April 1962, when Ernie was 21 and Pickette merely 18, their single, "Our Love," climbed to the No. 2 spot on the sales chart — at least the chart at Abe Livert Records in Jacksonville. The No. 1 track was Elvis Presley's "Good Luck Charm."

"Ernie had talent from the top of his head down to his feet," Pickette said.

They played a gig with Roy Orbison, met Patsy Cline, ran around with Skeeter Davis and Ralph Emery, and even bumped Brenda Lee off a live spot during Emery's broadcast from the Country Music Conference. Then, during a studio session, their manager got under Ernie's skin.

"He started cussing — went into a rant," Pickette remembered.

And their manager just told them, "That's it. Go home."

"We told people Ernie wanted to go to college, which was true. It just so happened to coincide that Ernie wanted to go to school when we got thrown out," Pickette said, laughing. When her smile ran out, she said, "I can't remember the last time I played my guitar." Her eyes moved toward a Guild acoustic near the front door. "It reminds me that he's gone."

After Ernie and Petie's foray into country music, Ernie moved to Atlantic Beach. There, he met Memphis Wood, director of Jacksonville University's art department. Wood could see a flare in Ernie, and she encouraged him to enroll.

"I'll be your counselor," she urged. "I can get you on the right line." In fact, the wings he wore on graduation day at Mills College were dedicated to Wood.

Pickette and I moved to a table in the kitchen strewn with Ernie Mickler ephemera. She showed me photos of Ernie as a boy with that same infectious smile, pictures of his family, and the old Palm Valley — Ernie's Palm Valley. Poring over images from their trips together — New Orleans, Mexico, California — she remembered how Ernie's charisma was inescapable, no matter the locale.

"He'd come into a room, and every head would turn," she said.

Two days later, I picked Pickette up early, and we drove down A1A to Palm Valley. We hooked west onto Solano Road, through a gated community, past retention ponds and manicured golf greens, to the home of Ernie's cousin, Faye Farace. Farace pulled out several albums and showed us photographs of Ernie in shows, his guitar draped around his neck. The two women shared quips about the people of Palm Valley 60 years ago, before golf courses enveloped the place and they started calling the area Ponte Vedra Beach.

Back then, "They didn't call the law," Pickette said. "They handled things themselves."

Shotgun shacks, fish camps, and moonshine stills set back in the sticks made up the quiet community.

"Of course, everybody knew everybody else's business," Farace said.

Stretching back to 1759, a land grant bears the name John Michler. As reported by Patricia Mickler, who penned an extensive family history, Jacob Mickler married Manuela de Ortega in 1831. And all across north Florida, you can find mentions of the Mickler family, whose roots run deep down here. Pushing down Mickler's Cutoff — the two-lane pavement that cuts through Palm Valley — Pickette mentioned how Ernie's taste in food reflected his family's Minorcan heritage. He adored pilau and fish and grits.

At the terminus of Roscoe Boulevard, where a bridge crosses the Intracoastal Waterway — or, as locals call it, "the canal" — we pulled into a gravel lot leading up to a restaurant on the water. This used to be Papa George's Fish Camp. More importantly, though, this land was also where Ernie grew up.

Across the canal, we could see docks marching off into the haze of an approaching squall. Pickette tried to place exactly where Ernie's house was.

"They had a really fabulous oak tree in their yard," she said, but all traces of that were long gone. When Ernie was 6, his father died. Left alone, Ernie's mother, Edna Rae, opened up a general store and gas station here. Gossip made its way through Edna Rae's promptly, inevitably becoming fodder for Ernie's stories.

Back in the car, we crept down a two-track plastered with "No Trespassing" signs.

"Yeah, the one that says, 'Keep out.' Go down there," Pickette told me. We reached a small compound of homes on a stunning finger of land pushing out into a nexus of creeks and cordgrass. At the end of the road, a sabal-palm cabin stood, a cypress addition tacked on, and a sliver of a screened porch out front. To my surprise, Pickette knew the old-timer who came out to greet us with his cattle dog and invited us to walk around the property — crystal clear ponds, wild grapes, and cypress trees sandwiched between the tidal creeks and untamed pine scrub. Leaned against a tawny pine, an oversize grave marker in the shape of a tombstone read: Here lies Palm Valley, Choked to death on a golf ball.

Soon enough, I realized this wasn't accidental. Pickette brought me down this road to see the Palm Valley of Ernie's youth. It was a place, as he wrote, "where you never failed to say, 'yes, ma'am' and 'no, sir,' never sat on a made-up bed (or put your hat on it), never opened someone else's icebox, never left food on your plate, never left the table without permission, and never forgot to say 'thank you' for the teeniest favor. That's the way the ones before us were raised, and that's the way they raised us in the South."

Food Stories

...

Oddly enough, the idea for *White Trash Cooking* first emerged in 1972 in a lean-to near Washington, California, a tiny town on the Yuba River between the Plumas and Humboldt-Toiyabe national forests in the foothills of the Sierras.

On 50 acres that belonged to Ernie's friend Laura, the two stayed in a little tin shack attached to a barn. Laura, a high-up in health education from Oakland, supported Ernie while he lived in San Francisco, and she thought he'd be handy in making the shack a home. She'd send Ernie out to local flea markets — where he was selling his own wares — so he could spiff up the place. While rigging it up, the spark happened. Laura pointed out an ability Ernie had. There was a simple elegance about everything he did, without a need for much money to live pleasantly. As Ernie would explain time and again, to be "White Trash" was something to be proud of. In the introduction to *White Trash Cooking*, Ernie laid out a distinction between uppercase "White Trash" and lowercase "white trash," claiming that "Manners and pride separate the two." To be poor, Southern, and White Trash was anything but shameful.

In October 1988, just a few weeks before he died, Ernie was interviewed by his friend Cal Yeomans. Ernie had rented a house in Crescent Beach to be near the Atlantic one last time, and there, he talked to Cal about the book's genesis.

"We got stoned out of our minds one night, and honey, we were seeing monkeys on the wall almost," Ernie said. "I can't take full credit for it; we all came up with the idea of doing a guide to the art of white-trash cooking on video." From there, Ernie labeled a folder and "started putting stuff in it from paper sacks — this, that, and the other." He took off from San Francisco en route to Jacksonville, where he had lined up a teaching job. But on his way through New Orleans in 1972, he remembered, "Halfway down St. Charles, I said, 'Shit, I don't need to go any further. This is it.'"

While living in New Orleans, Ernie met William "Bill" Fagaly, the former chief curator at the New Orleans Museum of Art. They took to each other, and part of *White Trash Cooking* was put together with Fagaly at

Ernie's side. Ernie didn't drive, but he didn't need to, Pickette says, "because everyone he met was willing to take him where he wanted to go." Fagaly was a staunch supporter of Ernie's and remained so even after their relationship fell apart. Then, Ernie met Robert Somerlott, and they set off on the road together. Ernie ultimately dedicated WTC to "Robert."

In 1976, Ernie ended up in San Miguel de Allende in Mexico. There, he literally ran into the author Edward Swift turning a corner. With 1,000 recipes brimming out of sacks and shoe boxes, he explained the idea to Swift — a Texan — and he agreed to help Ernie type it up and draft the introduction. The final introduction was their collaboration. Ernie said of Ed's role in the book, "That was a gift from God, and I'll never forget it."

Over four years in San Miguel, Ernie honed the material. Then, when his relationship with Somerlott fizzled, Ernie didn't want to return home just yet, and he settled on Key West, Florida, as his next home. In 1980, just as Key West was turning from a sleepy wartime remnant into a destination resort, Ernie arrived. He began cooking for all-male guesthouses and drank the place in. As Pickette told me, "If it weren't for Key West, WTC probably never would have been published."

While in Key West, Ernie met Anthony "Kit" Woolcott, an English entrepreneur with a foothold in the publishing world. Woolcott asked Ernie to make six copies of his manuscript, and he offered to send it around. Publishers in the Northeast immediately fell head over heels for the thing. The title, though, just plain terrified many of them. Ernie received a letter from David Godine, the head of Godine Publishing in Boston, that said he could never publish such a title, because it would offend three-quarters of the United States. After Jargon Press published the book, it sent an advertisement to The New Yorker, but the magazine sent the check and materials back — claiming it would offend the magazine's readership. Of that kernel, Roy Blount Jr. mused, "That just goes to show how much The New Yorker knows about anything involving gravy."

Nonetheless, Ernie's tenacity carried the thing to print and into people's homes. In a letter to Doubleday, Woolcott wrote, "It has been culled from a great knowledge of Southern cooking and is to a certain extent a historical statement of the development of American cuisine in the Deep South."

Food Stories

Then, Woolcott's partner — a Southerner, Joe Bailey — suggested publishers in New York might be unable to see the promise of *WTC*, so they sent the book to the Jargon Society, a rather obscure literary press in North Carolina, led by the poet and self-described "artisto-dixie-queer," Jonathan Williams. Tom Meyer, Jargon's executive director, recounted the story to me.

"Kit asked us as a favor to look at a cookbook a young 'caterer' he knew in Key West had written," Meyer said. "Kit sent the typescript, which sat on the desk for a couple months. Jonathan asked me to look it over before he returned it, assuming it wasn't anything our press would be interested in. I sat down, read it, and told Jonathan, 'This is fantastic — all the way through, the recipes, the presentation, the voice.'" And he added, "*WTC* was the only manuscript I recommended Jonathan publish, I'm proud to say. The rest is history."

Jargon's Williams called the Oasis guesthouse where Ernie worked. Ernie was staying down the block, and when word reached him, he ran over like a bat out of hell to take the call. Phone to his ear, Ernie listened: "My name is Jonathan Williams with Jargon. Joe gave me your book, and we want to print it." As Ernie recalled, "I almost fell off the end of the telephone."

After Jargon took the book on, they began raising the money to print the thing. But more than a year later, Woolcott grew frustrated with Jargon's glacial process, so he bought two tickets to Winston-Salem to crash the publisher's next board meeting. Mickler and Woolcott arrived as Jargon was hosting an art opening. Ernie felt out of place among the art snobs. But soon enough, someone screamed at Ernie, "I've seen you in drag!" And in a moment, the purported pretension fell away.

At the meeting the next day, a portion of Jargon's board members sat around the table with Ernie and Woolcott. After a bit of circumspection, they agreed to table the book for another year due to a lack of money, but Woolcott stood up and said, "If you people don't print this book, I'm going to print it myself." Woolcott offered $2,000 and typesetting right there. Then, Philip Haines — maybe the book's most ardent and unsung supporter — put down $5,000, followed by $10,000 from Don Anderson, an oil magnate. That day, $25,000 came to the fore, and *WTC* finally reached escape velocity.

On February 19, 1986, Woolcott and a group of friends hosted a release party for *WTC* at the Oasis. The culmination of 14 years of Ernie's work had arrived in an Eden-esque garden off Key West's Fleming Street. From there, he took off on tour, touting the book at conventions and bookstores from Ocala to Atlanta. In New Orleans, at the American Book Sellers Show, Ernie was promoting the book with Jargon. Walking around the booths, he recognized David Godine, introduced himself, and presented him with the Times review. Ernie waited for Godine to read through it. When Godine looked up, he admitted, "Well, you know, that was just a bad mistake I made."

Soon enough, Ernie's grin was strewn across magazines and newspapers. Food sections clamored to cover the book, photography outlets, too. Following the book's release, Ernie and his partner Gary Dale Jolley moved from Key West to St. Augustine, into a little shoebox of an apartment. They were looking to buy something more comfortable, but they were still living on piddling amounts. The royalties from Jargon hadn't shown up yet. And in December 1986, following a People magazine article that cited $45,000 in royalties, the Ledbetter family of Alabama filed a lawsuit against Ernie, because the front cover featured a photograph of their daughter. On photo trips, Ernie would ask everyone for their permission, explaining the book's purpose. Of course, nothing was on paper — just an agreement incised in emulsion.

Soon enough, the Junior League of Charleston followed suit, claiming that 23 recipes were plagiarized. And in the end, it was a delicate dance that cost Ernie immensely. When a royalties check came in from Ten Speed at the end of 1986, it totaled $180,000. Out of Ernie's half, $70,000 went toward legal fees and settlements. He remembered $50,000 going to the Ledbetters.

After Ernie appeared on a number of national television shows, he said, "The only thing I didn't like was they kind of made me feel like I was a buffoon. They just had me up there on a stick." He told Cal Yeomans he would happily return to television if the hosts would speak to him intelligently. But if it were another horse-and-pony show, "I ain't going through that again."

Maybe the most evident example was Ernie's appearance on David Letterman to cook chicken feet and rice. A trashcan erupted with roiling grease, and Ernie presented the dish to Letterman, who found it laughable — asking if chicken feet were just pure gristle, then refusing to eat it. Such incidents led to Yeomans' characterization of the book's rollout as "one fuck-up after another."

...

None of those incidents, however, kept Americans from embracing Ernie Mickler. Some thought him a prodigious folklorist, others thought him a roadside curiosity, but the friends, stories, and experiences Mickler collected while assembling the book are more than most collect in a lifetime.

He had also collected more confidence in the value of his work. And Mickler turned eagerly to writing his second title, *Sinkin' Spells, Hot Flashes, Fits and Cravins*.

Ernie and Gary found a modern house set on 1½ acres in Moccasin Branch, about 10 miles west of Crescent Beach. When the offer was accepted, Ernie persuaded Ten Speed to mortgage the house, with his royalties as collateral. And there, Ernie worked like mad to put together the next book, all the while hemming the place in with his charm, naturally.

He said of their Moccasin Branch home, "I don't think I've ever lived in a place that's just so gentle on your head."

Ernie worked with graphic designer Jonathan Greene on both books. Greene told me he sensed an undeniable urgency in Mickler's voice on their second go-round.

"I had no idea why [at the time]," Greene said, "but, of course, he wanted to see the book before dying."

When Ernie first set off to make photographs for *WTC*, he went to see Pickette, who then worked at Brandon's Camera in Jacksonville. She set him up with a rangefinder, showing him the nuts and bolts, and then he took off. Later, when magazines hailed Ernie as a Southern master of photography, Pickette said, she wanted to scream, "The man can't load the film!" But she added: "As long as he could be told how to point to something, he could compose a picture."

In his photographs, there's an affinity for his subjects that can't be learned, only lived. While he wasn't a pedigreed photographer, he had a natural inclination, and the rangefinder suited him. His photographs' likeness to those of Eggleston and Christenberry is uncanny, and to those of Walker Evans maybe more so.

Richard McCabe, curator of photography at the Ogden Museum of Southern Art in New Orleans, told me he clearly saw Walker Evans in Mickler's work, and talked about how his churches and interiors were reminiscent of Evans and writer James Agee's seminal vignette of Hale County, Alabama, "Let Us Now Praise Famous Men." (Playing off the same comparison, Southern Foodways Alliance Director John T. Edge in 2006 penned a piece about Ernie titled "Let Us Now Praise Famous Cooks" for Oxford American, and that piece was adapted for the foreword for the 25th-anniversary edition of *WTC*.)

"When you think about Eggleston or Christenberry, you think about sense of place and culture," McCabe told me. "Well, one way to define a culture is by the food they eat." McCabe said that as Christenberry used photographs of the same building, repeated over time, to register a sense of place, Ernie used food. He argued his case well, demonstrating how Ernie's photographs of cooking pans, signage, and buildings all point back toward the work of Eggleston, Christenberry, and Evans.

"In a way, he was more of a folklorist with a camera," McCabe said. Ernie's compositions, he said, shift between Eggleston's dynamism to Christenberry's and Evans' deadpan approach. While Ernie's work doesn't lie under the weight of an era of social documentary's scrutiny, as Evans and Agee's book does, it's become embedded in the narrative of the South, regardless of its notoriety. Ernie, like Christenberry or Eggleston, is one of the few Southerners who have represented the region with such acuity. And in 1986, he attracted the attention of prominent collectors. One wrote to him to let him know his work would be in good company next to the Christenberry and Eggleston prints in his home.

It didn't matter that Ernie had no idea how to use a camera; it mattered that he shot what he knew best.

The intimacy in his photographs spills off the page into the stories and then the recipes, and it all amounts to something home-grown and poignant. And undeniably, as with the aforementioned artists, there are strong connections to photographers like Clarence John Laughlin, William Ferris, and Fonville Winans — who all documented the Delta region (Winans actually began a project akin to Ernie's in the 1950s in Louisiana).

But maybe the most uplifting characteristic of Ernie's photography, McCabe said, is his understanding of his own region and its people.

"He didn't hate it," McCabe said. "He wasn't ashamed of it. It empowered him. People either reject or embrace their upbringing, but he elevated it."

Both books were ahead of their time, and both books still hold a strange, unmistakable relevance today as anthropological records of the South. And with each passing day, they accrue meanings. Who knows what additional meanings escape our notice today because we lost the books' maker, Ernie Mickler, entirely too early?

...

In St. Augustine this past summer, I parked in Lincolnville, where Ernie lived, swung up a narrow, brick-paved block, cut through an arch into a courtyard, then climbed a tiled staircase up to the St. Augustine Historical Society. The charm swelled as I passed through a glass door and met Charles Tingley, a senior researcher as loquacious as his bearing on the region's history is deep, and an encyclopedic storyteller.

He ushered me into a set of study rooms and recounted his memory of meeting Ernie at a book signing in St. Augustine. (He also remembered that event's sugar cookies made with Tabasco sauce.) He told me stories about how Ernie's work was treated after his death, how *Sinkin' Spells* was retitled *White Trash Cooking II* in an effort to sell more copies, and how family members penned subsequent books building off the *WTC* brand.

Looking down, Tingley paused, then, in a softer register, told me, "It was such a shame that Ernie died so young, because he was such a great folklorist."

Fortunately, Ernie Mickler's work lives and breathes in the annals of the University of Florida's Special Area Studies Collection in Gainesville, alongside the papers of Zora Neale Hurston, Stetson Kennedy, Marjorie Kinnan Rawlings, and countless other pillars of Florida's literary and artistic heritage. Fifteen metal-edged boxes ultimately stake out Ernie's life through correspondence, photographs, and manuscripts — many unseen.

On the second floor of the Special Area Studies library, I asked Florence "Flo" Turcotte, UF's literary manuscripts curator, what a collection like Ernie's offered students.

"You want people to go to the archive and understand something about themselves," she replied. "I think people are looking for connections to the past to help them move forward." And Ernie's archive, she said, might be particularly rich in that regard.

Turcotte told me she always goes to the correspondence in a collection first, because it's a window into people's lives that doesn't contend with the weight of posterity.

"It's just plain communication," she said.

"There's some things in there that are a surprise," Turcotte said. She explained how collections are often "sanitized" in order to mold the legacy that's left behind. But Ernie's, she said, is "really pure." Anyone can pore over his will, literary contracts, deeds, W-2s, love letters, or manuscripts.

After spending so much time with his papers, it gave me a deeper, more genuine understanding of Ernie Mickler; it was the covalent bond for this story ultimately.

Ernie's papers allow a researcher to see how a book comes together, the process, hardships, and rewards, but they also serve as a testament to his vulnerability, his resilience, and ultimately his grace — the qualities that carried him so far.

...

Food Stories

After I passed through a torrential downpour on my way east from Gainesville, out State Road 26 toward Melrose, the sky held back finally as I hit the edge of the city. I passed clearcuts next to conservation easements, Trump banners, and vestiges of "old-timey" Florida — things Ernie might have photographed. In Melrose, I hooked left on State Road 21 north to Keystone Heights to meet with the writer Andrew Holleran, who was a friend of Ernie's — and whose book *Ground Zero*, published in 1988, chronicled the earliest years of the AIDS crisis.

The air hung heavy as I stepped out of my car at Johnny's Barbecue — the way it does after morning thunderstorms in this fecund corridor of the state. Inside, Holleran sat on a bench, and when he looked up, his smile seemed to broaden from his eyes down to his chest. We sat down in a red Formica booth against the window. Holleran had the special: smoked chicken, lima beans, and coleslaw. I had David's Deal, a jumbo pulled-pork sandwich with baked beans.

Holleran's family moved to Keystone in 1961, shortly before he took off to college at Harvard University.

"Cal [Yeomans] and Ernie were to me the real Floridians, and then there was the rest of us, the late arrivals," Holleran said. "Both Ernie and Cal were small-town aristocrats. They had the same values. They knew they were from a state that everybody made fun of, yet they loved Florida, and they took it seriously. They had a kind of anthropological historian's appreciation for the outsider, and [yet] they were part of it. They had this double vision about Florida. That's what made them fascinating. We were all doing the same thing: We all had to leave Florida to be gay, but we never entirely severed the relationship, and then we ended up coming back."

Ernie told Yeomans that when he came out to his three brothers, "They were polite at the very best, but they didn't come see me, I didn't go see them. They wanted nothing to do with me 'cause I was queer. Simple as that." Finally, Ernie said, "They got the idea: If they gon' treat me right, I'll come see them. If not, they lost a brother." But in 1970, after they lost their mother, "everybody accepted Ernie," Pickette said.

In his soft voice, Holleran explained the predicament of being queer in a provincial place like Keystone. "I wasn't out to anybody for years.

In fact, that's why I moved up North and stayed up North." Pickette also remembered how dangerous it was to be out then, citing bars in Jacksonville being evacuated due to bomb threats.

Holleran remembered a young man he knew from Windsor, a small village hidden off some backroads near U.S. 301, who walked into traffic, killing himself, after he learned he had AIDS. But there were heartening stories, too — such as Ernie's own death in Moccasin Branch.

"What happened in small towns is the ... thing that's so marvelous about the South," Holleran said. "What came through and overwhelmed whatever homophobia was present was the indomitable strength of the Southern family. I was just driving through Keystone the other day by the public beach where families picnic. And I thought: This is the thing that the South really has going for it: It's this ability we have to celebrate family."

In Holleran's essay "Ernie's Funeral," published in Christopher Street in 1988, he wrote: "Even in the hospital, he could not stop removing his oxygen mask to introduce whomever had just walked into the room to the rest of the people there or ask a cousin to move to one side because Anthony, seated on the window ledge, could not see past her, and no one should be excluded like that, Ernie said. There was no reason for anyone in his view to be excluded — and that included, of course, himself."

Pickette recounted those last days with Ernie one afternoon in her backyard as thunder groaned and the sky turned moody. When the doctors told Ernie death was imminent, he asked to go home. In the living room, Ernie lay on a table made up as a bed. Beside him, his cousin Rosemary, his brother Hugo, Hugo's wife, and Gary stood vigil. Purportedly, Ernie died, but then a knock came on the door just before midnight. His brother Hampton and his wife, Dorothy, called out, and the sound of his brother's voice brought him back. Once Hampton reached Ernie's side, Ernie gave up the ghost.

Before they left the hospital, Gary had brought copies of Ernie's new book, which had just arrived at the house. Scrawled in what Holleran described as "the spidery, shaky, almost illegible handwriting of an old man," Ernie inscribed a copy to Cal Yeomans. The inscription read, "I guess we'll figure it out someday."

Ernie's wake was held at St. Ambrose Church down the road from his house. At the end of a long canopy of live oaks lies a cemetery, Sampson, that harks back to Ernie's roots — markers bearing Minorcan names like Solano, Sanchez, Rogero, and Lopez. In Holleran's essay, he wrote, "Ernie was contemporary. I watched him one night on 'The David Letterman Show,' but he was also connected to the past, and when he died, a connection between the two was lost. So, it was doubly startling, and doubly touching, to drive to his funeral one Friday afternoon in mid-November — a funeral he had planned down to the music and food — and find one more place in which they touched. The menu is barbecued pork, baked beans, hot sauce, cole slaw, rolls, beer, and Pepsi. Cal and I sit with Gary and the nurses from the AIDS Network who helped Ernie through his last months. We are the gay portion of Ernie's life, in a room filled with his other parts."

Pickette described the wake to me.

"People cried and ate and drank, danced, and carried on just like Ernie wanted," she said. "That's exactly what he wanted his wake to be like."

When Ernie died, he was cremated. Afterward, Ernie's brothers and their cousin, Ken, "buried Ernie's ashes right beside his momma," Pickette said.

At Sampson, where Ernie and 38 other Micklers rest, I visited during a hot summer morning with dark bands of rain looming above. At the gates, a soft, steady wind passed over the place. I could tell it must have changed tenfold since Ernie made his photographs here. Cookie-cutter cul-de-sacs spilled out all over the place, forming an endless array of terra-cotta roofs and manicured lawns. To get to the cemetery today, you pass through a country club development where even the speed-limit signs look ostentatious.

Winding down the four-lane promenade, signs pointed toward the cemetery, which sits at the end of a road littered with sterile-looking stucco homes. I hooked past two-track trails falling off into woods, and then I reached the gated cemetery, flanked by a border of sparse pinewoods that separate it from the golf courses fanning out all around — a place time almost forgot. As I got out, a young boy passed by in a golf cart, pink polo shirt and frosted tips beneath a visor. I wondered what a passerby might have looked like when the road was only a coarse, oyster-shell path through the pines.

Inside, it didn't take long to find Ernie's grave, sandwiched between his parents, William and Edna Rae. A tabby-concrete obelisk adorned with a silver plaque marks his place. I stood watch for a while, visited the places where Ernie stood. I thought about how he must have reckoned with death here where I stood, how he spent so much time over the years with friends and family, parents, and ultimately accepting that he might be interred here soon — Gary standing next to him as death crept in prematurely.

Out here in what was once the middle of nowhere — now tame suburbia — I thought of how grateful I was to know Ernie's work. All around, the state was vanishing, but Ernie preserved a chunk of it. The dimpled sugar sand and strewn pine needles conjured up Ernie's photographs, Ernie, too.

...

In an interview in November 1986, on a local San Diego TV news show, an anchor asked Ernie what the essence of Southern people was. Without skipping a beat, he told her in his honeyed voice, "Eating, laughing, and telling stories. They love that. They like life more than they like money," and that incomparable gleam stretched across his face, just as contagious today as it was three decades ago.

Retracing Ernie's footsteps this summer, I played Ernie and Petie's record over and over, memorized the lyrics, the chord progressions, the thin space between tracks. But one part stuck with me. Hell, it haunted me. About halfway through the 13th track, "Rambling Boy," Ernie croons in his light, confident timbre words that seemed to encapsulate his life:

Oh, when I die
Don't bury me at all
Just place my bones in alcohol
And at my breast
Place a white stone dove
To tell the world that I died of love

For me, Ernest Mickler's books, stories, and photographs gave me a sense of place, a well to return to. And for many, I believe Ernie forged a portal into the South — a South unto itself — proudly bound up in all its contradictions. He helped Southerners of all strata hold onto their roots, spanning the spectrum from blue-blood aristocrats to rednecks. But more specifically, he helped queer folks find that root in a place that — particularly during the AIDS plague of the 1980s — wanted to expel them.

The loss of Ernie and so many others like him in those years left a chasm in its wake.

As Edmund White wrote in an essay for The New York Times Magazine in 1991, "For me, these losses were definitive. The witnesses to my life, the people who had shared the same references and sense of humor, were gone. The loss of all the books they might have written remains incalculable." He continued, "The grotesque irony is that at the very moment so many writers are threatened with extinction, gay literature is healthy and flourishing as never before. Perhaps the two contradictory things are connected, since the tragedy of AIDS has made gay men more reflective on the great questions of love, death, morality, and identity, the very preoccupations that have always animated serious fiction and poetry. Or perhaps AIDS has simply made gay life more visible."

Following Ernie's death, some obituaries listed no cause of death or "bone cancer," possibly at the family's behest.

"There was a stigma about it," Pickette told me. "It was like anybody knowing you were gay, period. If you had AIDS, obviously you were." But some papers, namely The New York Times and the Key West Citizen, printed AIDS as the cause.

A few weeks after Ernie died, Pickette drove down to his house. She found it abandoned — just a cardboard box filled with *White Trash Cooking* press materials left inside.

"Gary let nature have it," she said. Out on the porch, there was one hanging plant — withering. She threw the plant and box in the car and took off.

In Pickette's backyard this past summer, the sky molted into a dark purplish-gray, threatening to open up. Just behind us, a 20-foot-tall bird of paradise plant stretched up into the troposphere, dwarfing the greenhouse behind it. The plant had grown as tall as the cabbage palms that line the perimeter of her house. This bird of paradise is the same plant Pickette rescued from Ernie's house 30 years ago. She called it her "Ernie plant."

I asked which of her memories of Ernie is strongest, 30 years after his death. She didn't furrow a brow or dwell on the answer for long. She just looked off toward the top of her Ernie plant and beamed.

"It's his energy," she said. "His spirit is what I carry with me — his smile." ◊

—

Michael Adno is a writer and photographer who lives in Sarasota, Florida. He won a James Beard Award for his profile of Ernest Matthew Mickler, and his work has appeared in numerous publications, including Oxford American, The New York Times, National Geographic, The Bitter Southerner, and The Surfer's Journal.

SOUTHERN HUSTLE: HOUSTON HIP-HOP & CHINESE CHICKEN

by Alana Dao

—

Photo by Marie D. De Jesús
This story was originally published February 9, 2021

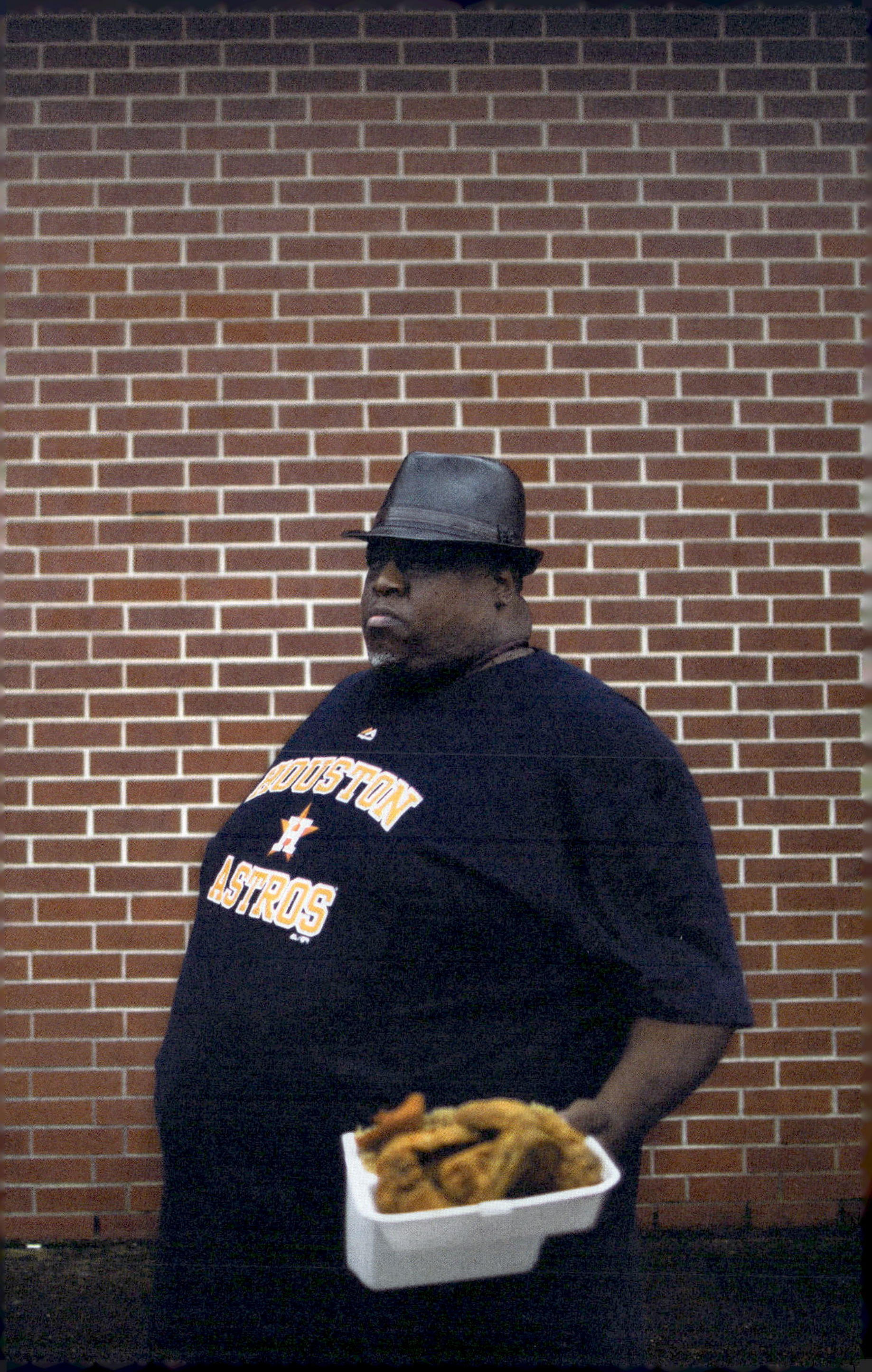
HOUSTON
ASTROS

Southern Hustle: Houston Hip-Hop & Chinese Chicken

*What you know bout Timmy Chan's,
what you know bout Cloverland*

—

"Southside," Big Mello

On my now-husband's first visit to Houston, my parents took him to see all the "sights." Sights for us anyway: Chinatown, our favorite dumpling spot, the strip mall where I took ballet lessons. On one car ride, my mother casually mentioned that she had managed a couple restaurants with my grandparents. And after my grandparents had sold their restaurants in the 1980s, the restaurant had become a well-known quick service chain that served fried chicken and rice.

As a child, I'd heard all this before. But this time, she elaborated, telling us that she'd heard a "rap person" talk about my grandparents' restaurant in one of their songs. That maybe it had been in a music video? My husband's interest was piqued. All he had to do was a low-key Google search, and he was shocked to find an Urban Dictionary entry:

Timmy Chans is a chain of restaurant[s] in Houston, tha land of the playas and pimps. The restaurants are a good place to go when you are broke and don't have enough dough. They can be found throughout the great land of Houston and they have become an integral part of the city. The food is not the highest quality but it is the experience of going and getting mountains of rice and chicken at rock bottom prices.

Food Stories

Writer Shea Serrano put Timmy Chan's famous chicken wing dinner in the Rap Food Reference Hall of Fame. And that "rap person" my mother was referring to was actually Bun B of the group UGK, one of the most well-known rappers from Houston. In the Paul Wall song "They Don't Know," we hear the lyrics, "Down here we got ghetto grub / Like Williams Chicken or Timmy Chan's."

Timmy Chan's was a familiar name in our household, but only because it was the restaurant my grandparents started when they moved from the East Coast to the Gulf Coast. Before its entrance into the Hall of Fame, Timmy Chan's was a restaurant that served Chinese American staples like egg rolls or fried rice and where my mother and her family spent their days.

Like Houston itself, the story of Timmy Chan's has become larger, intertwining itself with other cultures, urbanization, and hip-hop.

...

I grew up in Sugar Land, on the outskirts of the city. At the time, there were more grassy fields than houses, and cattle would graze by the railroad off the highway going into Houston. The first time I ever saw a Timmy Chan's was riding in a car — a 1990 Toyota Camry with my beloved MD Anderson Cancer Center Christmas tape in the cassette deck. I listened to those Christmas carols all year, every year, from age 5 to too long.

I was almost always listening to the sweet voices of children from the cancer center sharing Christmas wishes ringing out in the wet, Houston heat as my mother sped, stopped, pat-patted to stop and start along the highways of Houston. She was always kind enough to push the tape into the deck for me, even on scorching summer days as I sat in the backseat in a sticky sweat, shrinking away from the hot metal seat belt buckle. One time, she quickly pointed out the window as she drove past a building with a yellow and red awning and said, "That's a Timmy Chan's, but not ours."

Driving by, it looked smaller than I had imagined. In my child-mind, Timmy Chan's was where my mother had spent her own childhood, and it was the stuff of legend. In these stories, she was a little girl pulling pranks with her brother; or a college student quickly rolling egg rolls between classes, surrounded by chefs' knives flying through bushes of scallions. But as swiftly as she had pointed, Timmy Chan's flew past my window and we continued, speeding steadily through the city.

While I was probably listening to "We Three Kings of Orient Are" on my Christmas cassette or whatever pop hit 104.1 FM was playing (the morning DJ Roula of "The Roula & Ryan Show" had gone to my high school, so I felt loyal), the music playing out of cars in the Timmy Chan's parking lot, so loud the neighborhood around them shook, was primarily chopped and screwed. The historian and author of *Hip Hop in Houston: The Origin and the Legacy*, Maco Faniel, explains that DJs would slow pitch controls on a song then manipulate the entire thing by "mixing, scratching, and back spinning over it." The original song evolves into a foggy, unhurried, steady new thing. He tells me that oftentimes, musicians will release an album then drop a subsequent chopped and screwed version to offer more: a stretch in sound, slower lyrics where every word can be heard.

Chopped and screwed may be everywhere now, but in the 1990s, back when Timmy Chan's was first becoming a part of the hip-hop fold, DJ Screw made copies of his mixtapes and sold them from out of his home and at independent music shops — one of which happened to be close to Timmy Chan's on Martin Luther King Boulevard and Interstate Highway 610.

This serendipitous location gave way to a community hotspot where, as Cedric Hill (better known as E.S.G.), of DJ Screw's Screwed Up Click, puts it, "The price was good and the food tasted good as well." He remembers a $2 fried drumstick dinner that came with rice large enough to feed a family. The combination of good, hot food at an affordable price and geographical proximity began to create a place worth mentioning.

Faniel says that Timmy Chan's is now one of the "most referenced restaurants in Houston music" and that referencing places within a neighborhood is important in the culture of hip-hop. You are rapping and mapping, placing yourself within a larger history. Referencing Timmy Chan's was a way to tell of where they have been and paint a scene of where they are going, Hill says. He would mention it in his songs "because everybody loved it. If you came from the Southside, everybody would talk about it, because it was the place to hang out."

Food Stories

"Car culture is a part of Houston. Your car is an extension of yourself," says Dave Anthony, known as DJ Dirty Dave, of Street Pharmacy. He remembers Timmy Chan's being important for this very reason. With a large parking area to pull up and park, the restaurant lot would fill with "candy slabs, poppin' trunk, just bangin' music. It was like a car show." He tells me that at the end of the week, you could "take your car and go get a girl, go to the Galleria to get some new clothes, then the record shop to buy a tape, then drive over to Timmy Chan's for wings and noodles and fried biscuits. It was our place." For him, Timmy Chan's always felt "almost like a hub. They didn't disrespect you there, and it was the perfect place to park the car, blast the music so loud the buildings would shake."

Both Dirty Dave and E.S.G. explained that it became the spot to be because "it was really good." Different rappers even shot music videos in the parking lot or at other locations. E.S.G. wistfully wishes he had shot his first music video there. It was the place, they said, you took people from out of town to "really experience Houston."

> *Out of towner's be comin around*
> *Runnin they mouth be talkin down*
> *But you don't know nuttin 'bout my town*
> — Paul Wall ft Bun B, "They Don't Know"

...

My mother's parents, Larry and Lily Chu, or to me, Gong Gong and Po Po (the Cantonese terms for maternal grandfather and grandmother), knew a very different Houston. In reading through both of their autobiographies (which they wrote for their Southern Baptist church class), I learned what Timmy Chan's used to be and of their common struggles.

Born in Canton, China, my gong gong arrived in the United States to reunite with his father in 1937. According to family lore, Gong Gong's father, my great-grandfather, first came to the United States by way of a barrel on a boat. He arrived in New York where, true to the stereotype, he began a laundromat in Chinatown. The man remained an enigma; my mother recalls gambling in the back and a strong, stolid man. My gong gong must've inherited the swagger of his father, this man who floated the seas in a barrel to find his fortune, and to become a man whose funeral turned into a public parade in New York City's Chinatown.

When Gong Gong Larry arrived in the U.S. for the first time, he was immediately detained in a detention camp in Boston for six months. In his autobiography, he recalls, "I was a young man then, and it was the first time for me to experience discrimination. I resented the way I was being treated." He "saw no future for me in the United States," so he returned to China but came back in 1946, this time landing in New York, where he met my grandmother — where else but working in a restaurant.

In 1949, they married, and in a story straight out of a Western, or maybe just a soap opera, my grandfather met "the real estate man from Texas." Gong Gong and Po Po and a few other friends decided to move to Houston and invest in a restaurant. At the last minute, one of their friends, a professor named Fook Tim "Timmy" Chan, pulled out to return to New York. But my grandparents forged ahead.

Upon arriving in Houston in the 1950s, they opened their first restaurant, naming it after their friend Timmy Chan. They recall moving to Houston and struggling for years, as business was slow. As my grandfather wrote, "With the building of the space center and the development of the oil industries, Houston had become a very active city, hence, our business gradually improved," and they opened several other locations.

At the time, Chinese food was considered too foreign and not served regularly. My grandfather created a menu that catered to the local palate, featuring lunchtime specials like New England boiled dinner, chicken and dumplings, and liver and onions. The restaurant became known for its ribeye steak dinner. But slowly, they began to incorporate American Chinese cuisine into the menu, things we would consider chop suey. They began offering chow mein, fried rice, and all those egg rolls my mother folded; foods that Americans liked but that had little resemblance to the food they once ate in China.

Before Timmy Chan's became a part of American Chinese cuisine in Texas, Chan, aka Timmy, had actually been an educator of Chinese culture and culinary history. He once wrote, "the name 'Chop Suey' so familiar to the Americans is really unknown to the Chinese. To tell the truth, I have never had any such dish in my life in China." So while he was an expert on Chinese food and etiquette in its original form, his name carried on to become something else entirely. Chop suey is Chinese food of American terroir: invented, created, manipulated here in the United States. And like chopped and screwed, Chinese food is a reimagination, a way to adapt to the region where it finds itself, showing up and showing off for the communities it belongs to.

My grandparents had the foresight to expand into downtown Houston next, making their bread and butter on lunch specials and catering to businessmen. As business grew, so did their children. My mother and uncle eventually took over the management of a location each, and soon my uncle and grandfather decided to open Timmy Chan's on MLK Boulevard. This location would serve fast-casual food such as fried chicken and rice, the one now so famous in Houston hip-hop.

• • •

Beyoncé, one of Houston's hometown heroes, in her song "Bow Down/I Been On," honors another Gulf Coast fried chicken chain, Frenchy's Chicken. Frenchy's is sometimes mentioned in the same breath as Timmy Chan's. Frenchy's, however, was Black-owned, by a man from Louisiana, Percy "Frenchy" Creuzot Jr.

According to my mother and uncle, Creuzot was a customer at Timmy Chan's, and he and my grandfather became good friends. It was Creuzot who passed along a recipe for chicken when my grandfather and uncle decided to open the Timmy Chan's on MLK Boulevard. As my mother likes to tell it, my gong gong added soy sauce and other spices that made the chicken "more Asian," but she and my uncle won't divulge what's actually in it. As the story goes, Creuzot sampled the Timmy Chan's version and said it was better than the original Frenchy's recipe.

Outside businesses coming in and profiting off Black people is not new. And in a way, how an Americanized Chinese restaurant became a cultural icon and touchstone for Houston hip-hop reflects this. An incredibly intricate relationship emerges as cultures and communities bump up against each other and stories build up in a single place.

A place adapts to the palates of the neighborhood and new ways of living and eating are formed. For Timmy Chan's on MLK, it became, as Dirty Dave recalls, "their spot." New stories of survival also take root and grow. Family lore stands in to account for what happens to those who were left out of the larger narrative of urban cowboys, outerspace, and "progress."

My grandfather writes, "In May, 1982, God decided that we should sell our business and to retire." He leased the Timmy Chan's on Fannin Street to a Texas-based steakhouse, then sold the quick service locations to families that were already working for them. The MLK location was sold to the Dangs, a Chinese immigrant couple. A Vietnamese immigrant family, the Trans, bought the one on Richmond. The Trans had come to work for my grandparents by way of the Vietnamese refugee diaspora — yet another significant history woven into the city of Houston. From there, Timmy Chan's became what it is today: an institution in the Houston hip-hop community.

Timmy Chan's, under my grandparents' ownership, had been the quintessential high-end Chinese restaurant for (primarily) white, middle-class patrons. One replete with large banquet halls decked out with cloth napkins, red and gold decor, and dishes like shrimp with lobster sauce and egg foo young. Photos show my grandparents schmoozing with smiling regulars in front of a dazzling bar and shiny black and gold menus — a space with its own narrative.

While Timmy Chan's has been forever immortalized in hip-hop, there is another life in this yellow-and-red restaurant, another history. The history of grand banquet rooms, tableside dinner presentations, and shaking hands with local celebrity regulars like Creuzot, Marvin Zindler or the Moody family has all but disappeared and been replaced with counter service and menu boards.

What remains still leaves a taste of what my grandparents first started: a place to show up and show off, a place to be at ease. Dirty Dave remembers Timmy Chan's was the place to go because it "was our place for African American youth, where they didn't disrespect. ... People in the urban community felt welcome and they treated you with respect."

I think of my grandparents' tenacity: my gong gong's swagger, my po po's desire for grandeur and economic comfort, and the struggle against poverty and discrimination. I think it was with this same spirit that they started Timmy Chan's. What they first created has become a place of comfort for some, even if not in the way my grandparents had expected. It is also a place that rebels, adjusts, and adapts to change in its own way.

Houston hip-hop takes this concept further. Chopped and screwed, leaning into a slower sound, is a resistance against the harsh backdrop of capitalism and being stuck in traffic on Interstate 10. A way to connect and cope against larger systems. Hip-hop in Houston tells of a specific time and place, of lives lived in the face of hardship. In spite of natural and constructed forces, whether it be hurricane season, racism, or even the criminalization of simply being, the music declares: We are still here, still seen.

It is in the spirit of the Gulf Coast — the Third Coast as Bun B says — and Houston that, as things are destroyed around us, we build and rebuild. We, of the Gulf Coast, have grit, determination, and hustle. Dirty Dave, E.S.G., and Bun B are just several rappers from the Houston area that never forgot their roots, referencing and connecting others to their sense of place and, quite literally, putting it on the map.

And like them, my gong gong and po po had the determination to build and build and build. As Michael P. Jeffries writes about Southern rap, "The South is no longer the aggrieved underdog; it is king of the hill. Its climb was a beautiful and disjointed process, as piece by piece, cities and rappers with their own ideals of Southern authenticity scraped and clawed their way upward."

• • •

I never really experienced Houston hip-hop or the family business, but something of that grit and grease followed me. I left for New England after high school with the only piece of advice my mother often repeated to me: Never work in a restaurant.

But as I finished college in the face of the Great Recession, a restaurant was the only place I found work. Even after grad school, it was hard to find work. I landed in, of all places, a Southern-inspired restaurant in Maine known for its fried chicken. I was attracted to the energy that can only be found working in restaurants.

Not only did the anticipation of service, the beat of the kitchen, the rhythm and pace of a dinner rush as customers clanked away get me going, but I realized I was good at the work.

I believed fried chicken would define my existence. Food, fried chicken, and hot platters were in my blood, my family's blood, and no matter how hard we tried, this was my fate. Miles from home, I was destined to always be around the smell and sizzle of grease popping and food cooking.

Everything has a weird and winding road to get to where it's going, be it chicken, music, or who we are. So now, rather than thinking of restaurant work as some predetermined fate, I think of food as a way to place ourselves in history. A history ever changing and evolving, uncovered and revealed as buildings shake around us. I, too, can stretch a sound or explore a beat, resist by my own presence, at a pace where my words can also be heard. And I realize: It's not the chicken that is my destiny, it's the hustle. ◊

—

Alana Dao is a mother, writer, and restaurant professional. Her writing often explores race, contemporary culture, and food. Her previous writing has been featured in The Kitchn, VICE, and HuffPost, among other publications.

MY OLD FRIEND NATTY LIGHT

by Mickie Meinhardt

Photo by Gunner Hughes
This story was originally published August 14, 2018

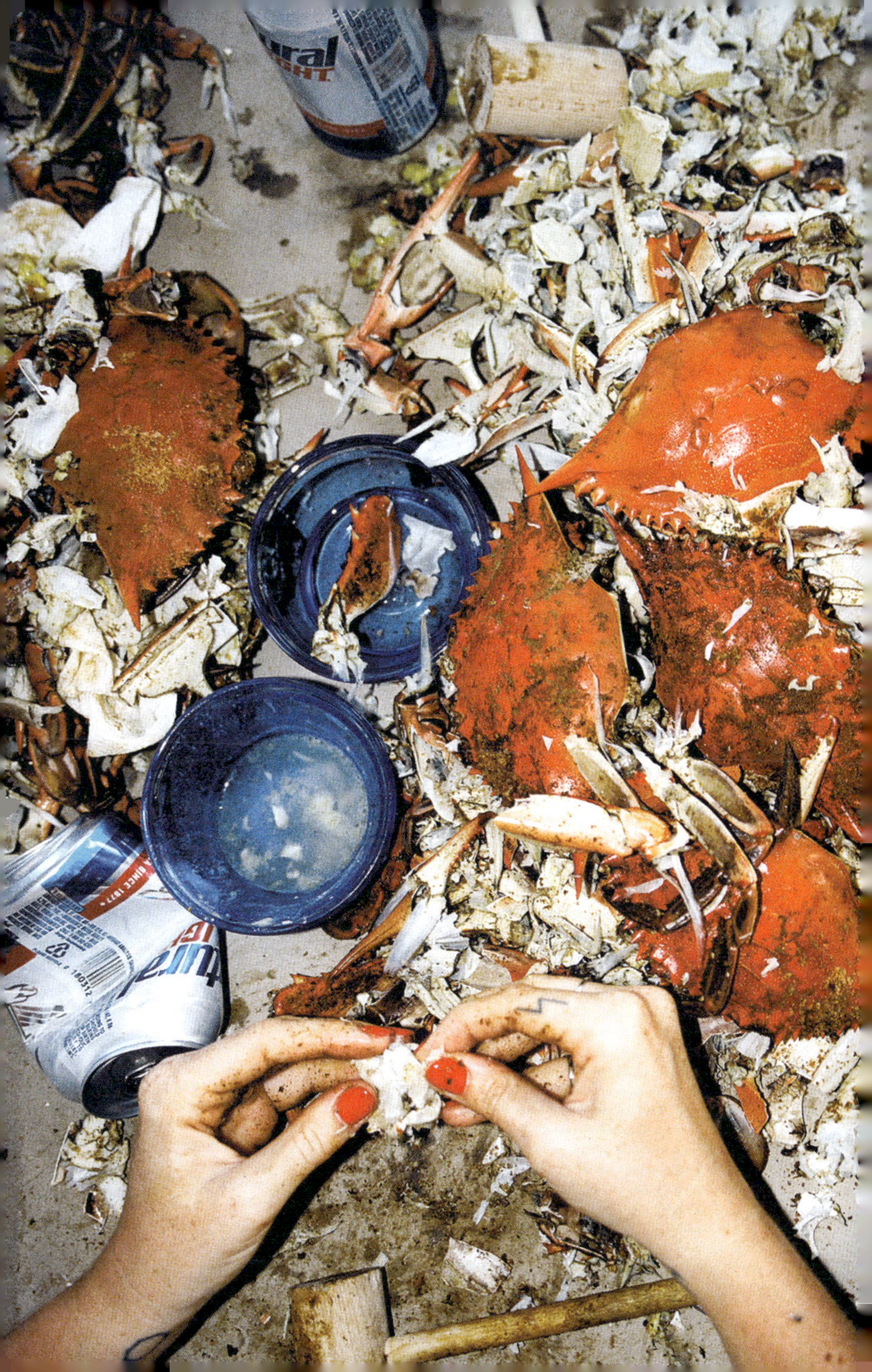

My Old Friend Natty Light

The night I lost my virginity, I special-requested Natural Light. The "nice" version: a six-pack of 12-ounce long-neck bottles.

"Are you sure?" my then-boyfriend asked. "That's really what you want?"

In his 17-year-old excitement, he surely would have bought me any beer I asked for. But I was a hardheaded 17-year-old, and when I imagined toasting what I naively thought would be a passionate, exhausting night, I knew only one beer would do.

"Um, yes. I like Natural Light."

I still remember him popping off the top with the end of a lighter, and toasting across the comforter and grinning at each other. I can't say I remember the beer tasting any different. It blends in with the memories of every other time I've had a Natural Light, innumerable ones both important and utterly forgettable. (Or forgotten thanks to too many Natural Lights in one night.) I can safely say I've consumed more of that easy-drinking, silver-and-blue-canned domestic beer than any beverage other than water, and the reason can be traced directly to my hometown.

If a mass-produced domestic beer can have terroir, Natural Light's is Ocean City, Maryland.

• • •

Food Stories

Ocean City is a beach town, a 10-mile strip of barrier island on Maryland's Atlantic and a summer destination for a large swath of the central East Coast. It's best known for blue crabs, seafood buffets, free public beaches, an insane bar complex called Seacrets, and a fantastic tropical drink called the Orange Crush. Like all beach towns, it's boom in the summer and bust in the winter — hosting up to 8 million tourists annually but with a local population of only about 7,100. The locals like life simple: Surfing and skateboarding are big subcultures, but so are hunting and fishing. And like all small towns, people drink. A lot. Domestic beer and cheap wine mostly, nothing you'd call a "cocktail." They drink at beach bars, pool bars, bars on the bay or the harbor or the inlet or the boardwalk. To celebrate the town coming alive in the spring and the tourists leaving in the fall. To cut the stagnation of long, dead winter nights when you can drive the length of town and see only two other cars, both of them driven by bored cops. And most — old and young, man and woman — drink Natural Light.

A resort town established in 1886, Ocean City was built from the start on the tourism and fishing industries, which are at their peak in the summer. Which means that in those hottest months of the year, everyone works double time; most make the bulk of their annual income from mid-May to early September and use it to live out the rest of the year, probably with a vacation to somewhere tropical in January, when everything in town is closed. Many jobs are labor-intensive. Construction, working the docks in the harbor, mating a ship, serving or bartending. Or they're outdoors: beach patrol, manning an umbrella stand, serving food at a to-go counter with a hot kitchen at your back and the sun in your face, cocktail waitressing at a beach bar.

There's a reason heavy IPAs aren't a Southern thing. It's too hot here for anything heavy; being bloated and beer-drunk in direct sunlight in 80-to-90-degree weather is a recipe for passing out. This is why my neighbor always had a Natty in hand when cleaning his boat; why it's omnipresent at dockside bars and in boat coolers; why many an outdoor bartender might sip one under the table during a shift. Refreshing, light, airy, and unfilling, it's the perfect beer to cut the perpetual heat. In those circumstances, the libation doesn't need to be trendy — they're not drinking for cultural capital. (No one Instagrams a Natty.) Folks down here just want something to sip on while they shoot the shit. Overwhelmingly, Natural Light is precisely that beer.

When I was in high school, an article in a local newspaper went something like viral (before viral was a word people used) for citing that Delmarva — a name for the combined Atlantic-adjacent peninsula of lower Delaware, Maryland, and Virginia — was the highest per capita consumer of Natural Light in America. This statistic cannot be verified anywhere on the Internet today, but then as now the lack of hard facts didn't prevent it from becoming lore.

Of course it is, we all thought. Duh.

Natural Light is served in every bar and restaurant in a 50-mile radius, even the fine dining establishments, and nearly required at every cookout, party, and wedding, in every boat cooler, beach bag, and golf cart. It is far and away the beer of choice, but not just because it's cheap. People from Ocean City, like me at 17, will staunchly defend their choice of light domestic beer. They like it. The taste, the high carbonation, the slight skunkiness, the way it goes down the hatch easy and quick. Even if most people think it has no taste, we know better. God help you if you — you high-minded individual — try to suggest folks here drink Bud Light (too expensive), or Coors Light (trashy), or something more millennial-approved like Miller High Life (for sissies). No National Bohemians, thanks, that favorite domestic headquartered in Baltimore — that's for Yuppies and their lax bro offspring.

"Shore Champagne," we often call it, but mostly it's just "Natty," that y-sound making it into an affectionate pet name, softening it with a fondness that other single-name beers lack. Bud is heavy, flat, muddy; Miller sounds like your dopey next-door neighbor; Coors is uttered like a question. Coors? Why?

But Natty, oh, Natty is your friend. Your oldest, most dependable friend.

...

Food Stories

I know what you're thinking: Is Ocean City the South? I've gotten this question since I left for college in New York City at age 18, decidedly not one of those who liked the simple life. Most of the early friends I made assumed I was from California — the beach-town vibes were hard to shake. No, I'd reply, Maryland, "a small Southern beach town." Invariably, I'd be met with the same reply I've been getting since: Is Maryland really the South? Or a scoff: Maryland isn't the South.

"My part is," I'd say, and still do. I ask the person if they've ever been — D.C. doesn't count, I say. Usually, they concede they have not.

The lines of what is or isn't the South are endlessly debated, and Maryland is a tricky state in that debate. Technically below the Mason-Dixon Line yet typically Democratic, dyed blue by D.C.-area liberals but redder and redder as you go farther toward its edges, it's a political hodgepodge.

Much of this can be traced to the problems Maryland had before and during the Civil War: As a largely agrarian state with a central capitalistic engine, its people often have directly contradictory needs and wants. During the war, it was one of those states that split itself, a border slave state not part of the Confederacy but filled with sympathizers. The first bloodshed of the war was in Baltimore. Massachusetts troops on their way to D.C. to protect Lincoln were set upon by unsympathetic Baltimoreans, which prompted a Maryland man named James Randall, then living in Louisiana, to write a song called "Maryland, My Maryland," still the state song, which includes the lyric, "Huzzah, she spurns the Northern scum!"

John Wilkes Booth was a Marylander, but so was Harriet Tubman; the latter is the one most prefer to remember. Maryland's Eastern Shore and southern Western Shore made their money on tobacco and slave labor and thus were on the side of the Confederacy (though not as heavily for secession). The center, around the capital, tended to be more abolitionist. The major port of Baltimore was crucial to the state's and the surrounding region's economies and couldn't afford to be sacked or occupied. Mostly, Maryland officials wanted to avoid fighting with both the state's southern and northern neighbors and thus voted not to secede — though they also asked Lincoln to remove the federal troops he had stationed there to protect the capital.

This rural edges vs. urban center debate makes it still somewhat a house divided. There are certainly parts of Maryland that are affluent and liberal, mostly around the D.C. metro area, and in fact, Maryland consistently ranks as having the highest median household income in America, mostly due to overflow from that metro area. But the Eastern Shore is not one of those areas, and anyone who is from there will say, unequivocally, that it is Southern. Consider a recent interactive map from The New York Times showing the voting precincts of each state in the 2016 election. Maryland is overwhelmingly red, red, red — except around D.C. and Baltimore, which swung the state in favor of Hillary.

The Eastern Shore is a solidly blue-collar, lower-middle-class and working-class area, small towns populated by hardworking, simple people. There are many backroads, pickup trucks, antique stores, farmers markets, and rundown trailers at the edge of every town, hallmarks of the South, yes, but also of small American towns everywhere. There are miles of farmland that provide sweet corn, ripe red tomatoes, asparagus, blueberries, peaches, and pumpkins, more cows than you would think, and acres of chicken coops; Perdue, one of the largest chicken-processing corporations, is headquartered a few miles from my high school. In the winter, those farmlands are leased for deer or duck hunting, another favorite pastime here; it was not unusual for boys I knew to be pulled out of school by their fathers in peak deer season. There are a few city-ish areas, notably Salisbury, perhaps Cambridge, but these are nothing anyone would call metropolitan. And it is, notably, more conservative leaning. Maryland was a Catholic enclave, after all, which prevails still, and those boys I grew up with will die for their Second Amendment rights.

Another Southern hallmark: the heat. Maryland is hot and humid in the summer, especially the Eastern Shore — flat as a board and evenly sweltering for miles north, south, west, and east until you hit the Atlantic Ocean. Trees, where there are any, are scrubby pines; you have to make your own shade. At the beach, the ocean breeze offers some relief, but even just 15 minutes inland the heat settles into the hundreds, thick and oppressive.

More than all that, though, there is a deep sense of pride in being from the Eastern Shore, the same type of stubborn pride one feels in most

Southern states — it runs deep, rooted firmly in hometown ground. It's in the dirt and it's in our blood, and we can't usually explain why we feel the way we feel. We just do. Having lived in the Northeast for a decade now, I have never gotten that same sense from anyone from Connecticut, or Pennsylvania, or Vermont, or California. Ours is a jut-your-chin-out kind of pride that comes from knowing you are part of a line of hardworking, resilient people.

The Eastern Shore has that in spades. It took me a long time to feel it, and when I was younger, I rejected it. Only as I grew older did I feel that familiar tug pulling me all those miles back home. This can put me at odds, sometimes; I'm quite liberal, and my home is very much not. I have a handful of old friends who feel the same but, like me, are drawn back year after year. Some end up staying. Maryland, my Maryland, for good or ill.

It's precisely that irrational, inexplicable pride that supports the enthusiastic drinking of Natural Light by Ocean City-ers. How else would you rationalize serving it at your wedding, or graduation, or ordering it at a white-tablecloth restaurant if you didn't feel deep down this beer was made exactly for someone like you?

. . .

Eastern Shore Marylanders are not the only people who feel this way. Natural Light is one of the best-selling beers in America; as of 2017, it was ranked No. 6 in sales, at $336.2 million, behind only Bud Light, Budweiser, Coors Light, Miller Lite, and Michelob Ultra. In 2001, Consumer Reports ranked it the No. 2 light beer in the country, and in 2006, The Wall Street Journal had it as the No. 5. Natty is overwhelmingly popular among college kids for its low price, and among light beer drinkers nationwide, also usually for its low price. As a strong presence at high school and college parties across the country, it's the gateway beer for many young Americans.

Following the craft beer revolution, the mixology era, and the rise of natural wines, it's easy to assume we are drinking better, more superiorly, than ever. But that type of thinking leaves out large swaths of the population; like our politics, it puts us in a bubble. In much of the country, populism reigns in alcoholic beverages as well as ideologies. Many Americans proudly consider themselves Not Fancy. They still love the U.S.A.-brewed light beers they started drinking young. They never saw the point in switching up, which is why many of my friends' parents still keep Natural Light in their fridge.

Anheuser-Busch introduced Natural Light, the company's first widely distributed light beer, in 1977. Created initially to compete with the 96-calorie Miller Lite and get Anheuser-Busch a foothold in the reduced-calorie beer market, it rang in at 97 calories (it's now 95) and 4.2 percent alcohol by volume.

It was in the market two years before Bud Light. Originally, Anheuser-Busch executives didn't want to water down the Budweiser name with a light option, hence the entirely separate beer. Of course, they changed their minds when Natural Light and other light beers took off; now, Bud Light is the best-selling beer in America by millions of dollars.

Unlike other light beers, Natural Light wasn't necessarily marketed toward women or the calorie-conscious when it debuted. Instead, taste, natural ingredients, and drinkability were the selling points, as well as a "refreshment for physical exertion" theme. In a 1977 television ad, "Airplane!" actor Peter Graves croons, "When you're thirsty for a beer or two, but what you're doing isn't through, that's the time to take a natural break." The actor notes it's "brewed naturally" and "won't fill you up, so it won't slow you down," a perfect marketing position. Very light, easy-drinking, and with absolutely no identifiable or controversial flavors like hops or sourness or fruit, Natural is exactly the type of beer you want to guzzle when you're doing something really terrible and hard, like moving or yardwork, but aren't necessarily done for the day yet and can't get tipsy. A print ad from the same time features a woman with Princess Leia braids and reads, "If I'm going to have a beer after a jog, it's got to be Natural. It's my favorite light beer. Because I like the way Natural tastes. Clean and smooth, it's really thirst-quenching."

Teenage me's idea of it as an ideal post-first-coitus beer wasn't far off the mark.

Until Bud Light was introduced, Natural was a star child, priced nearly the same as other full-calorie beers and selling well. Then it was shunted off, gradually lowered in price and given less attention until it hit its status of today: one of the lowest-priced, least advertised beers on the market. Today, a 30-pack of Natural is a mere $16.99 in Ocean City; when I was in high school, it was only $11.99. Bud Light and Budweiser currently ring in at $23.99.

Consider: Have you ever seen an ad for Natural Light? Probably not. Its marketing comes from prominently placed, towering stacks of 30-racks in package store windows, silver and blue cardboard gleaming in the sun, never dusty because it has such high turnover. It's an "economy" or "value" beer, the industry category for light beers or other cheap domestic lagers and ales. For the now-mega conglomerate AB-InBev (comprising Anheuser Busch, MillerCoors, and the many smaller brewing companies the two have swallowed over the years), the value beers include Natty's siblings, Natural Ice and the malt beverage hybrid Natty Daddy, neither of which inspire much fandom even in Ocean City; Busch/Busch Light/Busch Ice; Rolling Rock; Bud Ice; Hurricane; and King Cobra. The lack of marketing suits them fine; most sell well without it. (In 2008, for example, Natty received 0.0015 percent of Anheuser-Busch's advertising dollars but was still a top earner.)

The "natural" part quickly fell off as a selling point, though in that area it certainly isn't the worst beer you can drink. Natural's current listed ingredients are water, barley malt, cereal grains, hops, and yeast, the same as they were in 1977. It has no added sugars and is low-carb and low-calorie. Still, you won't find anyone who drinks it championing it as a healthier alternative, especially in the wellness era. Cheapness and drinkability remain Natural's stalwart traits, though opinions on the quality of the latter vary. If a person has any sort of palate for finer beers, not necessarily even a craft beer but just something that's not light, they'll likely call it garbage. Natural is ranked the No. 1 worst-tasting beer on RateBeer.com, and Beer Advocate's experts give it a 37/100 overall score (the Beer

Advocate public has it higher, but only by 10 points). Raters describe it as "piss water," "skunky," "stale," and "total crap." Often people say it doesn't taste like anything, or it's "like water."

This might be why the beer is such a success. It's inoffensive. Unmemorable. Sessionable, to borrow a craft beer term.

But speak to an Ocean City local, and you'll hear Natty is the preferred beer, not the last resort.

It tastes like home — pronounced, down here, as "hoehm."

So, what is that taste exactly? Popping a can to actually think about it, writing tasting notes like I'm considering a fine wine, I note it's first and foremost yeasty, a bready beer; those cereal grains make themselves known. "Skunky" is right on, but that's not a bad thing. It's more like a tang, one that dissipates as the beer's heavy carbonation turns to pure bubbles in your mouth, becoming almost gentle as it finishes. It tastes, in short, like a shaken-up can of beach foam, something that was once crisp but has happily mellowed. There's a total absence of sugar; in fact, Natural somehow manages to miss all the major taste buds. It's not sweet, not salty, neither bitter nor sour, and it certainly has no umami. From experience, it's best enjoyed when your lips are salty from the ocean, perhaps with a little sand on the rim for crunch. Don't linger over it; the carbonation leaves the can quickly, and flat Natty is no good. Also, about that: Always go canned. Natural is one of the few beers that is leagues better when drunk from a can rather than glass, something I didn't have the perception to realize as a teen. Bottled Natty is flatter. The zip of metal from the aluminum perfectly offsets the taste. There's something about the shining silver of the can, too, the retro blue type and thin ribbon of red above the cobalt base.

I am utterly American, it says, and so is anyone who drinks me.

It's a simple, humble, light beer, made for picking up and putting down over and over quickly until it's gone. It does not want the heft of a bottle, a fancy label, a TV ad on Sunday night football, a place on a big-city bar's bottle list. It doesn't need it.

•••

I returned to Ocean City and Natural Light last summer, living home again in a break after a master's program for the first time in seven years. I was there to write a book, funded by a side job waiting tables at a popular mid-range American restaurant and wine bar/store. Years in New York had turned me into an amateur wine snob. Concerned about my summer libations, I left Brooklyn with a case of natural wine in the back of my car, aware that Ocean City bars — except for the restaurant where I'd be working — served only sweet whites and rotgut reds. Establishments in Ocean City are built for tourists, stocked with loud Top 40 music, a drinks list of various "bombs," and 6-ounce beer-liquor mixes that will get you drunk frighteningly fast. The town's most popular drink is the Orange Crush, a cocktail invented by local bar Harborside in the '80s and made of freshly squeezed orange juice, orange vodka, orange liqueur, and Sprite. Delicious, certainly, but dangerous and not sustainable for a summer.

At the end of one of my first shifts at the restaurant, a waitress invited me to the pub next door for a nightcap. Standing at the bar, I realized nothing I normally drank was on hand; I don't drink much beer anymore, and hardly ever liquor. Everyone else ordered Natural Light, so I did, too. I laughed to myself, a condescending city girl slumming it with the locals, thinking, "This again?" as the bartender cracked the can and a burst of pure white foam engulfed the rim.

But with one sip, I was back — chastised and reconverted. There were the shotgun contests with my brother on the back porch, the high school flip-cup and beer-pong games, swimming in the bay at night and having friends on the dock throw beers into the water. The unopened beers float, bobbing and gleaming in the blackness, reflecting the moon.

I drank that first beer quickly, and had another, then another. It is possible to get drunk on Natural Light, but thanks to the low ABV, it's harder to do than with most beers; your evening can be long and relatively put together if you stick with Natty. It's perfect for talking long and late into the night, which is what I did that first night after work that summer and most nights after at that pub's lacquered bar, sitting under neon signs with a mix of waitresses, bartenders, chefs, and Hispanic line cooks, shooting the service-life shit. People tend to leave their manners

My Old Friend Natty Light

at home when they go on vacation, and beach-town service folk spend our nights gabbing about the hellish demands that come from Middle America families enjoying their one week off a summer. Every night, we looked forward to that first beer. We were bone-tired, hadn't sat down in hours, and when that first brush of bubbles hit our lips, we could suddenly, finally, relax.

By the end of the summer, I was drinking Natural Light at home, out to dinner, at all occasions. The case of natural wine sat languishing in a dark corner of the living room — I'd found quickly that in the heat of the summer, it just wasn't what I wanted. New York friends visiting for my birthday laughed at my fridge full of Natty cases, but they drank it, too. By the time I returned to Brooklyn in late September, I'd renamed it as my favorite beer, and when I went to my local bodega, I was saddened to be reminded they didn't stock it. Few stores in New York City do. I had one at a party months later, an errant can found and saved for a special moment. When that first foamy sip hit my lips, I instantly had a wave of homesickness.

In 2008, Natural Light won the bronze for best-tasting American-Style Light Lager at the World Beer Cup. People were outraged. That piss water? That skunky cheap shit? It offended their palates. I wondered if perhaps they had bothered to taste it at all.

In the wake of the long, exhaustive craft-beer boom, there's been a return to drinking more easygoing beers. Lagers and pilsners are acceptable again, and heavily hopped, high-ABV California IPAs get the bad rap; no one wants a beer that smacks you in the face with every sip. But that hasn't necessarily meant a return to the major domestic-beer-conglomerate beverages. The demand for local is unceasing. If you live in certain (urban, coastal) areas of the country, the idea that people wouldn't want small-batch over mass-produced, even if it is a pilsner, is bizarre.

But most of this country simply doesn't care. They don't want fancy. They want familiar, something that does the trick and tastes the same every time. Price matters, but they won't settle for just anything cheap — they want cheap and good. The irony isn't lost on me that my Hispanic colleagues at the restaurant loved it, too — immigrants, the people who are currently being cast as "non-Americans" and told to "go home" despite being the foundation of this nation. They take to this low-rent beer alongside good ol' boys — perhaps because it's not as loudly American as Budweiser or Bud Light. Maybe the non-marketing scheme allows Natty to occupy a niche as an American beverage without any of the aggressively patriotic overtones.

The flavor of Natural Light isn't memorable, but it is memory. It's the feeling of a cold can in your hand after a long shift on your feet. It's the day on the boat in the middle of the bay, all your friends swimming and sunning themselves around you. It's the shit-eating grin before you take your clothes off with someone else. It's beer pong in the backyard, a can in a tote bag going to the beach at night, a case presented proudly at a barbecue. It's simple, humble, comfortable. It's home. ◊

—

Mickie Meinhardt is a writer and sommelier and the owner of The Buzzed Word bookstore, natural wine store, and wine bar in her hometown of Ocean City, Maryland, where she champions diverse voices and community. She was formerly the Events Director for Guernica magazine and holds an MFA from The New School, where she was a creative writing fellow. She covers southern mid-Atlantic culture, beverage, and food, and teaches wine classes locally. Her work has appeared in Guernica, The Bitter Southerner, Eater, and elsewhere. When not writing, she is probably surfing.

THEY LIKE THAT SOFT BREAD

—

by Chelsey Mae Johnson

Photo by Chelsey Mae Johnson
This story was originally published January 15, 2020

DELI KORNER
MARKET & DELI
851-9812

They Like That Soft Bread

Nights when my mom only wanted popcorn and beer for dinner, she'd send us down to see Faye. We lived in South Knoxville, in a midcentury subdivision full of bad drivers — a dicey mix of old people and teenagers. I was always careful to stay off the shoulderless road, keeping my little sister corralled on the safe side as we tramped along on so many sticky Tennessee summer evenings, our light-up sneakers collecting cut grass. About a quarter-mile down the hill from our house sat a low cinder-block building shaped like a brick, its white paint speckled with adornments in always-fresh Volunteer orange. It was the first place we were allowed to go by ourselves.

The Korner Market & Deli was not a quaint country store. It was a purpose-serving place, anchoring the neighborhood in a way that was becoming dated even in the early 1990s. I learned the word "loitering" as soon as I could read, sounding out the hand-lettered rules on the side of the building while my mom ran in to grab an emergency bag of hotdog buns, or Cokes and Winstons for my visiting grandparents. Inside, Faye cashed checks, ran the grill, and recognized our phone number when it popped up on her caller ID. Underneath a halo of cigarette smoke, she gave hell to whoever else was posted up at the counter.

Faye would nod toward us as the door clanged and holler out, "Hey, girls. How's your momma 'n' 'em?"

"Momma says hi," we'd say, barely looking up on our way to the candy aisle. We'd hand over a 10 at the counter and head back up the hill with a heavy plastic bag smelling like fries, Styrofoam boxes squeaking with each step, a secret slab of Laffy Taffy tucked into the back pocket of my sister's cutoffs. Occasionally my mom or aunt would spring for a burger — occasionally my mom's friends made the trip out to our house just for that burger — but my sister and I never deviated: There was always a hoagie in that bag. Always ham and Swiss, on dark bread, mayo only. Always steamed.

With high school and a driver's license came the wild opportunity to make lunch an act of rebellion. I would grit my golden-child teeth and stroll confidently out into the parking lot at 12:20, as if I were a person who regularly did bold, adult things, like leave campus without permission. My best friend, Cassie, was usually along for this thrill, and we would bolt to the nearby gas station advertising *Cold Beer * Tobacco * Market * Deli*. Our high school sat just off a nearly empty seven-mile stretch of state highway between two larger and more important roads. The Bi-Lo was the only place near enough to grab a sausage biscuit on your way to first period. Its parking lots, where we held car-wash fundraisers or arranged off-campus fights after school, was the first place we ate on our own.

Back in the school's parking lot, we'd peel the foil off our sandwiches, gossiping and giggling, washing that stolen half-hour down with weightless frozen Mountain Dew swirled into giant foam cups. Imagine it in Kodachrome: two teenage girls enjoying gas station food without the intrusion of irony or Instagram. Week in and week out, our orders were an early exercise in the comfort of sameness. Always hoagies. Always steamed.

All Knoxvillians know about steamed sandwiches. In fact, all Knoxvillians know steamed sandwiches so very deeply in their consciousness that they rarely consider their standard hot-ham-and-cheese has, in fact, been steam-heated. It's so widespread — such a default — that most people seem puzzled if you poke around to find out why we do it this way. You get a lot of shrugs, a lot of "Well. I never really thought about it."

In Knoxville, we understand hot deli sandwiches are called hoagies; we understand they should be soft and squishy; we understand (at least implicitly) they should be made that way by a joyride in a Fresh-O-Matic steamer, which is about the size of a big microwave and retails for $1,370.

They Like That Soft Bread

In 2009, The New York Times offered readers a chance to fire questions about regional foods to foodways historian John T. Edge, executive director of the University of Mississippi's Southern Foodways Alliance. Of the 25 questions posed in the comments, two asked for an elucidation of the Knoxville tradition of steaming sandwiches. Edge dismissed the question by telling us, "Steamers are embraced elsewhere," then got back to a narrative concerning the nuanced terroir of barbecue sauce.

Steaming appliances may be embraced elsewhere, but I'm certain it is only in Knoxville that you could lift the lid of one and expect to find a hoagie there. While I am aware of the great power of the collective American consciousness to ruin anything regional and peculiar — last year, thousands of people lost their minds on Twitter when they found out that St. Louisans prefer to slice a bagel like Texans slice a brisket — I am here nonetheless to stand tall and tell you: This is special. There are half a million hillbillies in East Tennessee who have been steaming each and every one of their hoagies for over 50 years.

...

It took several years of moving around after college to grasp it: There were no steamed sandwiches to be found in the Carolina Lowcountry, or on the West Coast, or even in Nashville. By the time I moved back to North Carolina in 2019, I had gone from hoagie-curious to hoagie-obsessed. I wanted to know exactly when and why we started steaming hoagies in Knoxville, but no one I spoke with knew. If I wanted the truth, I would have to dig it up myself.

As Knoxville historian Jack Neely graciously warned me in the early days of my search for the steamed-sandwich big bang, it's often difficult to trace the paths of even the most well-known historical foodways. In earlier decades, Neely said, people didn't think low-culture facets of everyday life like mountain music, utilitarian clothing, or corner-store foods were significant enough to write about. As a result, there's often very little published on local restaurant trends in older newspapers and books. It's easy enough to find out when proprietors applied for liquor licenses or needed to hire extra hands, but it's rare to find pre-internet photos of menus or restaurant interiors. Keeping that in mind, I thought it best to start my investigation broadly.

According to *The Oxford Companion to American Food and Drink*, the term "hoagie" first appeared (sort of) in Philadelphia in 1936: "After witnessing a friend devour a large sandwich and thinking he was a hog to eat it all at once," sandwich shop proprietor Al De Palma introduced a pile of cold cuts on a long Italian roll and called it a "hoggie." Soon, "competitors in the Philadelphia area copied his sandwich and sold it under various names, including hoogie, hogie, and horgy. By 1950 ... the sandwich became commonly known as the hoagie." *The Companion* maintains this was the first instance of the "submarine" style of sandwich, which spread quickly throughout the Northeast and then the greater U.S., taking on many names. *The Companion* never mentions the term "hoagie" being used outside of Philadelphia and New Jersey; its only further specification is that the sandwich be made to order.

The first occurrence of the word "hoagie" in the Knoxville News Sentinel appears in 1961, in a help-wanted ad that would never fly today: "Waitress — Preferably unexperienced, age 19 to 22. Work near college campus in Knoxville's new and original HOAGIE HOUSE — Cumberland and Eighteenth." As best I can tell, the Hoagie House never opened. This does not render the listing insignificant; in 1961, Greek immigrants Sam and Andy Captain (née Kapitanopolous) were already operating a diner called The Tennessean at that same intersection on the University of Tennessee campus. And they had been since 1946.

Nine years into The Tennessean's existence, in 1955, the first superheated food steamer hit the American market: the Wear-Ever Fresh-O-Matic. After exhaustive research, I'm still unsure how the Fresh-O-Matic was first marketed, but the record clearly suggests it was always sold as a commercial product. (And the 1955 date satisfies my own nagging curiosity as to why no hoagie sellers are included in the abundant Knoxville café references in Cormac McCarthy's *Suttree*. The novel is set in 1951.) To Neely's earlier point, nobody thought to write an article for the News Sentinel celebrating the Fresh-O-Matic first hitting the foothills, so the dates of the earliest sales here remain a mystery. However, the first appearance of a used model for sale in the News Sentinel classifieds appears in April of 1963, in an ad for an auction closing out the old Star Drive-In in Sevierville. It is listed at $229.50, about $1,935.38 in today's dollars.

...

By 1967, Bill Captain, nephew and employee of the brothers, was tootling around campus in his Hoagie Wagon, selling "hamburgers, hot dogs, hoagies [and] all kinds of sandwiches." The News Sentinel reports steam tables, but by this time, I suspect there were also Fresh-O-Matic steamers involved. The building at 18th and Cumberland had been subdivided, and there, in 1969, the brothers announced the opening of a deli within their Roman Room Bar. In the 1970s, the deli became known simply as Sam & Andy's, and by then they were cranking out steamed hoagies by the thousands to feed the constant hordes of hungry, drunken college kids.

Every UT alum from 1965 to 2000 seems to remember (or, "remember") hitting Sam & Andy's for late-night fortification, and everybody remembers those soft, steamy, chewy sandwiches, but nobody seems to know precisely when the Fresh-O-Matic intersected with the hoagie. I asked Neely, hoping that as the doyen of Knoxville pop history, he would have some information long forgotten by other Vols of his generation.

"I had this romantic idea," he said, "like something from a Ken Burns story. ... I knew that before ever opening a restaurant, the Captains were hatmakers; therefore, they would have had steamers around the shop. I imagined that one day they just said, 'Hey! Let's try these steamers on some sandwiches!'"

Before I even realized that a folklore nugget of this caliber should be regarded with some suspicion, Neely let me down gently: "Unfortunately, that turned out not to be true." However, he handed off a vague memory of having read something about the origin in a 1990s newspaper column, and that was enough to get me as close to the truth as I'll ever get.

The on-campus Sam & Andy's closed in April 1997. A few months later, News Sentinel columnist and reported hoagie enthusiast Shannon

Stanfield ran an interview with their aforementioned nephew, Bill. Bill Captain had come over from Greece at age 16, and went from washing dishes at Sam & Andy's to piloting the Hoagie Wagon to running his own deli, Vic & Bill's, with yet another Captain cousin. Bill would have been 62 at the time of the interview, reflecting on almost five decades of making the sandwiches that would come to define his adopted city. Stanfield reported:

"Up in Yankeeland they like those cold sandwiches — and some of them up there heat the sandwiches up in the pizza oven or rotisserie ovens," Captain says from behind his counter. "Hillbillies down here, they like that soft bread."

Captain said (in the early 1960s) his uncle got a notion to put a cheese shop in the space behind the Roman Room and was checking out other such shops around the region.

"We went up to Asheville to look at a cheese shop, and on the way back saw a sign that said 'Pickle Barrel Deli,' so we turned around and went in there. The old boy had bagels and hoagie sandwiches that were frozen, and he would heat them up in a steamer," Captain says. "We had a hoagie, and it was pretty good. Before then, the only steamer we ever saw was the Blue Circle's, and they used them to warm up the hamburger buns."

"The first year we couldn't give them away, but after that, they were standing in line." And now almost every deli in Knoxville steams its sandwiches — although Captain says the best ones are at Vic & Bill's.

If you get the feeling this tidy origin myth sounds a bit embellished — a successful sexagenarian splashing an extra wash of sepia on the good ol' days — you might be right.

Linda Schandler Newman's father was the Pickle Barrel Deli's founder, Aaron Schandler. Newman managed the eminent Asheville, North Carolina, Jewish deli for a brief time in the '80s. She says — with great certainty — the Pickle Barrel never froze its sandwiches.

I can't argue with her: Who would freeze a whole, preassembled sandwich? The Pickle Barrel did, however, own a Fresh-O-Matic steamer and used it for its sandwiches, Newman confirmed. The Pickle Barrel piled slices of fresh rye high with meats — never cheese — and served up just what you'd expect from a classic kosher deli. But Newman assured me:

They Like That Soft Bread

They never had hoagies.

Thus, Bill Captain's recollection of the Pickle Barrel might have been the work of an aging memory or just playful trash talk between two midsize mountain towns. Take it with a few grains of salt. The bottom line is that inspiration strikes in unassuming moments. Who could have known that a carload of Greeks watching a Jewish Ashevillian pump the handle of a steamer in the 1960s would eventually move the collective culinary consciousness of the entire city of Knoxville?

• • •

Within this complicated and not-quite-traceable history, I found the predictable twists and turns you'd find in any business sector historically driven by small, family-owned operations. Families fuss and fracture along ideological lines, parents want to retire, and kids aren't always interested in taking over. Rent goes up. Entire neighborhoods transform. Buildings crumble or flood or catch on fire. Sometimes folks relocate, sometimes they rebuild, sometimes they just lock up and go home. Sam Captain spent his sunset years breeding bird dogs; Andy Captain died in Greece.

As best I can tell, Parton's Deli, established in 1974, is the oldest continuously operating family-owned deli in the greater Knoxville area, which extends eastward through Sevierville to the North Carolina line. There may well be others; sandwich shops of this generation rarely have a strong internet presence, and I haven't yet visited all 127 delicatessens listed in the Yellow Pages.

Parton's is in Gatlinburg — the bewildering wonderland of fudge shops and mini-golf hugging the eastern entrance to Great Smoky Mountains National Park. If you could pluck out every numbered traffic light along the Dolly Parton Parkway, you could probably make the 34-mile trip from downtown Knoxville's Sunsphere to Gatlinburg's impression of the Space Needle in about half an hour. On a bad day, for the hours you'll spend sitting in the car, Parton's might as well be in Nashville.

If you run the gantlet from the Dolly statue in Sevierville, past Pigeon Forge's Titanic Museum (a lifesize replica charging through a roadside spray of fountain meant to make you think, I guess, of the ocean), and, finally, through a small, disorienting patch of undeveloped forest, you're just about there. As you come into town, if you look closely between Hillbilly Golf and the Gatlinburg Mountain Coaster, you'll see an old building that looks like a gabled breadbox. That's Parton's.

Henry Parton opened the deli with his 18-year-old son, Dennis, in August of '74, right after Dennis graduated high school. They ran the place together for 36 years, but for the last nine, Dennis has worked alone — no employees, not even a pinch hitter.

Amid the chaos of the holiday weekend, the quiet of Parton's shop at 4 p.m. feels like an oasis, if one was to find an oasis in a grandmother's wood-paneled basement. A shelf along one wall holds an array of potato chips surrounded by vintage soda bottles, signed baseballs, signed Dolly Parton (no relation) photos, antique bee smokers, Costco-sized barrels of mayo and pickles, decorative baskets, a small radio that works, a set of speakers that don't, and a TV I'm not sure about. Hornets' nests and gourd birdhouses decorate the top of the Coke coolers. I count, hanging on the walls, at least four clocks, three of which are working but read different times, and five ball caps, two of which are UT orange. I have never seen Dennis Parton not wearing UT orange — neither in person, nor in a photo, nor in my imagination.

Dennis sells only hot dogs, hoagies, deviled eggs, and lemon pound cake. He's open for lunch five days a week. On Sundays, he goes to church; on Mondays, he goes to Walmart. All other days, he opens at 9 in the morning to bake the pound cake and sell early lunches to road crews and picnic packs to hikers. He runs with a single Fresh-O-Matic, capable of steaming two sandwiches at a time, and a separate setup he calls "the dog wagon," an elaborate steam table with separate compartments for hot dogs, buns, toppings, and condiments.

I ask Dennis if he has any insight on why we started steaming sandwiches so furiously in the greater East Tennessee area, and he doesn't, really. He guesses it came from down around UT campus, but it doesn't really matter now, does it? That's just the way Parton's always did it, and the way they still do.

I ask him if he has any trouble getting uninitiated tourists to try a steamed hoagie, and he doesn't, really. He can usually convince them to try it, and once they do, he says with a laugh and a bit of a growl, "They don't go back to cold!" He asks if I want to see a knife he's been using for

They Like That Soft Bread

45 years; I do, and his blue eyes twinkle as he shows off a wood-handled blade worn down into the shape of an icicle. He asks if I want to see his original lettuce holder, and he pulls out one of those old Jadeite-colored Tupperware crispers meant to hold a single head of iceberg. I'm struck by the familiar smallness of it, and how homelike this place feels.

As Dennis slices ham for my sandwich onto the old Simpson True-Weight scale his father used in the family grocery long before opening the deli, I ask him if he thinks anyone will take over when he's ready to retire. He doesn't, really. His nephew isn't interested, and he never had employees or children. He intends to keep making sandwiches in this shop, just him and the Lord, until one of them decides Dennis is done making sandwiches.

"My customers," he says, "if they love and enjoy this place, they'll pray for me, and we'll make it to 50 years."

I take to a booth in the corner with my ham and swiss on dark with mayo. It's a cold, gray day, and the glow of slow-moving taillights through the steamy windows makes the shop feel especially cozy. There is something holy in the humility of this place, in the work, in being uncorrupted through 45 seasons on and off, as the town swelled and morphed and began to close in on all sides.

"I do the very best I can," Dennis had said earlier. "Sometimes people have to wait. But I do it as fast as I can, and I do it well." He'd shrugged and laughed, then was quiet for a minute. "Well, you don't get rich doing it. You just meet a lot of nice people."

As I'm eating and thinking, a woman with a slight hitch in her get-along and a voice like a country-fried Fran Drescher comes in. She and Dennis greet each other like high school sweethearts, and she quickly thanks Jesus for Parton's still being open at this hour of the afternoon. She tells Dennis that even though she lives an hour away in Strawberry Plains, he's the only one she trusts not to over-steam her hoagie. She tells him about her new grandbaby, then fascinatingly segues into a recollection about the first time she saw a calf being born — its wobbly legs and saucer-sized eyes, the wonder and purity and heart-stopping thrill of it all.

She leaves with two turkey and hot pepper in a sack, and I'm left to try to reconcile this conversation with the steady stream of tourist cars rolling by on the Parkway a few feet from where I sit. I guess even in Gatlinburg, people just need a place to go. Somewhere to talk a little, to hand out blessings, and to get something good to eat — maybe even some pound cake to take back to the house.

• • •

Murky origins aside, the unquestionable, concrete foundation of all steamed-hoagie lore and legend is the Fresh-O-Matic. Without it, Knoxville's classic side-of-the-highway, quick-stop lunch might have been the same as anywhere else: your choice of a chili dog, Nip-Chee crackers and a Dr Pepper, or a biscuit that's been sitting under the heat lamp by the register for four hours. Fareed Nasser, the current owner of the Korner Market of my youth, put it to me straight: "If you don't have a steamer, you can't sell hoagies. And people here like their hoagies better than anything else."

Nowadays, the Fresh-O-Matic is sold as a thing to "re-therm" food, commercial-kitchen shorthand that brings to mind a "Star Trek"-style futurism reflected in the early aesthetics of the appliance. I could find only a handful of photographs of older models. The first Fresh-O-Matic had rounded corners and a spunky atomic font; an update I imagine occurred in the '70s produced steamers that look like station wagons, complete with wood paneling and Fresh-O-Matic spelled in elegant Oldsmobile cursive. The last update before a drastic modern redesign brought machines that look like squat little robots. There are still quite a few of these later models kicking around, but most are a little scuffed up and would look more at home alongside WALL-E than aboard the Starship Enterprise. Until recently, a pump handle controlled the steam action. In the last 15 years, a push-button replaced the handle. (I haven't been able to date the makeover that included the switch to push-button. The best clue I've found is the cover of a user manual dated 2014 announcing, "This is not your father's Fresh-O-Matic!" and heralding updates. However, the cover does not point out the button explicitly as an update; it only promises the steamer button will now prevent flooding of the hot plate.)

No one likes the button.

They Like That Soft Bread

On today's internet, although pump-handle models are nearly impossible to find, new Fresh-O-Matics are abundant. On the massive Knoxville-based restaurant supply site KaTom.com, there is an entire subsection for "Sandwich & Deli Steamers" listing 20(!) different options alongside the original, priced from $600 to $1,600, with suggested uses ranging from heating pasta to steaming clams. Most are shallow, with big, square surfaces — the type you'd see manned by a stoned undergrad gassing tortillas at your neighborhood Chipotle — but there are a couple of purpose-built sandwich models still in the mix.

The relative simplicity of the machine — and the lack of ambient flammable grease produced by it — is likely a key component of its proliferation, although this still doesn't explain why it gained such a foothold specifically in Knoxville. Peter Lanois, a former chef who went to UT in the '80s, laid out the basics of commercial kitchen economics for me: From at least the 1950s onward, to operate a flat-top grill, pizza oven, or even a deep fryer, a kitchen needed an industrial ventilation hood with a fire suppression system. Today, the ballpark price of such a system is around $1,000 per linear foot, with the average hood 10 to 14 feet long. Add this to the initial cost of those larger appliances, and your minimum equipment cost is well into the five-digit realm — most likely implausible for a midcentury immigrant start-up and definitely implausible for a neighborhood convenience-store owner today, already fighting the battle against grocery, gas-station, and fast-food chains. On the other hand, Lanois said, "The sandwich steamer was a [relatively] cheap and nonregulatory solution to traditional baked subs."

A Fresh-O-Matic, a slicer, and a refrigerated prep table, and you're in business for a few grand. You don't even really need tables; there are stories of market and deli owners refusing to offer seating. Customers just shrugged and ate their sandwiches off the empty shelves that once held groceries.

In 2019, the mythos of the machine itself could nearly stand alone. Dennis Parton said he has one steamer he's kept running for 45 years; no other deli owners could believe that's possible. Old-timers speak reverentially about the heyday of Ali Baba Time Out Delicatessen, a now-shuttered 24-hour joint in West Knoxville rumored to have blown through two steamers every six months, creating a trickle-down supply of cheap, refurbishable models for the little guys. I spoke with several civilian enthusiasts — including both my father and stepfather — who have put years of casual browsing into trying to track down old models on eBay for home use.

When you poke around Knoxville asking about Fresh-O-Matics, one singular, mythical figure rises above the chatter, again and again: Gene Kitts. If today's pump-handle devotees resemble that loose cadre of folks who keep old German diesels running on swapped parts and 50 years of healthful grime, Kitts is the guy with the garage full of dead-stock odds and ends, the guy you call when you've got problems too big for your own ingenuity. He's the one, and these days he's the only one. His company is Kitts Carbonation Service, but no one can really remember a time when he worked on soda fountains or draught lines or anything but Fresh-O-Matics. If you can manage to get your hands on three steamers that don't work, he can turn them into two that do, and you're in business. He covers all of Knox County, of course, but he also has a confirmed presence in Sevier, Union, and Blount counties. I wouldn't be surprised if the few folks still steaming in Johnson City and Kingsport make the two-hour drive to him for repairs.

Most folks I talked with guessed that Kitts is in his 70s, though, and that worries them a bit.

"Every time something breaks down, I hope Mr. Kitts is still alive when I call," one deli owner told me. "I pray he lives to be 100, because there's no one else."

• • •

Almost every neighborhood small business — hardware store, newspaper stand, whatever — struggles with aging populations and big-box suffocation. Any family that traffics in small-community necessities has lived that reality for decades. But now and then, you run across someone trying their damnedest to resist, or even shift, the oppressive tide.

In a far-northeast corner of Knox County, David Vandergriff and his dad operate Sunrise Deli. On an early-spring Saturday, I drive out to

They Like That Soft Bread

Corryton to see them. The area is not quite rural, but the hills out here do plenty of rolling, with whitewashed farmhouses bobbing alongside the occasional dilapidated barn. When I pull into the parking lot, I'm underwhelmed. Another cinder-block shell with a thick gum of new white paint, not quite dingy enough to have kitsch appeal. My curiosity is piqued, however, when I notice that Sunrise explicitly uses the word "steamed" in their shiny new vinyl signage. Nobody does that.

David has an East Tennessee accent like cane syrup, lithe and fast-moving but indulgent. The man is all business, with binders full of invoices and app-generated sales reports and — my eyebrows hit the ceiling — hopes and dreams of franchising.

"Everybody comes to Sunrise for sandwiches," he says. "Hopefully we'll have a hundred places one day, all over. Do you know how crazy it would be to take this stuff to places that don't have it? I mean, really. Do you?"

David is not a devotee of the early, pump-handle Fresh-O-Matics. David believes in warranties. The cashiers tap away on tablets, and bright LED menu screens display the full-color logos of available soft drinks. He's setting up online ordering so he doesn't have to hire an extra employee just to answer the phone during the lunch rush. Plus, he's tired of pickup orders ringing to his mobile, which they do when the store line is busy, which it is, very often.

David's dad worked at delis on the UT campus during the late 1970s heyday and opened Sunrise in 1992. He ran it for 20 years, then sold the business. When the new owners folded, David quit his cybersecurity job at Oak Ridge National Laboratories, and he and his father reopened the place in 2017.

Sunrise sources bread from the same place as everyone else; these days, the only acceptable provenance is Quality Bakers of Tennessee, operating out of East Knoxville since 1988. David drives out personally and loads his car with as many as 500 rolls every week. (No matter where you're ordering your sandwich, there are only two real bread options for hoagies: light or dark. Light is not French or sourdough, it's just light. Dark is not wheat, it's pumpernickel.) David says, "This bread is not made for cold. It's made to be steamed. It's a tougher bread so that you can steam it." He has a few folks he can recognize by their telephone voices, regularly hollering on the other end of the line: "Steam the hell out of that thing! I want it good and soggy!" Others ask for the cheese to hardly be melted, the sandwich just barely warm.

I will say, of all the sandwiches I ate while researching this story — so, so many sandwiches — Sunrise misses no marks. Its push-button steamers may be shiny and new, but they're blading their meats down to a katsuobushi thinness that allows cheese-and-mayo melding as I imagine God or Sam or Andy first intended it. David is weeks away from opening his second Sunrise Deli in the nearby Halls neighborhood. It's easy to imagine that it could be the second of many — that anyone, in any neighborhood, anywhere, would come to a place like this.

...

To be marked as an outsider in Portland, all you have to do is carry an umbrella, broadcasting your discomfort with the persistent mild drizzle. In Charleston, it takes missing the tiny orange flag in a crosswalk and stepping in what looks like an ordinary puddle but is actually a small, smelly lake created by a carriage horse. In Manhattan, you might stare at the subway map too long, or mispronounce "Houston." To announce to the world that you are not of Knoxville, Tennessee, you start hoagie flame wars on the internet.

I get it, to a point — after all, we make Reubens on submarine rolls. But on the review pages of Facebook, where people are free to be their worst selves, battles rage. Northerners, in particular, seem inclined to lob insults when they realize we do sandwiches a little differently ("Hoagies are NEVER served on soggy-ass bread").

Although he is more restrained in his criticism, UT professor James Plank has maintained a webpage roundly denouncing steamed sandwiches from an anthropological perspective for at least 20 years. Plank came from Delaware and was shocked upon his arrival in Knoxville to realize they only make the subs he likes best in the place where he came from.

They Like That Soft Bread

"The main hindrance is that local culture seems to encourage steaming the sandwich. ... Why? ... Maybe [because of] a lack of Italians? I don't know. ... It turns the bread into amorphous goo and the lettuce into mush." The highest honor on Jim's list of Knoxville sub shops "worth repeat business" goes to Jersey Mike's; this is where Jim loses me.

Peter Lanois, who earlier shared his expertise regarding fire suppression systems, also came to Knoxville from the Northeast, where, as he says, "they have some sandwiches and feel strongly about them." Like so many others, he is not sure about the specifics of the first steamed hoagie he ate, but he is sure he was in college at UT, he is pretty sure it was after midnight, and he is definitely sure it confused him.

"Hot subs were baked in my world — hearth, pizza oven, whatever. I just couldn't understand. I had never seen such a thing as this 'wet sub.' So humid." Lanois, however, gets brownie points for reassuring me he doesn't necessarily dislike steamed sandwiches — they've just served as a lifelong touchstone for a somewhat bewildered nostalgia. After all, where the hell but Vic & Bill's Rock and Roll Deli ("the Rock and Roll" is colloquial) could you get a tallboy and a hoagie, see a sweaty punk show, then get the full breakfast that you'd desperately need a few hours later? (The punk history of Vic & Bill's is a fascinating aside; in the mid-1980s, shows advertised included Black Flag, the Dead Kennedys, and Suicidal Tendencies.)

Tom Bayless, Nashville chef and steamed-sandwich apologist, offers a counterpoint just as punchy: "Toasted sandwiches have names, like BLT, Patty Melt, Club, Reuben, Cuban. Only bougie sociopaths order nameless toasted sandwiches, and the toasted sub sandwich is an abomination of the human spirit. A simulacrum. Suspect those who suggest."

Let's not get lost in the kerfuffle.

Hoagies are universally beloved by native Knoxvillians, but exploring the specifics of this love takes us to a special and tender place. Most responses I got in my straw poll of hoagie opinions around Knoxville were overwhelmingly positive; among the boots on the ground, "nostalgia," "satisfaction," and "favorite" were the most commonly occurring words. People I've never met responded to tell me about their late nights at Gus's Good Times Deli on the UT campus. Many said they could (or wished they could) eat a steamed sandwich every day. Before responding to my survey, several participants went out and ordered a sandwich so they could take a photo to send to me along with their answers. I assume they thought me to be hoagie-deprived in my current home in North Carolina, and they are correct.

My high school best friend pointed out that part of the appeal of the whole thing is that hoagies are prepared exactly the same no matter where you get one, and she's right. My stepdad likes steamed pastrami; my cousin dips his sandwich, bite by bite, in ranch dressing. My ex-boyfriend's sister gave me the name of the guy who operates the deli in the gas station near her childhood home in Blount County, just in case. Several of my 9-to-5 gal-pals now only eat hoagies on hangover days, ascribing a special revitalizing quality to rehashing the previous night over meat and cheese you barely have to chew. Another Tennessee alum theorized that maybe he preferred turkey and smoked cheddar on dark because of the classic orange, white, and brown colorway — perfectly matching the tones of the rifle-toting, coonskin-capped Volunteer screen-printed on so many vintage UT sweatshirts.

One of my dearest friends says his favorite thing about steamed sandwiches is that they remind him of the smell of human body odor. To state the obvious, he always orders his with onions. I made the mistake of adding them only once, at a deli touting signature homemade spicy onions in Elizabethton, Tennessee. When I unwrapped my hoagie, the steam released made my whole car smell like Krystals. Or armpits, I guess. Whichever you prefer.

My own platonic ideal of a hoagie has no vegetables, and I don't think yours should, either. This may have to do with the fact that I wouldn't touch vegetables as a child. But as an adult of distinguished taste, who now only eats gas station food sometimes, I will argue (at truly exhausting length, if beer is involved) that adding cold lettuce and tomato only interrupts the warm and perfectly mushy meld of meat, cheese, and condiments. According to my survey, I am in the minority here, but my sister agrees, and so do David Vandergriff and Dennis Parton, leaving me comfortable in my righteousness. Pickle spears and pepperoncini peppers are always served on the side, and that should be all the vegetables anyone needs.

They Like That Soft Bread

• • •

I worried the quiet corner store I wandered to as a child might have folded in on itself, crumpled by chain restaurants or reduced traffic or modernity in general. But when I revisit the neighborhood for the first time in a decade, the Korner Market still sits down the hill and around the curve from my childhood home, thrumming neon and fluorescence into the early winter darkness. I push the door open, the bell clangs, and I'm hit with that same old smell of scrubbed-down, Marlboro-glazed linoleum. There's a sweetness and a whoosh, and it's me and my sister, two sticky-fingered baby ghosts pushing past me, scampering out into the evening buzz of cicadas, our mouths crammed full of Bubblicious. I twist around, expecting to see the high crown of my grandfather's mesh cap as he waits for us in the parking lot, or the beat-up purple Saturn I drove as a teenager winking its one headlight, ticking as the little engine cools. Back inside, an awkward 13-year-old me winces as she peels her bare legs off one of the vinyl stools fixed along the counter; the 21-year-old heaves a sweating sixer of High Life proudly up to the register. In this abruptly flooded plane of memory, it is always summer, and every me exists at once.

A lightly accented greeting pulls me out of the sixth dimension, and I try to be normal as I introduce myself to the man behind the counter. Faye is retired, mostly. Fareed Nasser bought the place in 2010, but Faye still comes in from time to time to boss Fareed around.

"She's a good cook and a good person," he says when I ask about her. "But ... she's like Larry David. She says what's on her mind!"

He thinks for a minute, starts laughing at the comparison.

"But she's not as funny."

Fareed is funny, and he catches me up on the last 15 years of neighborhood happenings without much prompting: Most everybody around here's getting old, we think the Vols might really make it to the Final Four this year, one time the underground gas tank in the parking lot exploded and pieces landed half a mile away. He's rearranged the floor plan, ditched the groceries, and added tables. There are glossy orange-and-white menus and a dry erase board with specials. When he drops a basket into the fryer loaded with the same flat, mealy fries I remember disliking but always ordering anyway, I'm suddenly, stupidly, saddened that the smell of commingled hot grease and cigarette smoke is a thing of the past.

There's an important UT basketball game on the television mounted above the iced tea pitchers, and I post up at the counter to watch with Nasser. A delivery guy blusters in with a bag-in-a-box on his shoulder, hastily installs it below the soda fountain, and joins us to watch the rest of the game. For the next hour, the door barely swings — it feels like all of Knoxville is holding its breath this afternoon, hoping for a big win. A handful of people come in to buy beer, cigs, a Powerball ticket. A kid drops by and asks Fareed if he knows how traveler's checks work; he gives him an unimpressed look and sends him to Walmart.

At the half, Fareed brings me behind the counter and shows me exactly how to work the steamers. Cranking the pump handle does not, as I once imagined, pressurize anything. It's just as simple as the manual suggests. A third of an ounce of distilled water sprays onto a hot plate, and steam floats up through some holes and into a hoagie.

As the game winds down, Fareed talks about the neighborhood some more, how old everybody is, and how cranky these old white guys can be. He is from Jordan, but he waves me off when a slight hesitation suggests I'm about to ask a question about racism.

"They're nothing to worry about," he laughs. "They hate everybody equally. They're just old! Here, look."

He brings over a little acetate envelope; it turns out to be full of brightly colored funeral programs. He deals them out gingerly on the counter, eight in all, all from the last six months.

"My customers," he says. "Just this year."

The game ends, and on his way out, the delivery guy runs into a woman from church, or who used to be from church, whom he hasn't seen in 10 years, who sings like an angel. They catch up for half an hour. Fareed tells me, "Knoxville is kind of frozen in time, sometimes."

As I head back downtown, I try to take in all that is new along this once-familiar stretch of the major highway. It's hard; there is so much, but it's all just drive-thrus and big box stores and payday loan shacks. We've lost so many of our neighborhood institutions and icons, but I do notice one absence that's heartening. Down from the Walmart, there used to be a Quizno's, where so many of us South Knoxvillians first cut our tender mouths on toasted subs in the late 1990s. It has closed, but the Korner Market has not. The Bi-Lo has not, the Handy Dandy has not. We've still got the White Star and Victor's Lakeview and Jacob's and Sam & Jerry's. I am proud to think, at least in this matter, us soft-bread-lovin' hillbillies have made ourselves heard, loud and clear. ◊

—

Chelsey Mae Johnson earned a master's degree in Appalachian Studies and Public History from Appalachian State University in Boone, North Carolina. She researches and writes about food traditions, folk artists, and kitsch culture.

KILLINGS

—

by Daniel Wallace

Illustration by Daniel Wallace
This story was originally published March 1, 2015

Killings

Well, I killed a chicken. That's my news.
I cut its head off with a hatchet, the way people do. This chicken was the first thing I'd ever set out to kill, that I'd planned to kill over the course of many months, and the truth is it was weird, exciting, and sad. I didn't kill it to eat (though it was eventually eaten, in a soup); I didn't kill it because it was a troublemaking chicken (though it was a troublemaking chicken); and I didn't kill it because it deserved to die (whatever that means). I killed it because I'd never killed a chicken before and I wanted to have that experience on my list of things I'd done, sort of like going to Venice, to be able to say, as I'm saying now, I killed a chicken. So after talking about it, engaging a few friends in my pursuit (some of whom had a similar desire), hunting for an appropriate venue and, I hoped, a seasoned killer to accompany me, I did it. And though you, you who's reading this now, you who may be a hunter of some kind, a gun owner, a man or a woman who goes out in the woods early in the morning for the express purpose of finding something to kill — you might find this discourse silly and vain. I killed a chicken! But this news, more than almost anything else I could write, tells you everything you need to know about me. It explains who I am and the kind of life I've lived up until right now: the kind of life that not only can go on for almost 50 years without purposely shedding the blood of another living creature, even a creature whose existence is predicated on being killed, who is born not

only to die but born to be killed and eaten — not only that — but a man who felt there was something exotic in killing it, something magical and foreign that requires the assistance of something like a shaman, a guru, an ax-wielding sage.

It also describes my friends, some of whom understood my ambition, some of whom shared it, but none of whom, not a single one, had a chicken I could kill.

My sister had a turkey she said I could kill. But I could tell — even I who had never killed before — that killing her turkey would be an ordeal. That turkey was huge; it would put up a serious fight. I was scared of her turkey. I didn't tell her I was scared of her turkey. I told her I would kill it if I could find someone who had experience killing turkeys and who could be there with me when I did it and after a week of not trying even a little to find someone to help me kill the turkey I told her I hadn't found anybody so she would have to kill the turkey herself if she wanted it dead, which, in the end, she didn't. I think she was just trying to do whatever she could to help, and was willing to sacrifice her turkey for me. That's love.

Other than her, most of the people I mentioned it to thought I was joking, because no one really figured me for the chicken-killing type. When I told them I was serious, they didn't get it. What? Huh? What do you — ? What? Seriously? Why would you want to kill a chicken? Why would you want to kill anything?

Most often what I said was, I like chicken. I told them I eat it once or twice a week, which means over the course of my adult life I've eaten parts of thousands of chickens, chickens that were killed by someone else for me to eat, chickens that were once alive, who then were dead, and then — after all the posthumous stuff a chicken has to go through — found its way to my supermarket, my frying pan, my plate, my mouth.

So what I said was: I need to be able to kill what I eat. If someone else can do it, why not me? I need to be able to know what it's like to take a life because I've been dining on those lives forever. If I couldn't do it, I shouldn't eat them, and if I did do it, maybe I'd decide it wasn't worth it anymore, worth the killing, just so I can have a nice meal. I said to these people, I've never killed anything before — but in saying that, I realized, that's not true.

I've been killing things all my life.

...

To the best of my memory, the first thing I killed on purpose is something we in Alabama called a Chinese grasshopper. My friend Wade and I found a bunch of them at the edge of shade cast by the sour apple tree in my backyard, where we spent a lot of time in the summer.

Kids killing grasshoppers: no news here. But how we killed them, that was, as I would have said at the time, the cool part. With a length of sewing thread, Wade tied a small Black Cat firecracker to the grasshopper's back. I'd light it. Then Wade would set the poor grasshopper free. One hop, two, three ... bang! Smithereens. Wade and I probably killed close to a hundred that summer.

At roughly this same time, I discovered the magical properties of a hand-held magnifying glass. It wasn't about killing in the beginning; in the beginning it was all about fire. The sun's rays could be corralled as they passed through the magnifying glass into a stream of heat, like a laser. Old brown leaves glowed red and orange, smoking as the photons did their work. Then I discovered ants. Ants became ash in a moment. Little black cinders. One moment busily scurrying around, going left, right, back, forward — and then dead, incinerated by the malevolent god who was me. An ant's life is so fragile and evanescent that death must follow it wherever it goes, which would explain why an ant is always on the move. How easily their future is dismissed by a single swipe, a thoughtless flick or fire. Later I would date a woman who wouldn't kill the ants that found a way into her kitchen and marched in a wobbly trail across her windowsill. She'd wet a paper towel and gently scoop them up in it, then take the paper towel outside into her backyard and set it down in the grass somewhere, where the ants were free to go.

Plus which, on the insect front: Just the other day I poured tiki-torch fuel down a bee hole in the garden. We were about to have a party and I didn't want the guests being stung.

Food Stories

• • •

There were squirrels. There were birds.

Over the years my cats brought home many birds, ravaged but alive, always alive. Cardinals, wrens, rufous-sided towhees, I discovered them bloody, with broken wings, hanging on with the tenacity living things demonstrate near the end. I'd scoop the dying birds into a pillowcase, put the pillowcase in a plastic trash can full of water, and drown them. They'd struggle for a moment, but only for a moment.

Then they'd die.

I'm interested, of course, in other people, and things they killed — so I asked a few. These are a few of the living things they killed, but most, almost all of them, by accident: baby chicks, a buck, cats, more squirrels and raccoons while driving; lizards, a rat (after which the carcass was thrown on a fire ant mound), hamsters, birds with a gun, a ghost crab, possums, a hawk (again with a car), a classroom mouse, butterflies, copperheads (my wife has killed three), cockroaches, flies, granddaddy longlegs, fish (lots of fish), snails, lightning bugs (in order to detach their lights to make some flashy jewelry), dogs, and another cat, run over by a friend of mine on September 15, 2001. This one wasn't quite dead, though, so she carried it to the first public building she could find. It turned out to be a mosque, with a service going on inside. Women huddled around the edge of the prayer mats, men in the middle. And here was this blond woman, a crying, hysterical blond woman with a bleeding cat. They let her use the phone, and she took the cat to a vet, and had to pay $100 to have it put to sleep.

• • •

Now for the chicken. Like love, I found it when I wasn't even looking. I was in Brattleboro, Vermont, with my wife at a writers conference. My wife grew up in Brattleboro. I got to see her old haunts, her house, imagine what it might have been like to be her as she climbed trees, broke things, created fictional characters with a friend (hillbillies not unlike the one she would eventually marry). We went to visit some old friends of hers, Annie and

Killings

Rob. They have a small farm where they grow vegetables, raise a few sheep and pigs — and, of course, chickens, many, many chickens. They order the chickens from a company that does that sort of thing (news to me) but they only ordered hens because roosters were trouble. Somehow a rooster got mixed up with the hens in the last order and they really wanted to — What's that you say? You have a chicken you're interested in killing? What a coincidence: I'm a man who's interested in killing a chicken!

Thus it was arranged.

Laura and I drove over first thing in the morning. She went for a walk with Annie, while my shaman and I prepared for what was to follow. Rob gave me an old shirt of his to wear; he didn't want the blood to ruin the nice J. Crew I had donned for the occasion. How ridiculous all this seems in retrospect! Didn't I realize that death is messy, that one doesn't wear J. Crew to a killing? I was such a baby then.

Even with ants and Chinese grasshoppers under my belt, this chicken was different: I could feel it in my own blood as we walked to its pen. For one thing, it was bigger than anything I had killed before, and more alive, and it wasn't damaged in any way; it was, in fact, beautiful.

I stepped into its pen and, because it was a rooster, it walked right to me, and I picked it up, one hand on either side of its feathered body: a luminescent, dark copper this chicken was, and entirely agreeable. It didn't struggle a bit as Rob and I made our way to the chopping block, into which a sharpened ax had been driven. The chopping block was a section from a tree, an oak, I think.

It wasn't a long walk from the pen to the ax, but long enough, I thought, for the chicken to object. Only when I placed him on the chopping block itself — one side of his body flat against it — did he realize something was amiss. It tried to flap its wings but couldn't because one of them was pressed against the block and the other was beneath my left hand.

In the right hand was the ax.

Rob had shown me where to cut its head off, and it made sense: right in the middle of its neck between the bottom of its skull and the start of its body. But it wasn't a long neck by any means. It was about the length and width of half a Vienna sausage. I had an opening, briefly: For a moment, its head was still. I held the ax in the air above it but hesitated. What if I missed? I thought. What if I missed a clean shot at the neck and just injured it, nicked it. What would I do? Surely if this happened the chicken would go crazy and I'd freak out and let it go. Then I'd have to chase it down to give it another whack, and then have to live with the hard truth that I'd brought a world of pain to an animal who didn't expect it or deserve it. That's one of the big differences between a chicken and a man, though: A thought like this can race through a man's mind in a space of time briefer than a second. Fear, guilt, a notion of responsibility — the sensation of successfully killing what I set out to kill — all these emotions can occur nearly simultaneously in a man. I doubt anything remotely like that occurred to the chicken. I don't know what the chicken was thinking, or how a chicken thinks, or whether it thinks at all; I've read that only humans are capable of this trick. But if I were to go through with this, I knew I had to be more like the chicken was and stop thinking, stop feeling, and act.

I came down on it with all the force I could muster, which really wasn't very much: Just as I let the ax fall, the chicken turned its head to look up at me, and I pulled back, so the ax came down softly, and at an angle, and I thought I missed it almost entirely, because the head was still there. My nightmare was real: I'd only wounded it. It flapped, I held onto its feet, white-knuckled, and it flapped, flapped in terror, flapped for freedom, flapped because it didn't know what else to do.

But it was, in fact, dead. Its head was hanging on by a mere sliver of chicken skin. I could see how, had I let it, it might have run around for a while, the way they're supposed to do, but Rob didn't want blood all over the place, so he asked me to hold it by the feet while it "bled out." I did; it stopped flapping, became truly dead, and I had done what I set out to do.

My glasses were lightly spattered with blood, as was my borrowed shirt (how right he was about that). I have pictures of this, pictures from the killing, the plucking, the gutting and cleaning the insides out, until it looked a lot like a chicken you and I might buy at a grocery store. The only thing I didn't do was eat it, because I had to fly back to Chapel Hill the next day, but Rob and Annie did: They used it as stock for a soup. Turns out it was too scrawny for a main course.

That's it. And I'm afraid that sums it up, for at the end of a life, what else is there to say? That's it, it's over, done, finished. It would be the same from the chicken's perspective, if we allowed it one: I lived and then I died. Killed, actually, by a man who wanted to know what it felt like to kill me. Now he knows.

But I don't know, really. Even though I did it, I don't know what it meant to me to kill a chicken. I can't describe it, and the only way I know to understand something is to put it into words. I did what I set out to do, but I didn't learn any secrets. Killing a chicken didn't change me. No one has said to me, You've changed since you killed that chicken. Nope. I feel like I know what I've known all my life, or ever since I sat on the curb on the sunny cul-de-sac where I spent my childhood and roasted ants with a magnifying glass: There's a very thin line between life and death. Death can happen in a second. In fact it always happens in a second. Everything else, no matter how long and happy or sad the life is that precedes death, is all just preface. In that second, it will be over, you will be finished, whether I'm there to kill you or not.

Good luck, then, to all the dogs and cats, the snakes and roaches, the butterflies and the wandering buck. Good luck to all you chickens. Watch out for us. Not me — I have no plans to kill again. But there are others out there just like me and they want to know how it feels, and there are others still who don't want to know but will. It's a dangerous world. Good luck. ◊

—

Daniel Wallace is the author of seven novels, Big Fish, Ray in Reverse, The Watermelon King, Mr. Sebastian and the Negro Magician, The Kings and Queens of Roam, Extraordinary Adventures, *and, most recently,* This Isn't Going to End Well.

THE DRIEST STATE

—

by Alice Driver

Photo by Liz Sanders
This story was originally published October 12, 2021

COUNTRY SMOOTH
AMERICAN
PREMIUM WHISKEY
SMOKE WAGON
SMALL BATCH
STRAIGHT
LAS VEGAS

The Driest State

Wine is
Gun oil, graphitey, wet wool,
Water from the garden hose,
It's got fat running through it,
Blue plum skin,
Violets and lavender and heaps of dark rose

If I wrote this essay while picking beer cans out of the ditch on the road where I grew up in Johnson County, I fear it would never end.

In Arkansas, 34 of 75 counties are dry. The morality of a dry county, given how many people drive down the road drinking and tossing empty beer cans out the window, is lost on me. I wondered why dry counties continued to exist and why Arkansas has the most in the country.

When I started writing this essay a year ago, I wanted it to be about alcohol as a territory for exploration, about geography, soil, history, and the poetic language of wine and spirits. I wanted it to be about all the things I never learned growing up in a dry county where alcohol is sin. But my research took me in another direction. It led me to the Ku Klux Klan, to crystal collectors and anti-vaxxers. It left me even more puzzled about the spirit of this place.

I called Jake Lewis, a native of Texas and a sommelier, to get his perspective on dry counties. Lewis, who works as the beverage director for Momofuku, said of dry counties, "Our experience was, my grandparents lived in Lufkin, and it was, at the time, a dry county. It was a big Southern Baptist community, not a lot of drinking, temperance-forward-thinking people. When visitors came, they would all drive across the county, and there were three liquor stores on the line, and they would stock up. It never really deterred drinking." Studies have found that dry counties in places like Arkansas and Kentucky have higher rates of alcohol-related fatalities than wet counties. For Lewis, "The history of all of this from Prohibition is wild and outdated. A lot of the blue laws left over from Prohibition make it difficult to sell alcohol in the United States because every state and every county has its own law." He added, "It is weird and nonsensical."

Lewis Liquor, located in a vacation town called Crystal Springs, in Garland County, has been owned by the same family for roughly three decades. It was previously the last stop for alcohol in the last wet county heading west before the Oklahoma line. More recently, a second liquor store has opened up right down the road, even closer to the county line.

*I always picture
the Merlot
as the jelly inside
of the donut*

I talked to my cousin Rachel, also a sommelier, who had grown up with me in Johnson County. She said, "Just think about it. Imagine if we started a campaign for adults to drink wine instead of soft drinks in the U.S." She listed the benefits of drinking wine in moderation, like lowering bad cholesterol and increasing antioxidant levels. She mentioned obesity levels, tooth decay, and diabetes in relation to sugary-drinks consumption.

*It has a beautiful brightness,
lots of sea salt
and oyster*

In my early adulthood, Rachel had taught me to see drinking as a wild and creative territory. Traveling with Rachel, I began to keep a notebook that I titled "The Sommelier's Mother Tongue. I took notes of how Rachel and her sommelier friends described wine and spirits, arranging their words into poetry. In the notebook, I wrote down her description of a Sauvignon Blanc we drank together: "It tastes a little bit like elderflower to me which is like licking a sweaty girl." In high school, I had been a part of a group that preached to teens about the evils of alcohol. At the time, I wanted to fit in with my churchgoing peers. Sadly, those messages about alcohol and its evils stayed with me well into adulthood. When I began to drink in college, after my abstinent high school years, I drank like the rest of the students in our dry county — to get drunk. We drank Natty Light, Everclear mixed with fruit, or wine. For us, there were only two kinds of wine — white and red, and I knew nothing about either, nor did I seek such information.

After college, when Rachel began studying to become a sommelier, I observed her curiosity, her way of drinking, and her seemingly miraculous ability to do a blind tasting and identify the origin, region, climate, and age of a wine. Spending time with her, I became curious to try different wines and spirits, to map their regions, to trace their history.

Beer is
a sommelier's
water

Arkansas' war on alcohol can be traced back to the 1800s, the Temperance Movement, and Bible-thumping preachers. When I started researching the origins of dry counties, I couldn't get past this one fact: In Prohibition-era Arkansas, the KKK had over 50,000 members. They worked with local law enforcement to enforce Prohibition laws. For example, in the 1920s, when the U.S. created the Prohibition Bureau, agents in the bureau deputized volunteers from the KKK to enforce Prohibition laws. During that period, membership increased, driven by their ideas of cleaning up and purifying communities. Enforcement of

Prohibition law disproportionately targeted immigrants, Catholics, and African Americans.

After reading about the involvement of the KKK during Prohibition, I drove to Harrison, Arkansas. I knew I probably couldn't figure out how the KKK is involved in the politics of dry counties, but sometimes just driving and listening to the people I meet along the way helps me sort out ideas. Harrison has served as the national headquarters for the Knights of the KKK since the '80s, when Thom Robb took over as national director.

On my way into Harrison, I drove past a billboard featuring a white family sandwiched between words about "*White Pride*." Businesses on the central square had signs in the window that read *Back the Blue and Blue Lives Matter*. I walked around town talking to locals. One white man who I met on the main square near a Confederate statue said, "I'll say this about Harrison and racism — it has been known as a racist place; in fact, the most racist place in the country for a long time, mainly because of the Klan. But this is what people don't realize — here's the thing about it — there's racism all over the place."

Arkansans tell me it isn't fair to write about Harrison and the KKK — that it reinforces negative stereotypes about the state. But the White Pride billboard still graces the highway. The Harrison Community Task Force on Race Relations did launch a petition to take down the billboard, but I am waiting to write about the successful movement that finally removes it.

It was heavy
ripe
like raw meat
had the quality of blood

I sat on this essay for months thinking about Prohibition and racism and what remnants of that relationship live on in dry counties. In July 2021, after talking to Arkansas photographer Liz Sanders about our shared struggle to honestly document our home state, we decided to drive to Mount Ida, which is both in a dry county and the quartz crystal capital of the world. The truth is, I wasn't sure how to write about the KKK.

The Driest State

Normally, when I write about a topic, I interview sources and read related materials. However, with the KKK, I felt stuck, because I didn't want to interview KKK members or quote their publications. I hoped that by driving to Mount Ida to see crystal collectors, I would think of a way to write about the KKK that made sense. But perhaps the answer is that there is no way to write about the KKK that makes sense.

Arriving in Royal in Garland County, about 15 minutes from Mount Ida, we drove past a Baptist church with a sign out front that read: "ETERNITY SMOKING OR NON-SMOKING." On Yelp, a customer who visited a liquor store on the county line in the area wrote that it was "the only beacon of alcoholic availability in a sea of dry counties." When we reached Crystal Springs, we stopped at the first of its two competing county line liquor stores.

I asked a guy arranging bottles of bourbon outside the store why dry counties existed. He said, "I think because of the Bible." And then he walked over to his car and pulled out two half-empty bourbon bottles. He explained that Arkansas was a "good ol' boy state" that issued a limited number of distribution licenses, which benefited him as the only licensed bourbon distributor in the area. "Even Walmart isn't allowed to sell liquor," he said. In 2012, Walmart had thrown its weight behind a campaign to turn dry counties in its home state wet — and even with more money than God, it lost.

It tasted like a bonbon,
candy-ish, sweet
and then shifted to savory

At the second liquor store we visited, the woman behind the counter was engaged in a deep conversation with a customer about how COVID was just like the flu and had always existed. We looked at moonshine flavors: apple pie, hunch punch, lemon drop, sour razzin' berry. Liz told me, "My grandfather Lyman went blind drinking moonshine."

I wanted to know more about her grandfather Lyman and how his drinking had affected her family. Liz recounted, "My dad was a social drinker. He would go to The Vapors and other popular clubs in Hot

Springs. His favorite drink was a dirty martini with vermouth and two olives, and he had a glass of red wine with dinner every night. As soon as I reached the age of 2, he stopped drinking. He became a teetotaler." Liz thought that he didn't want her growing up seeing him drink. "He maybe had bad memories seeing his father drink and not be a good father. I never asked him," Liz said. Her father died in 2020.

Liz wanted to photograph individuals with their crystal collections. The lady behind the counter at the liquor store told us she had a large crystal collection, but she said she was worried her dogs would bite us if we went to her house to see it. She recommended that we visit the place across the road. Outside the store across the road, I saw an outhouse, wagon wheels, and all kinds of knickknacks. Inside, I found a room covered in bear rugs and stuffed snakes, another of pickled vegetables for sale, and one filled with display cases of Native American artifacts, crystals, and the head of a Black child — the type of object some people in the South used as a lawn decoration. The woman working behind the counter said that the founder of the store, now deceased, had collected the objects over 40 years from all over Arkansas.

Entering Mount Ida, we passed by Geode Place, Holistic Hollow, and Broken Rock Road. We stopped at every house or business that had a crystal collection outside. I talked to the owner of a crystal shop who had once been a truck driver, and he said, "What got me into this business was desperation." He didn't want me to interview him because, he said, it would be better for me to read two volumes of the history of Mount Ida.

He then pulled the books off a shelf and handed them to me, saying, "I could get it all wrong, so don't talk to me." Instead of reading the books, I followed him around the store as he showed me blush-colored rocks from Oklahoma shaped like tiny roses and phantom crystals where it looks like there is a ghost inside the crystal but it is where the crystal stopped growing. I thought I would talk him into an interview; instead, he talked me into buying some rock roses.

Outside his store, I met several crystal collectors who were traveling around the country in an RV to buy crystals. They talked about how COVID-19 was invented by scientists and drug companies so that they could get rich. I told them that in July 2021, only 35 percent of the Arkansas population was fully vaccinated, and the Delta variant was killing people in record numbers. I wanted to talk about dry counties, and, as someone who had survived COVID-19, it was hard for me to listen to conspiracy theories.

When I asked people about dry counties, they seemed to accept them as a fact and talked about making beer runs or driving to the county line. Although some people mentioned the Bible, nobody said they didn't drink, just that they had to drive farther to do it. We all agreed that we had been drinking more during the pandemic, and the liquor store owners and workers who I spoke to said that sales had never been stronger. According to a 2021 study, Arkansas liquor stores in select counties saw their sales tax revenue grow 35.9 percent between September and November 2020 on a year-over-year basis.

Aperol Spritz
is the sommelier's Gatorade.
You can drink them all night
and get up and go running.

When we stopped to get a Dr Pepper at a corner store, an older woman who was demonstrating a country line dance move and had manicured peach fingernails told us, "You look like the kind of girls who drive around and sleep in a tent." Liz and I looked at each other and laughed. A woman who came in the store told me that she had sold even more crystals during the pandemic, explaining, "If you ever have to sell your crystal collection, it's kinda like guns — they don't depreciate."

I was too busy
drinking sparkling wine
and didn't feel
the earthquake

Late in the afternoon, when we stopped at a house with crystals spread across the yard, we met a Reiki master who offered to speak to us in the language of light. Listening to her chant, I thought about the strange bedfellows that anti-alcohol sentiment produced — during Prohibition it was the police and the KKK, and during the era of dry counties, it has been county line liquor stores in wet counties protecting high profit margins and conservative churches. The messaging around alcohol — that it should be approached with fear and not curiosity — had shaped my Arkansas childhood. But despite growing up in the driest state in the U.S., I discovered alcohol in all its poetic glory.

> *The Syrah is a velvet curtain*
> *almost envelops you*
> *and makes you feel safe*
> *like you are in a library*
> *with old, well-handled books.* ◊

—

Alice Driver is the author of More or Less Dead *and the translator of* Abecedario de Juárez. *Her long-form reporting, radio segments, and essays have appeared in* National Geographic, Oxford American, The New York Review of Books, Time, California Sunday Magazine, Columbia Journalism Review, CNN, Reveal: From the Center for Investigative Reporting, CBC Radio, PBS, *and* Longreads.

The Driest State

COUNTRY COOKING: MINNIE'S CORN PUDDING & TAMMY'S BETTER THAN *SEX* CAKE

—

by Jennifer Justus

Illustration by Natalie Nelson
This story was originally published January 15, 2019

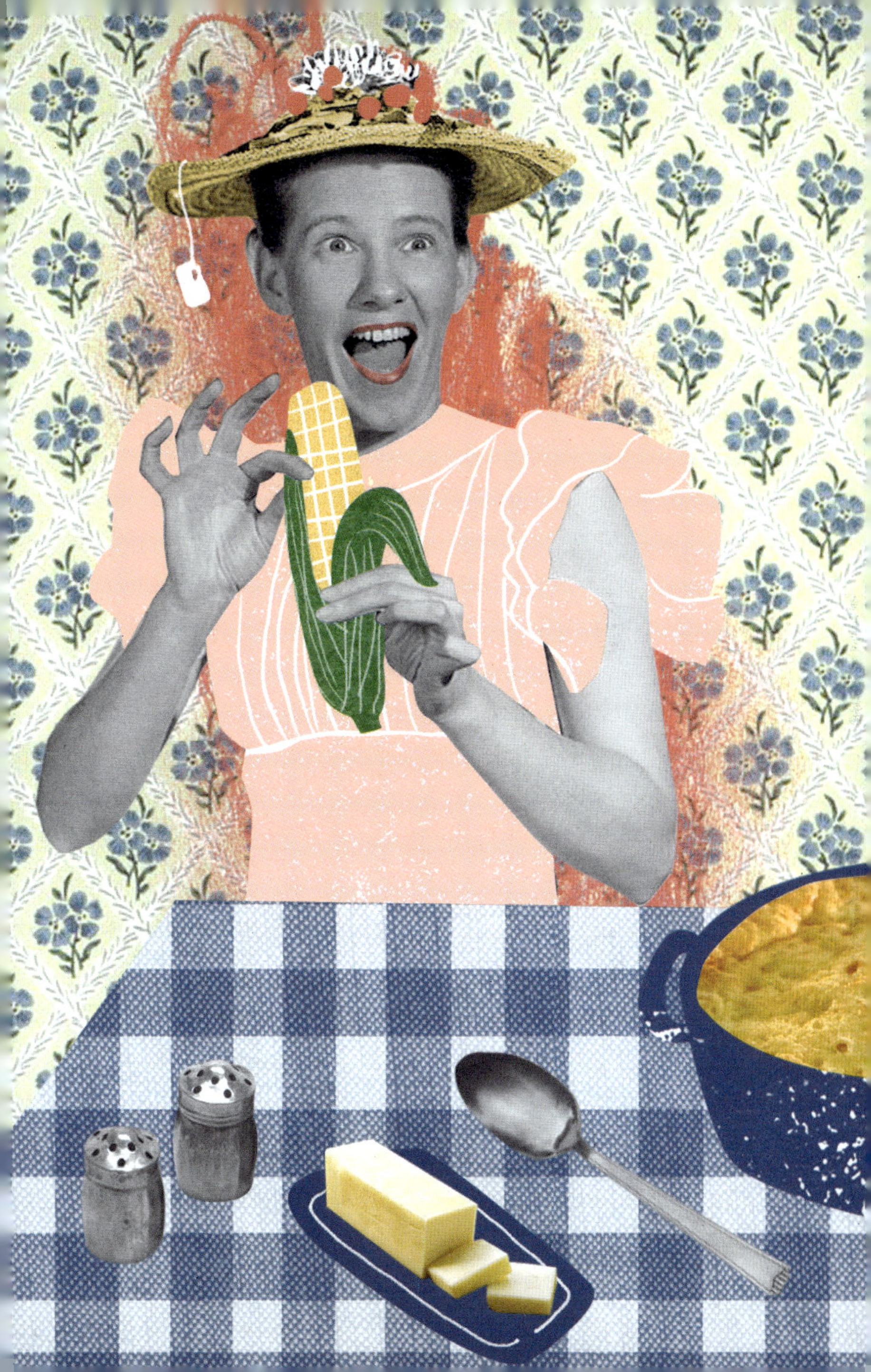

Country Cooking

I'd been married two years and 97 days when I finally got around to making Tammy Wynette's recipe for "Husband's Delight."

It starts with a pound of ground beef and a pile of garlic salt the size of an anthill. Top that with a couple of cans of tomato sauce, and then layer it in a casserole pan with spaghetti noodles, sour cream, and a blanket of melted cheddar. That's it. It costs about $16 for an entire pan. And not long after I served it, I realized Husband's Delight lives — at least partly — up to its name.

"This is stoner food," my husband said, scooping up another bite. "And it's great."

But that's not really how I would describe it.

First off, I'm not here to pick on Tammy or her cooking. Yes, I've worked as a food writer for many years, and I've eaten some pretty fancy dinners. But I'm not even close to a food snob. I grew up with a busy mom who warmed up Krispy Kremes in a toaster oven for our breakfasts. We regularly had fried Spam with canned white beans and cornbread for dinner. So when I read in Wynette's cookbook that she liked when her husband dropped Vienna sausage in the white gravy for breakfast? Didn't even flinch. I get it.

What I will say about Husband's Delight, though, goes beyond my husband's description. It's bold yet intimate and vulnerable in the same way Wynette delivers a line in "'Til I Can Make It on My Own."

Food Stories

Looking at the recipe's footnote, we learn she made the dish not so much to please her husband's tastes but to create something easy for him to pull out of the fridge and feed the kids when she went on the road. It's the kind of dish my Georgia grandmother called a "nasty bite," and I'd venture that many women have them. They're the quick meals we throw together that somehow work their way into the repertoire like a family secret or inside joke. They get the job done and help us get by, and we love these dishes for it. But while most of us probably wouldn't think of sharing these recipes, Tammy Wynette did.

I'd been on a tear lately making recipes from cookbooks by women in country music. I made Minnie Pearl's chicken tetrazzini and her mama's corn pudding. I made Wynette's cornbread and Kitty Wells' orange coconut cake and Mother Maybelle Carter's tomato gravy. As a grand finale, I baked Wynette's Better Than Sex Cake. Its layers of vanilla pudding, pineapple, and cherries coming in like one of her third-verse key changes — a little dramatic, maybe, and over the top. But I'm OK with that, too. I wanted to make these recipes to the letter, with zero tweaks or substitutions. Garlic salt? Fine. Cream of mushroom soup? No problem. Boxed cake mix, Cool Whip, Crisco? You got it. I wanted to do the work in the kitchen and taste the dishes just as these women had before me.

And I wanted to do this not for, but because of, the men. Here in Nashville, we have at least seven new restaurants with celebrity names like Jason Aldean's Kitchen and Kid Rock's Big Ass Honky Tonk & Rock 'n' Roll Steakhouse. It occurred to me that while country music and food have long had a special bond, the men are more apt to slap their names in neon on places of business, while the women work it out in the home kitchen sharing their recipes through books and cooking shows.

These days, for example, Martina McBride has a new cookbook (her second) and a Food Network show. Trisha Yearwood has three cookbooks and a show. Kimberly Schlapman of Little Big Town has a cookbook and show, and these women follow a deep history of country music queens with cookbooks — Naomi Judd, Loretta Lynn, Dolly Parton, Tammy Wynette, Kitty Wells, Minnie Pearl, and June Carter Cash, to name a few.

By reading and cooking from these books, I set out to learn more about what the recipes tell us and how they show us the special connection the country music genre — and especially its women – has to food. I'll also admit a bias upfront: I don't buy into cooking roles as domestic drudgery or any less important or powerful than a man's ownership of a restaurant. While I'm also not necessarily calling the woman who co-wrote "Stand By Your Man" a feminist, I agree with chef Nigella Lawson's notion that cooking provides a self-sustaining act of independence.

Recipes can be portals to our complex makeup — a reflection of our backgrounds, agriculture, traditions, and the nostalgia we cling to, as well as our aspirations and the way we want to be portrayed. Elizabeth Engelhardt, chair of the department of American Studies at the University of North Carolina at Chapel Hill and author of *A Mess of Greens: Southern Gender and Southern Food*, says women have long had access to kitchens as a channel for expression.

"Why wouldn't they use that for another tool for a public persona?" she asks.

Cooking is another avenue for storytelling, too, a hallmark of the country music genre. Because if Wynette's hit "D-I-V-O-R-C-E" tells a story, then so does her "Husband's Delight."

• • •

"I have collected recipes and cookbooks as far back as I remember. Collecting recipes must be one of women's oldest hobbies."
—
Minnie Pearl Cooks

Kimberly Schlapman of Little Big Town and author of the cookbook *Oh Gussie! Visiting and Cooking in Kimberly's Southern Kitchen*, has her own special copy of that 1970 cookbook by the legendary country satirist.

The photo on the original hardback's cover shows Minnie Pearl standing by a window seat, but it's also the same spot where Schlapman and her bandmates wrote their hit song "Boondocks." The recording studio owner, who found a copy of the book at his place, gave it to Schlapman. It has meaning to her in both her music and food.

Long before the cookbook existed, though, Minnie Pearl printed recipes in a 1940s fan newsletter called the "Grinder's Switch Gazette." Brenda Colladay, vice president of museum services at the Country Music Hall of Fame and Museum, says it's the earliest instance she's seen of a country star and recipes together. A 1943 issue, for example, includes "Mrs. Roy Acuff's Favorite Recipes for Hot Rolls." Minnie Pearl also hawked the foods of Grand Ole Opry sponsors like Goo Goo Clusters. Later, her Minnie Pearl Fried Chicken chain debuted (and bombed). But while her restaurants didn't last, her recipes did.

In the pages of *Minnie Pearl Cooks*, both Pearl and the woman who played her, Sarah Cannon, show up. Despite Pearl's hillbilly image, Cannon grew up in Centerville, Tennessee, about 50 miles west of Nashville, with a well-to-do lumber magnate father who later lost his fortune in the Depression. She graduated from Ward-Belmont College, Nashville's most prestigious school for women at the time. In her cookbook, Pearl reinforces her down-home brand with recipes like her mother's corn pudding, which has few ingredients, easy instructions, and no fancy garnish or serving instructions. Then, in other recipes, we can imagine Sarah Cannon serving the hot clam or Roquefort dip to Music City glitterati at parties.

In both recipe types, though, she shows a love for sharing family traditions and entertaining. And those sentiments might be part of why the country music genre has a strong connection to food.

"I cook for people to love on them," Schlapman says. "Country music at its roots is all about family and friends and taking care of each other. And when you sit down around a table, you're with family and friends."

Schlapman's and Pearl's willingness to share is where James Beard Award-winning author Ronni Lundy spots a difference in women with cookbooks and men with restaurants. Lundy has worked as both a music and a food journalist. Her first, much-acclaimed book, *Shuck Beans, Stack Cakes, and Honest Fried Chicken*, shares stories and recipes from the likes of Emmylou Harris and Brenda Lee and their mothers and grandmothers.

"Women's roles traditionally have involved a sharing, communal aspect — creating food and passing it along to another generation," she says. "When it becomes performative instead of collaborative (as in restaurants), men dominate."

Sure enough, by reading *Minnie Pearl Cooks* you get the sense Sarah Cannon doesn't just want to dazzle us with her trendy 1970s chicken tetrazzini; she really wants us to make it, too. She's sure to note that it comes from a personal, credible source: her husband's aunt Cynthia Fleming, who told her when she married "this dish would solve my entertaining problems, and she was right." In shades of beige with cream of mushroom soup, the olives and pecans dress it up, but it comes together quickly and tastes as comfortable as a wood-paneled basement on a chilly January night.

• • •

"I'm the happiest when I can be in my kitchen. To me, the most fun in the world is to work for my family."

—

Kitty Wells Country Kitchen Cook Book, Vol. 1

Look at the collection of country music cookbooks, and you'll notice they come from women who are "powerful and in control of their careers," says Engelhardt.

Kitty Wells had the first No. 1 hit by a solo female artist with "It Wasn't God Who Made Honky Tonk Angels," a rebuke of Hank Thompson's "The Wild Side of Life," which resulted in a radio ban.

She also wrote three volumes of cookbooks beginning in 1964.

But the style and delivery of her most famous tune — straight-up and without fanfare — matches the layout of her cookbook. It doesn't have long intros or cutesy illustrations. No headnotes to set up recipes. Just the titles themselves and bare-bones instructions. In the case of Wells, we can learn about her from what she included — and from what she left out.

Carrie Helms Tippen, a professor at Chatham University who wrote *Inventing Authenticity: How Cookbook Writers Reinvent Southern Identity*, says the bells and whistles of cookbooks can sometimes be an attempt to manufacture "realness."

"All these things we add now are about increasing authenticity in a skeptical public," she says. "But maybe you doth protest too much. The more evidence of authenticity, the less I'm inclined to believe it."

Wells didn't need to sell her song with theatrics, and she didn't need to sell her recipes either. Though some of her dishes have international flair reflecting a love of travel or a well-traveled image (sopapillas; "German" cornbread), the recipe that appears most often in her collections is orange coconut cake. Her husband's favorite, she writes, has been in her family for generations. It involves multiple layers and an icing made by boiling sugar to soft ball stage, a term used in candy making and fondant icing for wedding cakes. It's a sharing of family tradition, but it's pretty serious baking, too.

Of course, Wells didn't strip her books completely of personality and messaging. Her first volume has a gingham cover, for example, the unofficial pattern of "country." And though women in country music tend to publish cookbooks more often, it should be noted that men have published a few, too.

Men in country music can no doubt come to cooking authentically. John Carter Cash's new book, *The Cash and Carter Family Cookbook: Recollections From Johnny and June's Table*, brings together family recipes with his own, for example.

But look closely at the recipes from male stars in many other instances, and you'll likely find they actually come from women. In 1978's *Cooking With Country: Favorite Recipes From 32 Top Country Music Artists*, "Bill Anderson's Meat Loaf" comes from his wife, Becky. "Chet Atkins' Black-Eyed Peas" come from a woman whose husband built his guitars. "Buck Owens' Mother Owens' Banana Pudding" includes his mom in the recipe title.

In another example, a pamphlet from Merle Haggard called "Famous Recipes From Hag's Ramblin' Days" appears to feature the singer's recipes, until you spot the fine print on the back page: "Recipes from the kitchen of Margie Mille, 1981."

But if these recipes give stars an avenue for connecting with fans or appearing more down-home, maybe the restaurants hope to accomplish this goal in similar ways. Engelhardt says country music has always walked the line between conservative, family-centric definitions and rebellious, radical notions outside mainstream society.

"It would make sense to me that both men and women look for opportunities that allow them to move closer to one of those poles."

• • •

"When I was a little girl, cooking was what I did to escape the rigors of picking cotton. Today I do it to relax and express my love for others."
—
The Tammy Wynette Southern Cookbook

Tammy Wynette once called the hot dog her favorite food. But she also wowed guests with her ham dumplings and cobblers, stuffed peppers and pot roasts. When she dated Burt Reynolds in 1977, she says her banana pudding caused the heartthrob (who happened to have hypoglycemia) to literally pass out.

Like Minnie Pearl, Wynette shared the country recipes of her upbringing, such as basic vegetable soups to chess pie. But she also shared modern recipes — microwave peanut brittle, barbecue chicken with a cup of Coke and ketchup. A footnote to shepherd's pie says she ate the dish in London when she missed Southern casseroles.

Through her cooking, we get glimpses of all the lives she lived.

For instance, Wynette learned to make cornbread, she writes, at a young age to stay out of the cotton fields. She later lived on bread and beans while trying to make it in Nashville.

Raised on a farm and married at 17, she went on to have 20 No. 1 hits. She also had five husbands and four kids, and, according to her biography, *Tammy Wynette: Tragic Country Queen* by Jimmy McDonough, she kept a tuft of cotton in a $1,500 bowl at her Nashville mansion to remind her of her roots. Though McDonough indicates Wynette's downtrodden upbringing might have been exaggerated in places, she sure didn't waltz through life without trouble either.

So in her cookbooks, published in 1990 just eight years before her death, a sense of gratitude shines through. Rather than headnotes, she includes footnotes, every one beginning the same way: "Taught to me by … ," as a humble and respectful nod to the passing of knowledge from the women in her life.

"I think that was the hardest thing I've ever done," she said of writing her cookbook in a 1990 interview on the "Crook & Chase" television show. "I sat up at night and would make these things to make sure 'Well, it's a cup and a half of this' because I always just threw it in. … I tried to make it very easy to read."

And for the most part, it is easy — with plain text, and devoid of styled photos to represent the goal we're supposed to achieve. But still, Wynette leaves a few details out, like the size of sour cream container or can of tomato sauce. It's like we're supposed to know — or at least know enough to figure it out.

Overall, Wynette's book and the others I cooked from demonstrate the quiet power in sharing and knowing how to do things — taking care of yourself and those around you in the ways you choose. Even "Husband's Delight" shows her running the household and maintaining control from the road.

And though it's not a competition, cookbooks, which remain a best-selling category in publishing, go beyond the performative nature of restaurants.

"I would argue that a published cookbook is both," Tippen adds. "It's a private domestic document packaged through commerce. [Cookbooks] have these ways of crossing boundaries that a restaurant cannot do."

They come into our homes, and their recipes sometimes become a part of our lives, too.

...

With a fridge full of country queen leftovers, I texted my husband one night to remind him I'd be home late:

" … but there's Husband's Delight in the fridge," I wrote.

Then we cracked up in a flurry of laughing emojis, because despite my love of food, I'm no domestic goddess, and I had not yet explored what lay behind the simplistic image the dish's name conjures.

But indeed, I learned later that he did pull the casserole from the fridge. He ate straight from the pan until he'd nearly made himself sick.

"OK," he texted later, "never make Husband's Delight again."

Duly noted, I thought. But then he knows as well as I do: I'll be making the call on that. ◊

—

Jennifer Justus is a freelance journalist who writes about food, music, and life. She is the author of Nashville Eats: Hot Chicken, Buttermilk Biscuits, *and* 100 More Southern Recipes From Music City. *Her work has been published in two editions of* Cornbread Nation: The Best of Southern Food Writing, *and she has received national awards from the Society of Features Journalism, the Society of Professional Journalists, and the Association of Food Journalists. She worked as food culture and lifestyles reporter at The Tennessean newspaper and has written for outlets including The Bitter Southerner, Time, Rolling Stone Country, Southern Living, The Boston Globe, Garden & Gun, and more.*

THE CREATURE COMFORT OF AUNT JEMIMA

—

by adia victoria

This story was originally published October 29, 2020

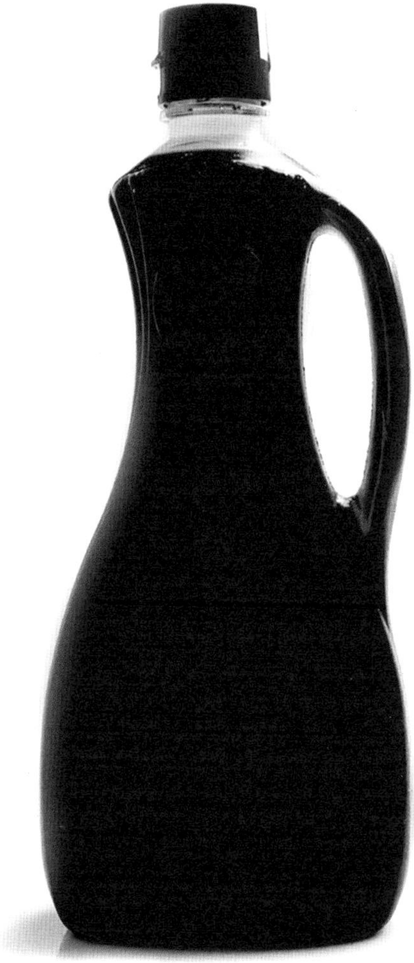

The Creature Comfort of Aunt Jemima

There is little that leaps from white mouths on the issue of racism that surprises or even moves me. How could it? For 400 years my people have existed alongside white folks in the Deep South. The same excuses, evasions, and justifications of white supremacy that deeply informed their lives still give hue and color to mine.

I had known racists of the venomous set — the one who spits "nigger!" with such spittle-laced passion you could imagine there's a strange love, like one might love a passed-down family heirloom, for the word. I knew well the ability of the preening millennial ally to rain mosquito bites of microaggressions onto folk of color.

At 7 years old, I took to heart my great-grandmother's advice to "know your whites, sweetie." It had been her way of teaching a young Black girl, whose body would grow in and on the Deep South, to manage her expectations and feel accordingly. It was the gift of protective armor that a Black woman born in Little Rock, Arkansas, in 1903 knew would be required.

This summer, however, over sweet tea, I was caught without my armor. An elderly white man I count among my closest friends admitted that he was saddened to see Aunt Jemima vanish from his pantry and polite popular culture. He labored to explain that Aunt Jemima's ever-available, smiling Black face reminded him of his ever-available, ever-jovial Black nanny from his own Southern childhood. A silence sprang up between us.

I felt my mind in hot pursuit of words my mouth failed to form. The tea was suddenly too sweet, too syrup-thick, to swallow.

For the first time I had encountered a white person willing to admit what every Black person knows: Racism persists because it is a comfort to white people. It is not a naturally occurring phenomenon beyond the control of men. Racism exists because it feels good. It feels useful. More precisely put, racism, for many white people, feels familiar.

Aunt Jemima had achieved what any successful brand must do: She tapped into a vulnerability and a nostalgia and created an emotional connection with consumers that ties into the larger stories of their lives.

Don Draper, infamous advertising Svengali of "Mad Men," explained the potential of this branded emotional manipulation. "Nostalgia — it's delicate but potent. ... It's a twinge in your heart far more powerful than memory alone. ... It goes backwards, and forwards ... it takes us to a place we ache to go again."

The Union had only recently been sutured back together following the Civil War when Nancy Green, a formerly enslaved American, made her debut as the spokesmodel for the Aunt Jemima brand at the 1893 Chicago World's Fair. White Americans were primed for a collective misremembering of both slavery and the Civil War, which measured in flesh and blood the nation's addiction to Black subjugation. The call for collective amnesia was felt strongest in the South. The white elite class — from bankers, politicians, and academics, to advertisers and artists — labored in concert to whitewash the legacy of slavery.

The goals of these men were twofold: maintaining and justifying a racialized other required for the existence of centered white identity, while simultaneously downplaying the violent sausage-making required to create the playground for the white imagination that would become the Jim Crow South. They needed a way for white Americans to feel strong emotions beautifully.

From their efforts bloomed a propaganda campaign where the Confederate states were recast as Dixie — an agrarian, bygone era peopled by high-mannered Southern gentlemen hell-bent on familial honor, genteel Southern belles, and "Happy Darkies" who perfumed the air with Negro spirituals and a sense of contentment and complacency with their station. Aunt Jemima, with her consumable smile and winking approval of Jim Crow social order, would be the sort of coddling psychological embrace white Americans would need in order to sop up the fragments of their own shattered post-antebellum identity. She would prove endlessly useful in ensuring white Americans that their nostalgia for Black oppression was righteous, justified, and sweet.

This emotional bond and yearning for an ideal and wholly fictionalized past ensnared not only my white friend, it also ensnared the psyche of some of the South's sharpest minds. William Faulkner admitted in an interview, "If it came to fighting I'd fight for Mississippi against the United States even if it meant going out into the street and shooting Negroes." Flannery O'Connor put this strange addiction plainer still, confessing in a letter, "I'm an integrationist by principle & a segregationist by taste."

For too many white Americans, against their better judgment, the trappings of white supremacy simply taste good. And feeding these good feelings was the Aunt Jemima brand. They could pour their taste for Black subjugation right over their pancakes. White supremacy became their daily bread, and Black subjugation sweetened the aspects of their life deemed too shameful to face head-on. White supremacy lives, still, belly-deep within the souls of white folks. The expectation and desire for Black women to comfort and coddle remains as inbred in their social cohesion now as it did when Nancy Green made her first appearance nearly 130 years ago.

My white friend's face was the portrait of the confusion, complicity, and shame that I hope white Americans harbor. They are, perhaps, the true victims of white supremacy. Robbed of their ability to relate, empathize, and grow in their humanity, so much of their life is spent justifying and denying their own perceived superiority. It has left them psychologically split and diminished and totally reliant upon the buoying effects of the racialized "other."

In "'B' Movie," Gil Scott-Heron says:

The idea concerns the fact that this country wants nostalgia
They want to go back as far as they can
Even if it's only as far as last week
Not to face now or tomorrow, but to face backwards

I know the work staring down white folks to confront, address, and exorcise their past will be generations long, much like excising kudzu that takes hold of a forest, or the toil required of my foremothers to keep white folks' homes an immaculate and impossible clean, so deep is the work needed to uproot their perceived supremacy. But I also understand this is work that I cannot and will not do. My own Black liberation has freed me from cleaning up their mess, from sweetening their bread. I gave myself permission to let my white friend wrestle with the funk of his own fractured psyche. I cannot carry that burden for him. I will not work to dress up and play down his own internalized white supremacy.

The kitchen is closed. ◊

—

adia victoria is a Southern gothic blues poet, musician, and storyteller from South Carolina currently based in Nashville. Her latest album, "silences," was co-produced by The National's Aaron Dessner and released in 2019 on Canvasback. When not making art, she dedicates her life to her family, silence, brooding in Paris, and mothering her four cats, bot, dot, nancy, and Shelby Foote.

The Creature Comfort of Aunt Jemima

LEMON MERINGUE PIE: A LESSON IN LOVE, HATE & BRAVERY

by Kathleen Purvis

Photo by Kenny Louie
This story was originally published July 1, 2020

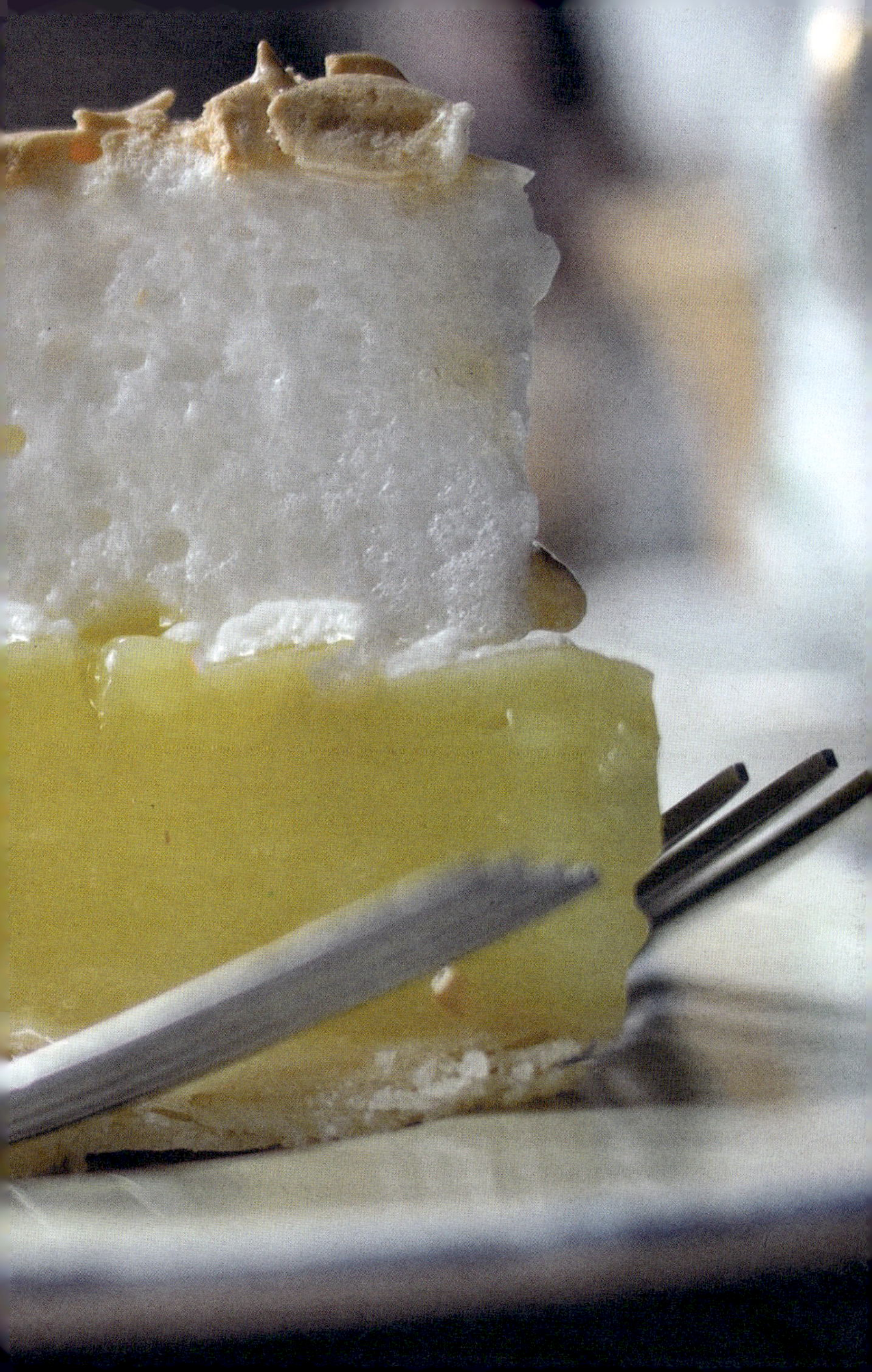

Lemon Meringue Pie: A Lesson in Love, Hate & Bravery

There it is: a single perfect slice on a plate, enough noon light coming through the windows of the café to make the yellow lemon layer glow and brown-tipped waves of meringue as high as my pinky finger shine ethereally, a thick cloud of dream foam.

It's lemon meringue pie, and I despise it on sight.

It isn't the lemon, most beloved of all flavors to me, even above chocolate. Hand me a slice of icebox lemon pie with whipped cream or a pan of lemon squares, and I might not wait for a fork.

The problem is the meringue. I'm good with crispy meringue, like Pavlovas and those little cookies you dry in the oven overnight. The trouble is soft meringue, the kind made from egg whites and boiling syrup. Just the thought of forcing a forkful into my mouth brings a gag response, built on years of hating the not-solid/not-liquid sensation.

It brings up more than disgust: guilt, that I'm a Southern food writer who can't abide a classic of the Southern baking arts; sadness, that I could never appreciate my late mother's lemon meringue pie, allegedly one of her highest achievements.

And there's another layer of emotions under there, as important to the proceeding as my mother's flaky pie crust. That layer is all mixed up with love, trust, and the lesson in bravery my parents taught me.

Like my only other food hate, liver, I test myself every decade or so. Our tastes change as we grow, and sometimes things we hated as children suddenly click: Mayonnaise, plain buttered rice, and grits were all suspect to me once, but all worked their way into my palate as I grew.

I've reached a détente with chicken livers. Hate them fried, love them passionately as chicken liver pâté or mousse.

But not the lemon meringue pie.

The last time I gave it a try was a decade ago in a classic meat-and-three in Albemarle, North Carolina, the Rosebriar Restaurant, famous for housemade pies and particularly for lemon meringue with a layer of meringue at least twice as deep as the lemon filling under it.

As a food editor on assignment, I treated the pie with respect: ordered it, admired it, took a picture of it. I interviewed the restaurant's owner and wrote a column about it. Before doing all that, though, I took one bite. Nope, still couldn't swallow it.

Food can be fraught when you have parents who knew hunger. Both of my parents, born in Georgia in the 1920s, knew shortages in the '30s, nights of government cheese, plain boxes of spaghetti with no sauce or butter, squirrels brought back from the woods.

For actual starvation, though, we had our father, the Marine veteran who came back from the South Pacific with no physical wounds, just emotional ones, shoals mostly hidden by his cheerful zest for life that could surface suddenly and dangerously.

My father's experience with starvation was the stuff of actual history book: He was dropped on a swampy mess in the Solomon Islands called Guadalcanal, with limited supplies for what was supposed to be a short battle with the Japanese. It turned into a six-month slog and a stand-off between the U.S. and Japanese navies, leaving 6,000 or so Marines and a few thousand Japanese soldiers scrambling with so little food they turned desperate.

My father survived with a disturbing nostalgia for grilled snake — even my food-adventurous mother wouldn't indulge him in that one — and stories of getting so hungry he and his buddies once went back to a Japanese encampment they had captured weeks before. When they had originally taken it, they had piled up the captured stores of rice and pissed on it, their idea of a protest against General Tojo. When they returned, just

Lemon Meringue Pie: A Lesson in Love, Hate & Bravery

to check, the pile of rice was inedible, of course, laced with blue mold and maggots. They still dug into the center of the mound, just to check.

Being a picky eater didn't carry much weight with my dad. If you said you couldn't eat something, he would pin you down with a hot stare and declare: "If you're hungry enough, you can eat anything. You can eat bugs. You can eat rats. I know."

Try arguing with that when you're 7 and you don't want to drink your milk.

After a few epic battles over liver, Dad and I established peace over food. I was mostly willing to try anything once. And no lemon meringue pie for me meant more for him, so we could co-exist.

But all peace requires a test.

In our Florida suburb, our family stuck out for our sheer Southern-ness, a trait beloved by our neighbors, Fred and Pearl Townsend. Fred and Pearl were retired people and actual snowbirds: They had a home in Canada where they retreated in the summer, and a stucco house right next to us for the winter.

They loved our Southern ways — our boiled peanuts, our spare ribs, our barbecue. They loved everything about us — my dad and his bighearted embrace for life, my mother and her cooking, my brother and his motorcycles, my own gawky adolescence.

Fred and Pearl were getting on in years, so when I was 14, Dad roped me into tackling the hedge between our houses, climbing up and down a ladder all day to trim it up. Neighborliness has its reward, so Fred and Pearl invited my parents and me for dinner.

I made sure to sit up straight and remember my "sir"s and "ma'am"s. I cleaned my plate as expected. And then Pearl announced she had a surprise, she had worked on it all day, and she hoped it lived up to our Southern standards. And she stepped out of the kitchen with a lemon meringue pie.

My parents heaped her with compliments. And they fixed me under their steady gaze, the one that says "you know how you were raised."

I did. I said, "thank you, ma'am," picked up my fork, and went to work. I fought back the gags and ate as steadily as I could, trying to breathe through my mouth and focus on reaching the crust. The whole time, my parents covered for me by keeping up a steady stream of "mmm"s and compliments, trying to divert attention from my struggle.

Once, pausing to let my gorge settle, I looked up and saw them both looking at me. To this day, when I think of what it means to be looked at with love, I think of that moment. They were both gazing at me with pride and unspoken encouragement. They knew how hard that slice was for me, how hard it is to choke down something while appearing to enjoy it. With their eyes on me, that silent rain of praise and pride, I got through the slice. Even picked up the crust crumbs with my fork.

And Pearl stood up, saying how much she loved watching me eat, and declared: "I know what you want." She cut another slice, bigger than the first, and plopped it on my plate.

I looked down and knew I was defeated. I couldn't do it again. I just couldn't. And that's when my father picked up his fork, making up a joke about trying to guard that pie from him, and reached across the table. My mother joined in, insisting she couldn't resist another bite and taking three.

My parents teamed up and made that pie go away so smoothly, Pearl never guessed a thing.

So what did I learn that night? I learned that you can do anything if you have to. And I learned that if you try hard enough, the people who love you will know it and hold you up through the last steps. I learned that love doesn't have to speak, it just has to act.

Yeah, it's a sentiment as sticky sweet as a slice of goddamn lemon meringue pie. But at least I didn't have to eat a rat. ◊

—

Kathleen Purvis is a longtime journalist and food writer and was food editor of The Charlotte Observer until 2019. She is the author of three books for UNC Press, Pecans *and* Bourbon *in the Savor the South series, and* Distilling the South, *on Southern craft liquors. Purvis is a member of the Southern Foodways Alliance, a member and executive officer of the Association of Food Journalists, and served for many years on the awards committees of the James Beard Foundation.*

Lemon Meringue Pie: A Lesson in Love, Hate & Bravery

TAMALEANDO *EN* TENNESSEE

—

by Keitlyn Alcántara

Photo by Keitlyn Alcántara
This story was originally published July 21, 2020

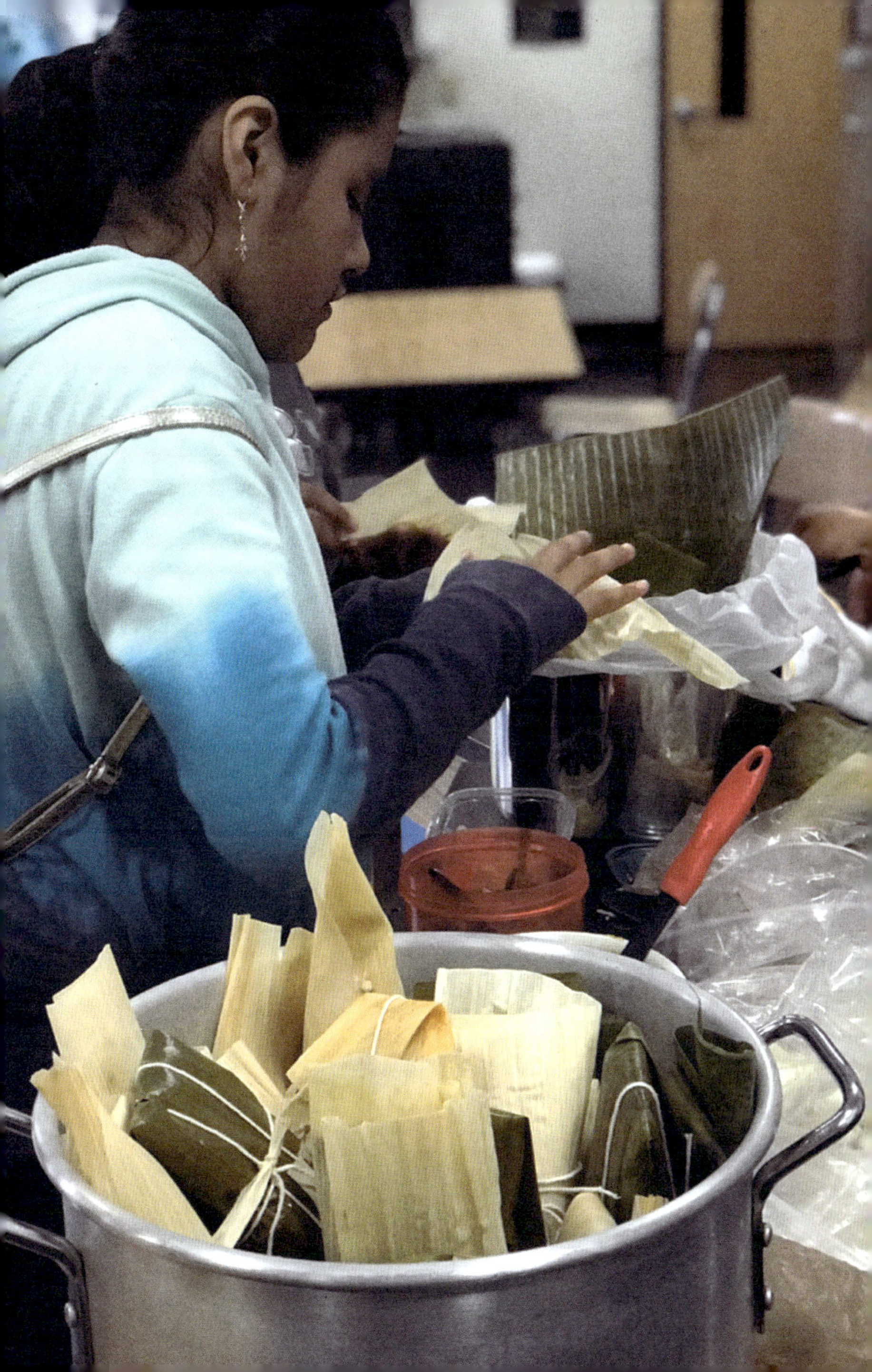

Tamaleando en Tennessee

At first glance, a tamal may fool you with its innocence. The simple cornmeal masa, grains united by steam until they sit as one, firm within the leafed wrap. Yet its wisdom, its capacity to feed and nurture, is thousands of years old. A simple portable and filling comfort food, tamales originated in Mesoamerica and were adapted by cultures throughout the Americas. And now, in Nashville, the tamal is my accomplice, a Trojan horse that has allowed me to breach the formidable emotional barricades ingrained in the average middle schooler.

In the fall of 2019, I entered my third year of Sazón Nashville, a series of cooking workshops I had slowly been cobbling together, propelled by a feeling I didn't quite understand yet. Teaming up with an after-school program hosted by Conexión Américas and the Nashville After Zone Alliance (NAZA), once every few weeks I would join these groups of Latinx middle schoolers to chop up delicious ingredients, filling the drab classrooms or cafeterias with a bright and pungent palette: the juicy gold of ripe mango, the sharp emerald nip of fresh-cut cilantro.

I started these workshops when I was a graduate student in anthropology, studying the ancient worlds and foodways of central Mexico — my country of birth. Nose deep in well-worn library books (F1219 my aisle of preference), I was worlds away from the country I loved, struggling to remember why I had done this to myself. During semesters spent at a predominantly white, elite private institution, my spirit was reduced to citations on a page, caricatures of what drove my heart. I spent my summers escaping back to Mexico, relishing the chaotic Saturday morning walk to the street market to fill my cloth bag with pungent yellow guayabas, big reams of crisp greens, damp earth still clinging to their stalks. Even walking through Walmart, salsa and bachata rhythms fill the dairy aisle, and my satisfied smile finds company in the millions of babies and toddlers everywhere. In Mexico, I was sister, daughter, prima, salsa dancer, la antropóloga. In Nashville, my shrunken world was a sallow hipster monochrome of meals eaten alone in front of a computer, Red Bull-flavored sighs escaping my lips as I tried to get through yet another arduous reading, or write a final paper that no one will read. I felt invisible. I felt collapsed. Instead of "hello," one friend would greet me with, "You look tired," which I repeatedly explain does not, in fact, assuage the fact that I am mentally, emotionally, and physically depleted.

Yet when we cooked, the peeling gray walls and dingy linoleum of that middle school cafeteria impossibly brightened.

...

Energy and excitement bubbled up past my end-of-day exhaustion as I bustled between cooking teams, each arranged around a plastic cutting board. As we chopped ingredients for mango salsa, I felt a joyful thrill seeing students' deeply guarded personalities begin to peek out. Silent, other than the swish of the knife, one polo-uniformed student with a mohawk fade minced cilantro with skills on par with the best-trained chefs. From beneath the emo shadows of a black-hooded sweatshirt, another casually demonstrated to his partner how to dice whisper-thin onions. My arcane archaeological knowledge found new life as I explained the proud history of maize, food of the Mesoamerican gods. We joked and told stories while they worked, finding a familiarity in the shared tasks and a confidence I had seen in Mexican family kitchens — everyone with a task, everyone with a place. Sazón was a program I had designed for the students, but it ultimately bloomed into exactly what I needed, too. Sazón became a space of finding myself, of existing exactly as I was; a healing that embraced many of those who became a part of it.

Tamaleando en Tennessee

My ability to shrink myself into a palatable unit of convenient existence was a skill that had slowly accumulated throughout my life. But in graduate school, I found academic professionalism and turned it into a full-time job. As part of the ebb and flow of the global Latinx diaspora, the boxes used to corral us shift with time (Check one: Spanish, Hispanic, Latino, Latinx), despite experiences that have always been an elusively diverse historical smattering of Indigenous, European, Black, Asian, Middle Eastern, mestizo, and criollo storylines.

Among those diverse stories, there is mine. My mother came from a poor, white missionary family with roots in the Midwest. My grandfather was a fighter pilot who moved his family of nine to 1960s Panama to proselytize. Growing up bilingual, my mom left home at 16 to travel the world on mission trips until she met my father through a church group in Mexico. My father grew up in Puebla, Mexico, selling bread on the colonial-tiled streets as a child. In a one-room home, one wall was the bread oven, and the remaining space housed his mother and her five children. His curious mind earned him scholarships and a path toward the world of academia (and Marxism).

Together, they formed a pseudo-religious hippie-esque pair, moving to Seattle for my dad's education, joining 1970s protests, working for a season as farmworkers in a Wenatchee apple orchard, birthing my older sister at home with the help of a midwife. A decade later, they returned to Mexico, my father as a professor of Spanish literature, my mother a photographer. Both maintained a passion for social justice, and as a kid I played happily in the dirt of forgotten fringes of Mexico City as my parents sat with community members, brainstorming how to build grassroots change from extreme poverty.

I was born amidst the slow unraveling of their relationship. After my parents' divorce when I was 5, my mom and I moved back to the U.S., and I spent the '90s seasoning my childhood with the taste of perpetual new-kid-dom, ricocheting between bustling cities (Vancouver, Philadelphia, Milwaukee, Seattle) and lesser-known locales (Valparaiso, Indiana, and Danville, Pennsylvania). I would arrive mid-school year to defend my existence, fighting against the woefully elemental understandings of what it meant to be me.

"No, I'm not from here. ... Yes, I speak Spanish. ... No, I don't eat tacos every day."

How could I possibly encompass everything that I contained in such clipped curiosity? My mom, tall, fair-skinned, and blue-eyed, didn't know and didn't have the vocabulary or lived experience to help me navigate what it meant to have my petite, brownish body incessantly met with the question, "Where are you from?" A question whose answer was only accepted when reduced to a caricature of all that I was: "I'm from Mexico." My dad, an "alien" in the United States, had long ago learned to detach and ignore — not an option for a kid whose heart yearned to fit in.

Once, returning from Christmas break in Mexico, my dad suggested I take my third-grade classmates some Mexican candies; a cultural exchange or something. He picked his favorites from when he was a kid in 1940s Mexico. "Glorias," a goat-milk-based, fudgelike candy wrapped in dark red cellophane twisted shut on each end like a bow. Delicious, but after traveling eight hours squished in a suitcase, the texture and appearance were suspiciously poop-like. I watched my classmates squeal in disgust, the trash can bursting with unopened cellophane bows. After this failed offering, I stopped speaking Spanish, stopped offering pieces of myself to people who would never get it.

Nearly two decades after those rejected cellophane offerings, I would once again take a chance at sharing my full self, finding an unexpected refuge in the lush green bluegrass and hot-chicken red of Nashville, Tennessee. Walking through the sticky blanket of August air and the towering magnolia trees of Vanderbilt's campus, I searched for any vestige of familiarity. A new kid yet again, I had moved to Nashville to start graduate school in the fall of 2013, my first time living in the unfamiliar South. On a bulletin board layered four deep in ragged pin-pricked posters, a tagline caught my eye: "Spanish-speaking volunteers needed." This poster led me just three short miles southeast to a middle school on Nolensville Road, a corridor lined with a hodgepodge of businesses, signs brightly painted in the colors and prose of the Latinx diaspora.

I first joined the NAZA and Conexión Americas program because I missed the rebellious banter of Spanglish, but as I helped the students with their homework, I was quickly drawn in by the mischievous familiarity of chile and mango candies students snuck surreptitiously out of backpacks, the jumble of beautifully chaotic, vibrant personalities, the mix of students who traced their roots to Venezuela, El Salvador, Honduras, Guatemala, Nicaragua, Mexico, Peru, each with their own origin story. We were united by the cafeteria scent of bleach and over-steamed vegetables, the aroma of after-school programming — still the same as I remembered 20 years later. But amidst my rapture at having found this community, I would also experience a flashback of shame.

Following homework time, the students rotated through "enrichment activities," like science experiments with Mr. Bond the Science Guy, or film critique with the Belcourt, a local independent movie theater. Once a month, the enrichment activity was a workshop on nutrition, led by a tall blond woman whose Southern drawl held no space for Spanish. Thinly cloaked in good intentions, she lectured about how to make "healthy pizzas" out of a Triscuit and cucumber, or "yogurt parfaits" with fresh $5-a-pint strawberries. The students sat glassy-eyed, the theme song of "La Rosa de Guadalupe" drifting up from under someone's desk as they caught up on the telenovelas they'd missed during the school day. The thing is, they weren't bored. What I saw, I recognized from my own childhood. They had given up.

Implicit in the speaker's lecture about health was the idea that these poor public school kids ate junk out of ignorance, out of brownness, rather than culturally devoid school systems that counted Tater Tots as a vegetable, entrapping students in an over-processed food hell that spanned from 8 a.m. to 6 p.m. I sat, simmering in polite silence, trying to identify where my anger should land. These students were not a charity project. Nor were they impotent and abandoned. Through casual conversations, I knew the wealth of nourishment they received at home. Thick steaming caldos floating rich with carrots, tomatoes, chiles, greens. Beans, nopal cactus, avocados. These foods would never show up on any USDA Food Pyramid. Yet these ingredients told the complex stories of Latinx history — the rise and fall of ancient civilizations, persistence through colonial traumas, the massive human ebb and flow across space and time.

Pettily productive, I decided to counter this whitewashed idea of health with culturally relevant cooking workshops. The first year of Sazón, I bumbled. Excited to share myself, the inaugural session was all about my favorite food: the elote, a boiled cob of luscious corn covered in mayonnaise, cheese, chili powder, and lime, found on any downtown Mexican street corner. It was fun to share, but when I asked students to reflect on what they were learning, more than a few responded, "We are learning about Mexican food!" If I continued on alone, I would risk trivializing the wealth of varied Latinx experiences. Stepping back, I sought out friends from other parts of the diaspora who could give examples of worlds I didn't know. Two colleagues, fellow graduate students who identify as indigenous Maya women, taught the students how to make handmade corn tortillas. Three of the quietest students, recent immigrants whose first and dominant language was a Mayan language, isolating them from both their English- and Spanish-speaking peers, beamed in recognition of the thick-bodied patties: "Las tortillas ... los de GUATEMALA!" Through cooking, and hosting guest chefs, we were learning to listen and to be curious about the secret lives we each contained — the stories, the knowledge, the shifting and complex identities.

The decision to end the year with a tamalazo (a tamale feast) was one based in intention. It was a way for everyone to say, "I know what MY tamales look like. But what about yours?" Before going ingredient shopping, we asked the students what they put in their tamales. "Chicharo!" Yelled one student. "Salsa verde!" exclaimed another. In an effort to not screw up the ingredient prep, I ended up in a deep internet rabbit hole of recipes and found that there are in fact 500-5,000 types of tamales in Mexico alone. Tamales have been adapted for thousands of years, spanning the length of the Americas. In Nicaragua, nacatamales are filled with potato, tomato, and pork. In Peru, the choclo-based humita rules. More recently, the hot tamale has been adapted and spread through the Mississippi Delta, the result of meals shared by African American and Latinx laborers, perhaps with roots in Native American practices.

In my hunt for guest chefs, I found kindred souls who were also fighting to exist in their complex and multifaceted brilliance. One

Tamaleando en Tennessee

volunteer, Bety, has been our resident tamal expert since 2017, when a mutual friend put us in contact. In her 16 years in Nashville, she's been a full-time mother and grassroots organizer. From her kitchen, she infuses her days with the colors, smells, and sounds of her hometown of Oaxaca, Mexico, running an informal tamal business among friends. Each tamal is a remnant of the home she left behind — a home she hopes will somehow be absorbed by her Nashville-born son and daughter.

In preparation for the tamalazo, the two-day affair that concludes our cooking season, we spend day one filling a big metal pot to the brim with raw tamales, masa filled with cheese, chicken, rajas, loroco flower, and red and green salsa, all rolled into ridged yellow corn husks or the sleek green of banana leaves.

It's a Wednesday evening and Bety stands at the front of the classroom, the angled neckline of her white shirt embroidered with bright red and orange flowers that radiate sunshine under the neon-bulb gloom. Three long tables form a U. Bety stands at the center, while the students have self-sorted; boys on the left, girls on the right. Every one of them leans forward, propped on eager elbows to watch as she explains how to make a tamal. As her mouth rolls over words like "loroco" and "hoja de platano," one of the boys turns to his friend worriedly. "There's only four boys!" he says, alluding to the table opposite him, crammed with nine girls from fifth to eighth grade. "That means you'll have to step up your tamal game!" I joke. They giggle and huddle to create a tactical plan.

Luckily, tamales are hard to mess up. Students begin timidly, but gain confidence, one making a "mega tamal" filled with every single ingredient, salsa dripping from a body barely contained by several banana leaves. At the end of day one of the tamalazo, Bety lugs the overflowing olla home. She returns the next afternoon, steaming tendrils escaping the lid to fill the room with the savory scent of fresh tamales.

Students eat their creations with pride. They hoard tamales to smuggle home to share with family and run to offer tamales to faculty, staff, or the odd parent early for pickup.

They sit, full in tamal-coma contentment.

Over the three years of Sazón, 13 different guest chefs shared their recipes and their stories. They were fellow graduate students, friends from salsa dancing, activists, and nonprofit employees, and came from Guatemala, Honduras, Mexico, Puerto Rico, El Salvador, and Peru. With each guest came new ingredients and new stories that expanded the possibilities of what it could mean to be Latinx.

There are many ways in which we can propel ourselves to move beyond the lazy question of "Where are you from?" For us, it was cooking. Immersing ourselves in smells, tastes, and sounds awoke crevices of our identities that had been dormant for years in strategies of survival.

What fantastic macrocosms are lost when we only brush the surface, when we are led to believe that our differences are anything short of magic.

Cooking created space to not only ask, but listen, watch, and relish the parts of each other that we bravely chose to reveal. To once again dare to share our full selves, and to encourage others to do the same. ◊

—

Keitlyn Alcántara is a professor of anthropology at Indiana University. Drawn to the role food plays in community resistance and resilience through change, she uses archaeological and contemporary case studies to explore how foodways shape our bodies and social networks.

Tamaleando en Tennessee

HE COULD HAVE BEEN A COLONEL

by Keith Pandolfi

Photo by Helen Rosner
This story was originally published June 26, 2018

WHAT'S AN *Ollieburger?*

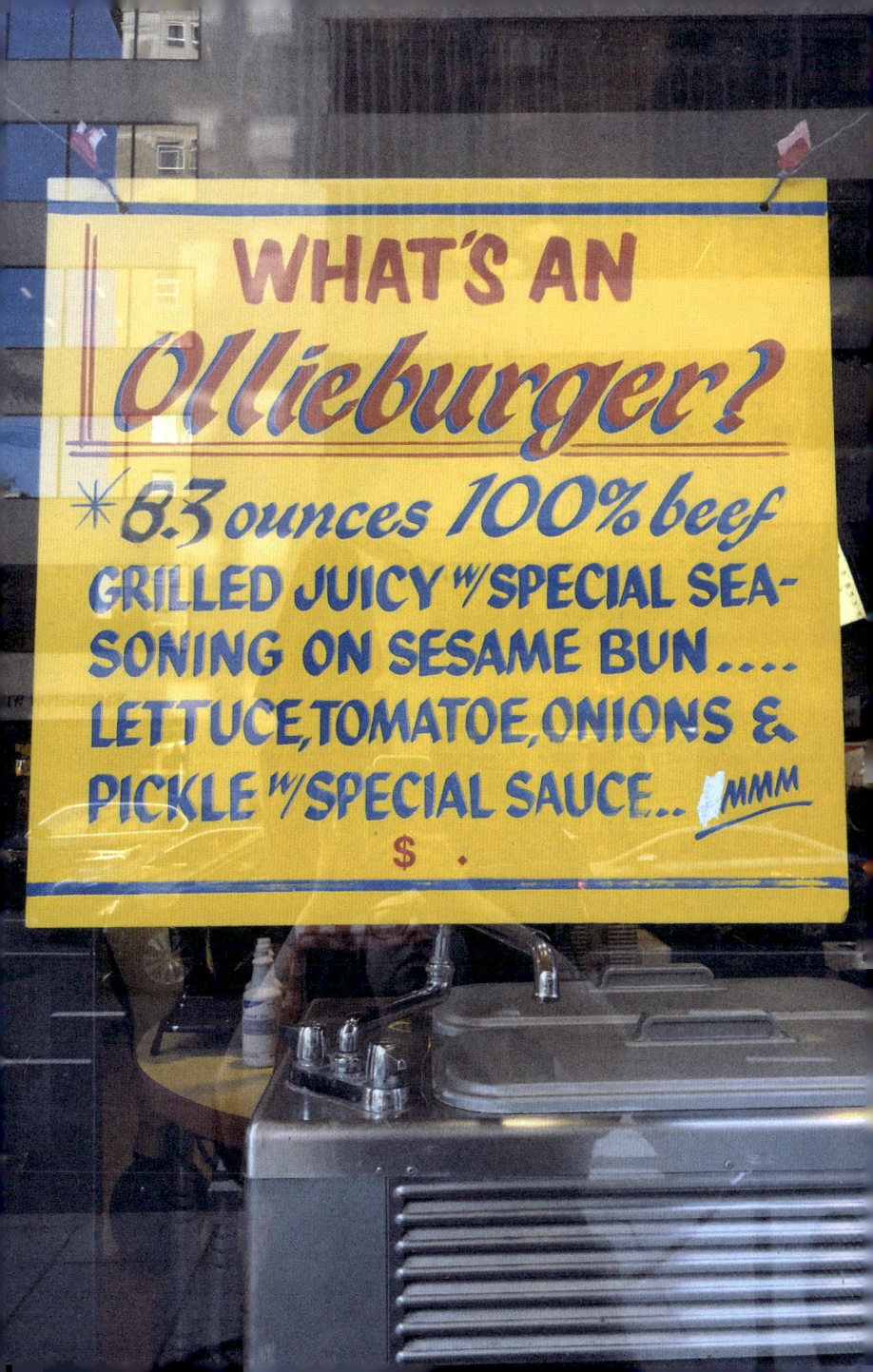

*6.3 ounces 100% beef GRILLED JUICY w/ SPECIAL SEASONING ON SESAME BUN..... LETTUCE, TOMATOE, ONIONS & PICKLE w/ SPECIAL SAUCE... MMM

$.

He Could Have Been a Colonel

During the lunchtime rush at Ollie's Trolley in Louisville, Kentucky, I sit in the parking lot, listening to the radio, waiting for the rain to die down, so I can make a run for it.

Through the sheets of water flowing down my windshield, I see a skinny white kid smoking a cigarette out front of the place, not giving a damn about the rain, it seems. Three highway workers come roaring into the lot in a GMC pickup, its bed full of orange barrels and cones. One gets out and rushes toward the door, but courteously holds it open for a sharp-dressed senior citizen in a baby-blue blazer who's on his way out. In one hand, he's holding a grease-stained paper bag, in the other, a big cup of soda.

That bag reminds me just how hungry I am. I turn off the ignition, pull the brim of my Reds cap down tight, and run like hell.

If you've never been to Ollie's Trolley, it's a curious thing to stumble across. Yes, it looks like a trolley — albeit one marooned on a sea of asphalt and cinder blocks since it opened 45 years ago. It's painted red and yellow. Its interior, to venture a guess, could not be more than 250 square feet in size. Every time I come here, it reminds me of the trolley from "Mr. Rogers' Neighborhood." And while it can't get you to the Land of Make Believe, it delivers something even better — one of the best hamburgers in the world. At least, that's what I think.

Inside, shaking the water from my cap, I notice there's enough room in the kitchen for the five women working that day to perform their duties in relative harmony. One shares an update about a sick friend as she fries burgers on the flat-top, while another listens as she tends a basket of fries sunken in hissing, hot oil. All in all, it seems like the platonic ideal of a family-owned restaurant, all "how you doin', honey?" and "please come back soon." I don't bother looking at the menu before telling the smiling woman behind the register my order, because I always know what I want. An Ollieburger, Olliefries, and a Coke, please. Five minutes later, she hands me a grease-stained bag of my own, and I dash back to my car to eat it. Given that Ollie's has no seating inside, there's no other option.

Eating an Ollieburger is like having a McCormick spice warehouse explode in your mouth. There's a magic mingling of oregano and garlic, cumin, rosemary, and Old Bay — an Italian pot roast and a Maryland crab boil all in one. There are other flavors in there, too — some I recognize, like onion powder, paprika, and cayenne, and others I don't. The same seasoning coats both the fries and the burger. And the more I eat, the more my taste buds re-acclimate themselves to those flavors, and the more convinced I am that the Ollieburger is the most underappreciated burger in America.

Part of the reason for its low profile is that Ollie's Trolley in Louisville is little more than a remnant of what it was four decades ago — a full-blooded nationwide chain of restaurants dreamed up by the fast-food restaurant entrepreneur John Y. Brown.

Yes, that John Y. Brown — the same guy who helped transform Kentucky Fried Chicken from a fledgling, regional chicken joint into one of the most iconic fast-food franchises in the world. Ollie's Trolley arose from Brown's partnership with a cigar-chomping, straw-hatted grouch named Ollie Gleichenhaus. Today, only three Ollie's Trolley locations survive — this one in Kentucky, one in Cincinnati, and the other in Washington, D.C.

But if Brown and Gleichenhaus had it their way, Ollie's Trolleys — thousands of them — would still be thriving.

• • •

Our nation's most famous burgers have good stories to tell. Stories like the time in 1937 when members of the Glendale High School Orchestra stopped by Bob's Pantry, a modest little diner in Glendale, California. They asked owner Bob Wian — a man who in high school had been voted "Least Likely to Succeed" — for "something different." Seeing as the kids were all regular customers, Wian decided to indulge them by adding an extra patty to his single mainstay burger, slapping on a few toppings, and inadvertently creating what would become the heart of a billion-dollar restaurant empire — Bob's Big Boy.

Three decades later, to goose sales at his fledgling McDonald's franchise in Uniontown, Pennsylvania, a former Bob's Big Boy employee named Jim Delligatti created a variation of that sandwich. Delligatti piled two beef patties, some "special sauce," lettuce, cheese, pickles, and onions on a sesame-seed bun. He christened the burger "The Aristocrat," but when he realized how difficult a time his customers had pronouncing the name, he came up with a new one — the Big Mac.

But those origin stories pale in comparison to the grandiose ambitions of Ollie Gleichenhaus, who professed an almost erotic connection to the burger he created.

"I started out to make the best hamburger," he once told the Palm Beach Post. "It satisfies me ... it turns me on."

The Ollie's Trolley in Cincinnati sits beneath a huge mural of President Barack Obama.

Gleichenhaus was born in New York City near the turn of the 20th century but migrated to Miami, where in the 1930s he and his wife opened Ollie's Sandwich Shop in South Beach. The place was small, just seven stools and a couple of booths, but it quickly became a hit among tourists, locals, and some celebrities, too, including Dean Martin, Joey Bishop, Rodney Dangerfield, and Don Rickles.

"The biggest people in the country ate in my place," Ollie once boasted to the Palm Beach Post. "If you didn't go to Ollie's, you didn't know nobody."

Most of the old newspaper reports about the Sandwich Shop make it clear that what drew those celebrities wasn't just the burgers, but Ollie himself, whose caustic demeanor both entertained and, if what Gleichenhaus says is true, inspired them.

"Rodney Dangerfield used to write material in my place," Ollie told the Post.

"He got all his material from me," Ollie said of Rickles.

Maybe Ollie wanted to be a comic himself. Maybe he dreamed of stand-up gigs in smoky nightclubs and TV studio sets, a life far away from slinging burgers. No matter. Those burgers were his ticket to glory. It took him more than three decades to perfect the recipe, adding a new spice here, a different type of cheese there. He'd change up the bun, or grind up a new cut of beef. He used his customers as guinea pigs until he finally felt he'd nailed it. And once he nailed it, he was happy with himself, just frying up burgers and basking in the Florida limelight.

That is, until John Y. Brown came along.

• • •

John Y. Brown was just 37 years old in 1971, the year he and Gleichenhaus first crossed paths. But he'd already achieved what amounted to a lifetime of experience in the fast-food business. In 1964, along with his business partner, Jack Massey, Brown acquired Colonel Harland Sanders' fledgling Kentucky Fried Chicken company for $2 million. By the time he sold it to Connecticut-based Heublein Inc. for $284 million seven years later, it was a multibillion-dollar business with more than 3,500 locations.

Along with scoring Sanders' secret recipe for what's now America's most iconic fried chicken, Brown's genius was turning Sanders (who'd been given the mostly symbolic title of Kentucky Colonel by the Commonwealth itself) into not just a mascot, but also a goodwill ambassador. Brown would send him on tours around the country, where he evoked images of country cooking and Old South charm.

"The Colonel wasn't merely the face of the company; he was the company," Brown once told the late writer Josh Ozersky. "I used to tell people inside the company, there's two reasons we're all rich — because the Colonel came up with a good product, and because he looked good on that sign."

John Y. Brown and Col. Harland Sanders visited the New York Stock Exchange in 1969.

He Could Have Been a Colonel

Part of the reason Brown sold KFC was because he wanted to run as a Democrat for the U.S. Senate. But after a favorite Republican candidate received his party's nomination, he thought it might be best to wait a while. To bide his time, Brown used part of the profits from the sale of KFC and bought a fledgling Florida chain called Lum's, known mainly for its beer-braised hot dogs. Brown knew he couldn't rely on the masses to flock to Lum's for hot dogs alone, so he decided to add something else, namely a burger that would be the beef-patty equivalent of Sanders Original Recipe chicken. And so, according to Time magazine, he "recruited a platoon of young executives and told them to scour the country until they found the perfect hamburger."

Around the same time his troops were deployed to find a burger for Lum's, Brown and his family traveled to Aspen, Colorado, for a ski trip. As they took a lift to the top of the mountain, Brown told me in an interview last year, he spotted a small trolley down below, selling popcorn. That trolley, he said, triggered something: a memory of the trolleys that used to navigate the streets of his hometown of Louisville when he was a child.

"Well, it was just sort of cute," he said.

He decided that, along with selling burgers at Lum's, he'd also sell them from small, replica trolley cars. There'd be no seating inside, only takeout, just like the popcorn stand. He figured it could be the kind of place men pop by at lunchtime for a sack of burgers to take back to the factory, a place moms pull into to grab dinner for the kids.

Not long after, Brown's platoon reached South Beach, found Ollie's Sandwich Shop, and declared their mission accomplished. They said Gleichenhaus' burger — a third of a pound of lean beef seasoned with a blend of 32 spices — seemed destined to be a sure-fire hit, not unlike the Colonel's spicy chicken. After hearing about the Ollieburger, Brown flew to Miami to try one himself and knew right away it was the one. In fact, when we spoke, he remembered eating four of them in one sitting. That the man who'd created them had a name that rhymed with "trolley" was almost too much, serendipity verging on the miraculous.

But there was a catch. Gleichenhaus was irascible. According to Ozersky's book *Colonel Sanders and the American Dream*, Gleichenhaus called Brown a "slick-talking sonofabitch" when he first broached the idea of buying him out. After Brown offered Gleichenhaus $1 million for his recipe, suggesting that he could turn him into the next Colonel Sanders, the burger-maker was unimpressed. According to a 1976 story in the Appleton, Wisconsin, Post-Crescent, his response was resolute.

"I told him we was doing just fine," Gleichenhaus said, "and he could get the hell outta my store."

"He had an infectious personality, for sure," Brown told me. "He swore like a sailor and had quite a routine; if anyone came into his restaurant and asked for ketchup, he'd say, 'Get the fuck out of here!'" Ollie wanted nothing to do with this rich man and his vision of an America dotted with trolleys. "He was seen as sort of a hero down in South Beach," Brown said, and part of that heroism was his bravado, an arrogance that could sometimes spill out into a destructively big head.

Still, given the success he'd had with the almost-as-petulant Sanders, Brown kept hounding Ollie, calling him several times each week with the same offer, but the exchange was almost always the same. "You'll be the next Colonel Sanders." No dice. "You'll be the next Colonel Sanders." Not interested. "You'll be the next Colonel Sanders … " And then — "He finally got to me," Ollie told the Post-Crescent. "With all the talk about the fun I'd have and the traveling, and how my name would be up in lights. Yeah, that fed my ego."

...

With Ollie on board, Brown's first step was to send him to Texas, where he trained the cooks at Lum's on how to make his burger. In the meantime, Brown got to work on the trolley concept, asking his old friend Ronald Dukes, an artist, to come up with the design. When the burgers received rave reviews during their test marketing in Lum's Ohio restaurants, Brown knew he had a hit on his hands and got to work promoting it.

"Brown intends to go nationwide with Ollieburgers within a year," Time reported, "and has prepared 63 television commercials featuring Ollie in 'an Archie Bunker kind of approach.' The rest may someday be history."

The first Ollie's Trolley, the one I visited on that rainy Thursday afternoon, opened in Louisville around 1973, selling Ollieburgers, Olliefries, and a simple menu of hot dogs, chicken sandwiches, and milkshakes. Shortly after, there were openings in Memphis, Nashville, and Atlanta. For each grand opening, Brown would send Gleichenhaus out to perform, selling not just the burgers, but also his grouchy, old-school, Archie Bunker-like persona (a wise move, since at the time, "All in the Family" was among the most popular TV shows in America). Gleichenhaus always delivered, showing up with a cigar clamped between his lips and an endlessly entertaining scowl. The reporters sent to cover the openings ate it up, especially because he always gave them a great sound bite or two.

By 1976, there were almost 100 Ollie's Trolleys nationwide, most of them east of the Mississippi River. But despite its rapid growth, the place had yet to find its footing among customers. Transitioning the Ollie Burger from the open grill Ollie used in Miami to the clamshell versions employed because of the trolleys' tight kitchen space "compromised the experience," according to Brown. "It was better when you could put it over an open grill," he told me. "You had the aroma and the smoke coming out." But it wasn't just that.

Despite the positive feedback during test markets in Ohio, many Americans, whose collective idea of an ideal burger was focused more on ketchup and mustard than thyme and oregano, found Ollieburgers a challenge to their taste buds. And as each new location opened, Brown heard more and more discouraging feedback from customers who complained the Ollieburger was too spicy and too salty. While Americans were quick to embrace spicy fried chicken, spicy hamburgers were something else entirely.

Even Gleichenhaus admitted to several reporters his exuberantly spiced burgers weren't for everyone, but predicted more customers would come around in due time. "When ya get hooked on an Ollieburger, it's like dope," he said. "Ya need it." People weren't crazy about the trolley's take-out-only concept, either, especially since other burger joints were starting to introduce drive-thrus, where you didn't have to get out of your car to order your food. In other words, things weren't looking good, and Brown was already thinking of pulling up stakes.

• • •

It's hard to say when Gleichenhaus first realized Brown's plan wasn't working out — that he would never be the next Colonel. In researching this story, I came across a 1975 photograph of him taken in Atlanta during a July 4th "Salute to America" parade that also featured Flip Wilson, Alex Trebek, and Frankie Avalon. When I scrolled down to the picture of Gleichenhaus, he was riding on the back of a convertible wearing a red velvet blazer, a flat-top hat, and a red hanky tie. His sideburns were salt-and-pepper; his black-rimmed glasses pure Nixon. He had a cigar in one hand, a can of Coca-Cola in the other. He was flanked by two young women — the sort your grandfather might call "nice-looking gals" — each wearing Styrofoam boater hats with bands that read "Ollieburger."

Staring at that photo, I tried to read the expression on Ollie's face and glean something from it. His mouth curls into something resembling a frown. His eyes are cast downward. I couldn't help but think that he knew where the whole Trolley thing was going and that it wasn't going far. And he was right. In 1978, Brown sold Lum's to a Swiss holding company and pulled the plug on Ollie's, too. Most of the trolleys were demolished over the next few years, though Brown sold a few — some to private owners who kept them running as burger shops, others to people who repurposed the little restaurants for other clientele. One morphed into a Bolivian restaurant. Another became a tiny tavern. On Columbia Pike in Washington, D.C., you can still find one, since converted into a burrito stand called Pedro and Vinny's.

And so we are left with three ghosts of Trolleys past. The Cincinnati location is known more for its soul-food selections of barbecued ribs and collards than for its Ollieburger (though it serves a damn fine version of it if you want one). The D.C. location does continue to sell an exceptional Ollieburger (now elevated with 100 percent locally sourced Angus beef). In a recent article in the Washington Post, writer Sadie Dingfelder wrote a story headlined "Ollie's Trolley: On Par With Shake Shack?" Other than the burger and fries, however, the menu comprises very un-Ollie-like dishes such as pastrami sandwiches and hot smokes. Only the Louisville location maintains the original menu — the one Ollie, if he were still alive, would still recognize.

...

He Could Have Been a Colonel

For Brown, Ollie's Trolley was little more than a bump in the road. In 1976, he bought the NBA's Buffalo Braves (now the Los Angeles Clippers). In 1978, he purchased the Boston Celtics. And in 1979, Brown ran as a Democrat and won the governorship of Kentucky, a post he held until 1983. And he couldn't shake the restaurant bug, launching other, more successful restaurant chains after he sold off Ollie's, including Kenny Rogers Roasters and Roadhouse Grill.

Brown's life history is vivid and public, but I had a hard time finding what became of Gleichenhaus after Lum's and the trolleys closed. When I asked Brown, he said he didn't know. No one seemed to have any idea. Through Facebook, I tracked down two of Ollie's cousins, but neither of them seemed to know much about their briefly famous relative. In fact, the only thing I could find about post-Ollie's Ollie was his New York Times obituary, from 1991. The headline read: "Oliver Gleichenhaus — Burger Maker, 79."

The obituary is brief, just four short paragraphs: The sandwich shop, the million-dollar payday, the Ollieburger and the restaurants that sold it: "a new chain called Ollie's and mobile restaurants called Ollie's Trolleys." It's true the restaurants were trolleys, complete with wheels, but the Times makes it sound like they rolled around town, a red-and-yellow precursor to the food trucks and pop-ups that would take the country by storm a generation later. But that's not how it was; the trolleys stayed in one place, anchored to the ground by solid foundations and water pipes and gas lines, real restaurants — if tiny ones.

They weren't meant to move; they were meant to stick around. ◊

—

Keith Pandolfi is a James Beard Foundation Food Journalism Award-winning writer and editor. His work can be found in publications including The Wall Street Journal, Saveur, Cooking Light, and The New York Times Magazine.

BS publishing

FOOD STORIES: Writing That Stirs the Pot
Published by The Bitter Southerner, Inc
Athens, Georgia

©2023, The Bitter Southerner, Inc.

ISBN: 978-0-9980293-6-8

—

Cover & foreword photography by Whitney Ott